Elements of Speech Communication

THIRD EDITION

David M. Jabusch
The University of Utah

Stephen W. Littlejohn
Humboldt State University

COLLEGIATE PRESS

Collegiate Press
San Diego, California

Executive editor: Christopher Stanford
Senior editor: Steven Barta
Senior developmental editor: Arlyne Lazerson
Design and Typography: John Odam Design Associates
Cover art: Paul Slick
Printer: Malloy Lithographing

Photo Credits
Page 8—Kirk Schlea/Zephyr Picures; pages 24, 290—Kris Kleine; pages
54, 128, 145, 209, 310—Jackie Estrada; page 106—Marc Pokempner/
Tony Stone; pages 154, 156, 160, 328, 343—Stephen Dunn; page 194—
Chuck Keeler/Tony Stone; page 205—Russ Gilbert/San Diego Union;
page 217—Bob Daemmerich/Image Works; page 248—Jeff Albertson/
Stock Boston; page 305—Mimi Forsyth/Monkmeyer Press Photo Service.

Courtesy Public Relations Office of the University of Utah—pages 6, 11,
14, 32, 34, 40, 42, 48, 51, 60, 69, 72, 76, 85, 91, 101, 124, 153, 165, 169,
176, 188, 199, 220, 228, 234, 245, 256, 261, 268, 313, 338.

Library of Congress Card Number 95-69717

ISBN: 0-939693-37-2

Printed in the United States of America

10 9 8 7 6 5 4 3 2 1

For Susan and Karen

Contents

Preface

With the publication of the third edition, *Elements of Speech Communication* is fifteen years old. We are gratified that our work continues to serve introductory students after a decade and a half.

Since its inception, *Elements* has been predicated on several beliefs about teaching and learning in communication. We think that good communication pedagogy combines insights gained from scholarship of all types as well as personal experience. We believe that communication competence cannot be achieved by precept, that it is a combination of understanding, sensitivity, skills, and ethical responsibility, and that it is developed by a combination of theory, practice, and analysis.

Our approach rests too on the assumption that communication is a complex process that infuses all aspects of human life, that communication is more than a tool for transmitting information. As the means by which we construct our experience, communication constitutes the very environment in which we live.

People understand and practice communication in many ways, and since the first edition of our book, the field of communication has expanded immensely its offering of useful concepts and ideas. Since then, we too have come to expand our awareness of the ways in which communication can be understood and practiced. This edition, then, has been affected by the growing literature in the field and by our own expanding awareness of possibilities. Still the book maintains what we consider to be "oldies, but goodies," insights that our most modernistic colleagues would call dated but that still ring true and help students in their effort to master their communication environment.

Continuing adoptors will see a stronger constructionist orientation, especially in Chapter 3; the influence of dialectics, especially in Chapter 5; recognition of public speaking as invitational rhetoric, especially in Chapter 8; a reflection of our growing concern about the quality of public discourse, especially in Chapter 9; and contributions from critical theory, postmodernism, and cultural studies, especially in Chapters 1 and 10.

A textbook revision inevitably will contain some structural changes. Such changes are minimal in this edition, though we have split the old chapter on interpersonal communication into two. Some sections have been dropped, and new sections have been added. There are some organizational changes within chapters. Still, the book retains the same general approach, organization, and style.

We have retained many of the features that have always given *Elements* its character, so that the "feel" of the book is about the same. Every chapter begins with a story or provocative allusion. Relevant photographs add interest and give pause for thought. The previewed section titles and summaries remain. And, of course, the image shifts, which have been unique to this book from its inception, still challenge students to look at the subject in new ways. We have added a complete glossary, to make the text easier to study from. All glossary entries are set in boldface type in the text.

We would like to thank all of those who helped create the third edition. Special thanks to Arlyne Lazerson, our editor and all those affiliated with Collegiate Press who literally "made" the book. Thanks also to our reviewers, whose names appear on the following pages.

Editorial ReviewBoard

PART ONE

Concepts & Principles

1 *Communication and Society*

On April 19, 1994, a two-thousand pound car bomb ripped in half the Federal Building in Oklahoma City. Nearly one hundred and seventy people died. At the time of this writing, the details of the story behind the bombing are still unfolding as three American citizens, members of the militia movement, are in custody.

One thing is certain. Acts of violence such as the Oklahoma City bombing result from the inability of certain individuals and groups to deal with their differences. The evidence from around the world is compelling: The tension and anger of people who cannot accept differing attitudes and actions often accelerate out of control, much like the behavior of a frustrated child. And the consequences are often staggering.

The character of a society is determined by the quality of its communication. Democratic debate is a kind of communication, and so are car bombings. A married couple working hard to settle a disagreement is a kind of communication, and so is domestic violence. A group of co-workers meeting to create a new company policy is a kind of communication, and so are the gun shots of a disgruntled employee.

The tools of communication are symbols like words and gestures, bombs and guns. The most important question for society today is whether human beings can interact creatively, constructively, and peaceably to construct a better world. In this book we explore the spirit of creative, constructive communication in public and private settings— in interpersonal relationships, groups, and society at large.

This book is about the processes and skills essential to communication in modern society. People's complex lives demand that they create and comprehend diverse messages, function in a complicated network of relationships, and possess the adaptability to survive physically and mentally in a multidimensional environment. In short, people cannot escape communication. It is the heart of all social life—the essence of being human. The success with which society as a whole addresses its problems depends in large measure on the quality of communication.

COMMUNICATION COMPETENCE

Being a competent communicator is no simple matter. **Communication competence** combines four important qualities: Competent communicators *understand* the process of communication. They are *sensitive* to needs and demands in communication. They have *skills* in reading, writing, speaking, and listening. And they are *ethically responsible*.

Understanding

The communication process involves many physiological, psychological, social, cultural, and physical variables. Too often people fall victim to the "conveyor belt" theory, assuming that if they state or write the message clearly, it will be neatly conveyed to the receiver's brain. Such reasoning leads to the "I told them" fallacy: "I don't know why they didn't do it; I told them to." For example, both authors of this text own home computers with word processors. One of us quickly taught himself, but the other, slow to learn how to use complex mechanical and electronic devices, was having trouble. The problem seemed to be solved when a representative from the university's computer center agreed to hold an hour-long orientation session for several faculty who had new computers. The representative quickly explained the basic procedures for word processing. She then turned for the next forty-five minutes to more sophisticated procedures of pagination, footnoting, and printing. Her students' heads throbbed as they struggled to understand the explanations and at the same time search for the "on" switch!

When you realize the complexity of the communication process, you will be well on your way toward avoiding such situations and toward understanding how the process operates.

Sensitivity

Understanding is a matter of knowledge, but sensitivity involves awareness, consciousness, and attentiveness. A person may have excellent knowledge of communication theory but lack the sensitivity to apply it in an actual situation. Sensitivity is the hardest of the four elements of competence to define, yet this attitudinal dimension is crucial to communication. Good communicators not only need to be in touch with their own feelings and needs but also must be sensitive to the feelings and needs of others. A competent communicator realizes that the message will always be filtered through the listener's screen of

Caring and openness are important to ethical communication

feelings and meanings. Clearly, the computer representative described earlier was insensitive to the needs of novices.

Competent communicators are also sensitive to the demands of the physical and social situation. Human communication is strongly affected by the environment—much more than most people realize. Public speaking classes, for example, stress that students need to adjust to what is happening right there in the classroom. If the class begins early in the morning or in the evening, extra effort will be required to wake the audience up. If multiple speakers address the same topic, they should adjust their talks accordingly. Student speakers are responsible for paying attention to how the room is set up and making whatever accommodations are necessary.

Skills

A skill is a learned capacity to perform an action. You can know what needs to be done without having the skill to do it, as we have so often realized trying to wire up a fixture in a tiny switch box. A student who begins driver's training has a pretty good idea of what drivers do but little ability to actually do it.

Communication competence requires mastery of sending and receiving skills: speaking, writing, listening, and reading. Good communication requires the ability to produce and receive clear messages. One advantage of taking English and speech classes early in your college career is that they will help you to develop the communication skills you will need in other courses as well as later in life.

Our computer example also illustrates that people learn skills somewhat differently at novice and expert levels. Whether using a computer, playing a musical instrument, or cooking gourmet meals, novices need much more time to work on the fundamentals, while experts move more easily to higher levels of competence. The same is true for any type of communication, whether written or spoken.

Ethical Responsibility

Most groups have rules of ethics so that their dealings with others will be constructive rather than destructive. The Old Testament has its Ten Commandments; groups such as Rotary International have published codes of ethics; the armed forces have established a Uniform Code of Military Justice. Many people are comfortable knowing exactly what is right and wrong. The problem with this approach is that once you get out of your immediate culture or organization, its rules may not be accepted by others as universally correct, and you may find that they don't work all the time.

Traditional codes of ethics tend to focus on the means used to achieve a goal. In communication, such a code would resemble a list of dos and don'ts, but situational exceptions can be found for almost every rule of conduct. We prefer to use general principles that, if applied intelligently and empathically, foster concern and responsibility. Using these principles leads to **ethical responsibility**. Specifically, three principles are important: (1) the principle of concern, (2) the principle of shared responsibility, and (3) the principle of equal access.

The Principle of Concern. The first principle is **concern** for all participants in the communication event. It is little more than the golden rule: Your communication will be more constructive if you are concerned about the well-being of all communicators, including yourself.

Your communication behavior will have consequences. You may affect the way others define their world, the images they have, and the decisions they make. You shape your own feelings about ideas and

Baseball players have an ethical responsibility when they communicate with young fans.

people, and you will often determine your relationship with others by what you do and say. Ethical communicators are concerned about these consequences. They care, not just for getting what they want in the immediate situation, but for what happens to themselves and others in the long run as well.

The Principle of Shared Responsibility. Although you may care a great deal about the outcome of the communication, you cannot always control it completely. In fact, because you have a limited perspective, taking complete control is often a mistake. You don't have to be humble to realize that if you always got your way, certain outcomes would be disastrous.

Actions do not always have the wonderful results you expect, and actions often have unintended negative consequences. People with different perspectives are sometimes able to help achieve a more positive result and anticipate the negative consequences you cannot see in advance. Allowing others some power to affect the situation is a healthy thing to do.

Now, this does not mean that you abrogate your own responsibility for the transaction. Indeed, in the face of disagreement you may argue vigorously, but in the spirit of respect, you also listen to the arguments of others. You insist on being heard, but you also listen to other points of view.

Ideally, all communicators in a situation should partake of **shared responsibility** in this way, but responsibility cannot be shared unless information is also shared. You cannot expect others to take any responsibility if they don't know what is going on. Openness, therefore, tends to be more constructive than concealment. The more clear and accurate you are about facts, feelings, and experiences, the more opportunity you give other communicators to participate on an equal footing.

Shared responsibility means that you take other people seriously and listen to their points of view, even when you initially disagree. It's true that some people use power to override disagreement, but this is not a very ethical way to communicate. Because people disagree with you does not mean that they are stupid, uninformed, crazy, or immoral. It is simply a fact of life that equally well-meaning and intelligent people can come to opposing sides on an issue. People have different opinions because they have had different experiences, have different interests, and view the world from different perspectives.

The ethical communicator, then, listens in a new way, trying to determine the experiences the speaker has had, the speaker's assumptions about reality and knowledge, what interests are being promoted by the speaker's point of view, and how an intelligent person could come to hold this position. Ethical communicators listen so well that they could make a good argument in favor of a point of view they personally oppose. That's what sharing responsibility means.

Although completely shared responsibility is ideal, people do not always enter a transaction on equal terms. A clear-minded and informed patient may be able to make decisions about a treatment plan, but a disoriented one may not. In the first situation, the physician shares responsibility for outcomes with the patient; in the second, the physician must assume more responsibility, acting on behalf of the patient.

If you have a great deal more power than another communicator, you should use that power responsibly. If your experience and knowledge enable you to see what another person cannot, you must use that knowledge on behalf of the less experienced party. If you have privileges not enjoyed by another, you should use them to help the less privileged person.

A Congressmember has more influence over legislation than ordinary citizens and must take that influence very seriously. A parent has more maturity than a child and must use that maturity to ensure the best outcome for the child. In each of these cases, one communicator assumes a portion of the responsibility the other one might otherwise take but, under the circumstances, cannot.

The Principle of Equal Access. The third ethical principle says that people should work to help other points of view be heard. **Equal access** means freedom of speech but more than the First Amendment of the U.S. Constitution can guarantee. The stricture that Congress shall make no law abridging freedom of speech does not guarantee that speech will indeed be free. Notice that the First Amendment does not say that Congress shall create laws ensuring that all opinions are aired. Indeed, the history of the world (even in the United States) is a chronology of attempts by various groups to silence other ones. The typical strategy is to further one's own interests by gaining speaking opportunities for oneself and denying them to others.

Who is heard in the general communication of a society? Those trained in articulate speech are often heard. Those with sufficient funds to buy air time are often heard. Members representing large groups are often heard. People with connections are heard. People who echo the dominant interests of society are heard.

Who is not heard? Marginalized peoples are heard less frequently and taken less seriously than speakers from the mainstream culture. People whose interests are not profitable are rarely heard. Uneducated people are seldom heard. People who do not speak with the customary level of eloquence are not often heard. These groups are not heard because they do not have forums from which to speak or because other people do not take their forums seriously.

The third principle says, then, that people should be conscious of the many subtle ways in which important perspectives are cut out of the ongoing conversation of society. Although you may vigorously express your own point of view, you should make opportunities for others to speak as well. You should seek the airing of interests divergent from your own. And you should listen openly for the good reasons people have for their ideas, even when you disagree with those ideas. Always ask, Who is left out of this conversation? And why?

The Ideal Speech Situation. The three principles of ethics discussed in this section constitute an **ideal speech situation**.[1] In such a situation communicators are concerned about the outcomes of the communication for everyone involved. They share the responsibility for the outcome as much as possible and act in the best interests of one another when sharing is not possible. And in such a situation communicators bring as many voices into the conversation as possible.

In an ideal speech situation, communicators are concerned about the outcomes of the communication for everyone involved.

The ideal speech situation is the forum for real democracy. It is a place in which people are truly free to speak and, when they do speak, are heard. It is a place where the will of the people is worked through and public judgment is formed. It is a place where the will of the majority is fulfilled, and the rights and interests of the minority are protected.

The ideal speech situation is most often thought of as a public situation, but it can be private as well. The spirit of the ideal speech situation can be sought in the workplace and in the home. It is an ethical ideal that cannot always be achieved but should not be forgotten.

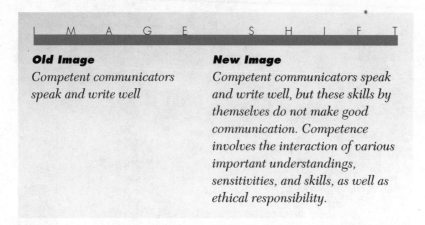

I M A G E   S H I F T

Old Image
Competent communicators speak and write well

New Image
Competent communicators speak and write well, but these skills by themselves do not make good communication. Competence involves the interaction of various important understandings, sensitivities, and skills, as well as ethical responsibility.

TOOLS FOR IMPROVING COMMUNICATION

In developing your communication competence through understanding, sensitivity, skill, and responsibility, you will find three tools helpful: theory, analysis, and practice.

Theory

A **theory** is an explanation based on systematic observation and research. Over the years a substantial body of theory has been written about communication. Theories can help people understand what happens when communication takes place. They help us become aware of important variables in communication, thus aiding our sensitivity to important factors in ourselves, in others, and in situations. Finally, theory can be a useful guideline for developing skills, pointing the way to areas for fruitful personal development.

It is obvious, however, that theoretical involvement alone is not sufficient for improving communication. The gap between knowing and doing can be cavernous. How, then, do people make their theoretical knowledge work for them? Two other tools, analysis and practice, are essential.

Analysis

Analysis is the careful scrutiny of actual communication situations. Using theory as a basis, you can observe communication while it is happening, suggest some reasons why a particular exchange has occurred, and make some useful suggestions for improvement. Competent communicators do this regularly in their daily contacts with others. In your communication class, you will be given a variety of assignments to be analyzed. These exercises will help you understand the process better, become more sensitive to occurrences in communication, and see areas where increased skill or responsibility may be necessary.

Practice

The third tool for improving communication is practice. **Practice** enables people to become more proficient in producing and receiving messages. Besides being essential to skill development, practice helps people become more knowledgeable, sensitive, and responsible communicators.

In a sense everyone is a practicing communicator, but practice without theory and analysis is much less useful than a combination of all three. Without theory we cannot know what to do when we practice, and without analysis we cannot know how well we have done it.

THREE BASIC PERSPECTIVES ON COMMUNICATION

In everyday living people tend to take things at face value. People go about their business without really questioning their assumptions. They act as though everybody sees things about the same way, even though a moment's reflection tells them that this is not the case, because people can look at the same thing from vastly different points of view.

The phrase "points of view" best describes what we mean by **perspective**. Look at the photo on page 14. You can look at this picture

Perspective makes a difference. What is this?

in a number of ways and see something different every time. What is really there? Everything you can see in the picture is really there, of course, but you have to look several times from various perspectives to make it out.

Communication, too, can be looked at from several perspectives, because there are many different ways to define and explain it. Each perspective highlights some important aspect of communication and downplays others. No perspective is all-inclusive, but all of them help us understand communication.

Does this mean that all perspectives are equally valuable? No. But it is important to recognize the particular assets of each. In this section, we will summarize three important perspectives and some representative models and definitions. In the following section, we will provide a more detailed explanation of a fourth perspective, which is the one we prefer.

We have arranged these perspectives in order of their complexity. Each perspective overlaps a bit with the next, and each borrows from its neighbors. Each focuses on certain aspects of communication without necessarily denying the existence of the other aspects. Reading about these various perspectives should you give an increasingly complete picture of what is involved in the process of communication.

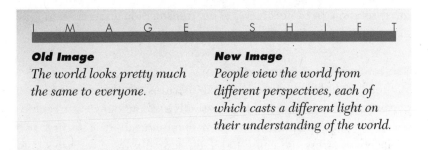

I   M   A   G   E   S   H   I   F   T

Old Image
The world looks pretty much the same to everyone.

New Image
People view the world from different perspectives, each of which casts a different light on their understanding of the world.

The Individualistic Perspective

The **individualistic perspective** of communication is psychological and focuses on the individual. It stresses how people behave in response to messages. It emphasizes the ways in which people are affected by messages and by other communicators. The individualistic perspective is interested in the manner in which people's attitudes, values, and behaviors change as a result of communication.

This perspective mostly pertains to how individuals process messages. What happens in the mind when a person gets a message? How is the information in that message treated? How is it integrated with other information? And how does it affect the person's orientations toward the world and behavior?

This perspective, then, stresses how people respond in communication.

The Transmissional Perspective

When most people are asked to define or describe communication, they say something like, "Telling another person something." This kind of statement expresses the **transmissional perspective**. The transmissional perspective stresses two important dimensions of communication: (1) the transmission of information and (2) sequential elements in communication. This perspective is primarily linear, suggesting that communication is like a line from point A to point B.

The transmissional perspective also highlights the elements that must occur sequentially for transmission to occur. In this view, communication is "the science and technology by which information is collected from an originating source, transformed into electrical currents or fields, transmitted over electrical networks or through space to another point, and converted into a form suitable for interpretation by a receiver."[2] The transmissional process can be diagrammed as in Figure 1.1.

The Interactional Perspective

Without abandoning the essential features of the previous two perspectives, the **interactional perspective** widens our view to capture a more nearly complete picture of communication. The first two perspectives stress the cause-to-effect, source-to-receiver aspects of communication. The interactional framework stresses the two-way, back-and-forth nature of communication, focusing on reciprocal response and interdependence.

Reciprocal response refers to the fact that two communicators respond to one another. In other words, communication is a two-way process in which communicators both send and receive. Even when

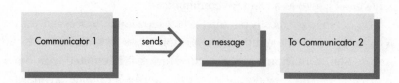

Figure 1.1
Transmissional model.

one person does most of the talking, the other provides nonverbal feedback. Thus, the communicative act "denotes a reciprocal social relationship between a sender and a human receiver."[3]

Communicators constantly give and take feedback. The process rarely ends with the reception of a simple message. Feedback tells communicators whether they are understood, whether they are believed, and whether they have captured the interest of the other communicator. Communicators constantly adjust their words and actions to feedback from the other person.

People in interaction are interdependent—the actions of one are determined partially by the actions of the other. In this regard, communication is like a ping-pong match. When one player hits the ball, the other will draw back and move the paddle into place. A slight letdown by one may elicit a hard drive into the opposite corner from the other. The interactional perspective is illustrated by the simple model shown in Figure 1.2.

These three perspectives are not contradictory but complementary. Each brings a different aspect of communication into focus, and together they define communication as a process of message sending and receiving in which individuals respond to and affect one another. Still, we believe that even this complementary view is not adequate to capture the most interesting aspects of communication. For that we turn to the fourth perspective.

A FOURTH APPROACH: THE TRANSACTIONAL PERSPECTIVE

We believe that the fullest approach to communication is the **transactional perspective**, which highlights the dynamic, interrelated nature of the feelings, meanings, behavior, and situations that enter into communication. As M. P. Anderson has defined it, communication is "the process by which we understand others and in turn endeavor to

Figure 1.2
Interactional model.

be understood by them. It is dynamic, constantly changing and shifting in response to the total situation."[4] The transactional perspective emphasizes three important aspects of communication: context, process, and function.

Context

Communication occurs in **context**. Just as you cannot understand how a word is used out of context, you cannot fully understand a communication event without knowing when, where, and under what circumstances it occurred. "I used to be terribly critical of how parents deal with their children," one parent admitted. "But now that I have kids of my own, I understand how it is. People have no right to criticize unless they know the whole situation." This parent came to realize the importance of context in communication. What people say and do in communication with others is always affected by a number of contextual factors, including history, the sociocultural situation, the physical setting, and the psychological context.

History. Every communication event has a history. Your communication at any moment is always affected by your previous experiences. In turn, every communication event adds to the backdrop for future interactions. How you respond to a television commercial, for instance, depends on whether you have seen it before, whether you have used the product, your feelings about the product, the opinions of your friends about the product, and a host of other feelings and perceptions from your experience.

Sociocultural Situation. Every act of communication also occurs in a social and cultural situation. A **culture** is a large community that shares common beliefs, values, and norms. Anthropologists frequently contrast the ways in which people from different cultures interact. People from Arab cultures, for example, tend to stand very close when they talk and even savor each other's odors. Americans, on the other hand, stand or sit at a distance and do everything possible to avoid body odors.

All communication is governed by such subtle rules. Some rules relate to how people use language; others govern nonverbal behavior. These rules can vary from one social situation to another. For example,

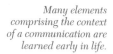

Many elements comprising the context of a communication are learned early in life.

a secretary who had worked for the same man for many years never hesitated to call him "George" outside the office but felt more comfortable using "Mr. Smith" during business hours.

Physical Setting. Communication is affected by people's surroundings, and people manipulate surroundings and objects to suit their communication needs. Studies show, for example, that a circular seating pattern elicits more discussion in a classroom than does a straight-row arrangement. When an office worker's desk is placed so that it faces the door, it is easier for the worker to see people as they enter. But it also sets up an authority barrier between the worker and others.

We authors had our own experience with the negative effects of a physical setting when we presented a seminar for management personnel in a local hotel. When we arrived, we were shocked to find that our setting was an old bar. Besides being long and narrow, the room was hot, crowded, and dark. We disappointedly saw our many hours of preparation go down the drain because the poor physical setting overshadowed our carefully designed program.

Psychological Context. Your psychological context is the frame through which you view what is going on in a situation.[5] It is the reference point by which you understand your experience—the mental categories you employ when deciding what something means and how to act.

The communicator's psychological context consists of those aspects of context (history, the sociocultural background, and the physical setting) most relevant to the communicator in a situation. Because it is the focal point of context, the psychological context is crucial to how events are understood.

Communicators understand and respond to messages from within a psychological context that makes it possible to understand and create messages. People's messages, consisting of words and actions, in turn reinforce the psychological context. If someone comes up and socks you on the arm, what do you do? It depends on how you interpret the action. Within the psychological context of a long-term positive relationship in which the hitting was done many times in fun, you will interpret the hit as play, and you will probably hit back. If the hit comes from a stranger on a dark street, your interpretation will be entirely different, and you will probably fight or run.

People usually interpret events easily. Events are coherent when you can understand them. Sometimes, however, you do not readily understand what is being said or done because you do not have a sufficiently clear psychological context. At these times, coherence is lacking. Everyone has seen situations in which one person seemed to find an event coherent while another did not. It happens all the time.

Because different communicators can have different psychological contexts, communication can fail. For one communicator, the history of the relationship may determine the meaning of a statement. For another, cultural values may be most important. One communicator may understand an event in terms of a personal goal, while another communicator may understand the same event in terms of something entirely different.

Examples of differing psychological contexts are frequent in male-female communication.[6] Sometimes a woman will share a problem or difficulty with a man, and he immediately will advise her on what to do about it. This common exchange often ends in hard feelings when the couple has differing psychological contexts. If the woman's main context is the relationship, she will want sympathy and support, not advice. She will be frustrated because he did not give her the quiet attention and time she wanted, and he will be frustrated because she did not appreciate his intelligent suggestions.

On the other hand, communication often succeeds precisely because the communicators do share a common set of meanings. People's psychological contexts are not something they work out privately by themselves. Psychological contexts are created socially through communication. Husbands and wives see some things differently, but they also come to see many things in similar ways. Parents and adolescents are often at odds, only to discover after the children grow up that they shared more than they realized. Good public speakers, professional writers, and media producers are successful because they take the psychological contexts of their audiences into account.

Communicators' psychological contexts are not static but are constantly changing. Your point of reference can change; when it does, your meanings will change too. You will act differently at different times because your psychological context changes. The same woman who wants her partner to listen sympathetically at one time may want him to provide advice at another. The same man who is so quick to solve his partner's problem at one time may prefer just to provide comfort and support at another. Constantly changing contexts are a sign that communication is a process.

Process

The third aspect of the transactional view is **process**. In talking of communication, it is sometimes necessary to treat it as an object. But it is not an object. Communication is a process, implying change, relatedness of events, simultaneous action, and social construction.[7]

Change. As a process, communication is a dynamic set of occurrences that never repeat themselves in exactly the same way. Communication events occur as a continuous flow through time. Each feeling, act, or event leads to another. As the old saying goes, you can never step in the same river twice.

Consider the following scenario: Tired from a long day of classes and work, you flop into your easy chair, determined to do nothing. In a few moments you feel, ever so slightly, a creeping boredom. You reach over to the table beside you and pick up the newspaper. Too exhausted to concentrate on serious news reports, you flip the pages, glancing at pictures and ads. Suddenly you spot the television listings. Yes, that's exactly what you want right now—a little passive viewing. You turn on the television and sit back. With your remote control, you flip through the channels. After a few minutes, a small child on the screen screeches, "I got a Nintendo for Christmas!" You mutter, "I'm sure tired of that stupid commercial." Then your roommate calls. Time for dinner. As you sit down to eat, you comment, "By the way, we're nearly out of toothpaste."

Relatedness. We could analyze the above scene by isolating the kind of day that made you tired, which newspaper you read, the television commercial, your interaction with your roommate, or the connection between food and toothpaste. In reality, however, these events form an inseparable flow of communication events. Thus, process also involves a relationship among events. What you think, feel, and do at any moment is related to what went on before and what you expect to happen in the future. What occurred in our example was not a string of isolated events but a series of interconnected ones.

One of the most dramatic scenes in recent history occurred when the former Soviet Union fell apart in 1991. Millions of people around the world sat in amazement as a staggering series of events unfolded. Each revelation seemed more dramatic than the last. As the days progressed, television viewers saw the spinning of a large web, each strand of which was connected intricately to every other. None of the communication events of the Soviet breakup could be interpreted adequately without a view of the whole, and the consequences are still unclear several years later, at the time of this writing.

Simultaneous Action. Process involves simultaneous action. In the communication process, people respond to one another at the same time. Failure to recognize this fact is one of the important omissions of the individualistic and transmissional perspectives. A public speaker, for example, simultaneously creates a message and interprets the behavior of audience members. Thus two or more people engaged in communication should be viewed as a unit.

Social Construction. In the transactional perspective, communication is never a solitary act. It is always something that people do together.[8] It is therefore social, but it is not just a social tool. It involves more than transferring information from one mind to another. In a transaction something is created or accomplished by the participants: a new meaning is created through **social construction**.

The most fundamental accomplishment of communication is the creation of meaning. How human beings understand their world depends upon the meanings of language and nonverbal behavior developed through interaction among participants. Children come to understand the things around them in terms of the vocabulary learned in interaction with adults and other children. A group of friends or work associates use speech to create a set of understandings about the things they have in common. Churches, schools, and organizations create meanings through communication. Even in society at large, people's interaction with the media determines what is believed to be real and significant in their lives. The creation of meaning, then, is one of the chief functions of communication.

Function

The transactional perspective recognizes that communication is a means to important personal and social states—in other words, it is functional. Communication does not simply happen; it leads to other ends. It is instrumental in making people what they are: thinking, social beings.[9] Communication has four broad and interrelated functions.

Creating Meaning. The first function, which is basic to all the others, is that communication creates and maintains symbol systems. How do symbols come into being, and how do they come to have special importance in certain situations? Symbols, both verbal and nonverbal, are created by people in the course of interacting. They are validated, sustained, and modified through communication. Through transaction, symbols come to take on common meanings for the people using them. These meanings are developed out of the actual give-and-take of everyday communication.

Symbol systems must develop and must be sustained on two levels. First, a group must create and sustain its own symbol system in order to survive as a group; then the individual, in order to become a member of the group, must internalize the group's symbols and meanings. In other words, the symbol system has a life both in the group and in the person,

The flag is a prime example of a symbol.

and only through communication does the symbol system live on. College students are a perfect example of this phenomenon. A fascinating dictionary of college slang, developed at the University of Kansas, contains sixty words for getting drunk and about the same number for sex, beautiful woman (or man), and good experiences.[10] Students in California recognize many of these terms, but they have never heard of others, and they can probably come up with words the Kansas students have not heard.

Linking the Person and Environment. Most animals confront the world directly, without conceptualizing or questioning, but human beings cannot do that. People are symbol-using beings, and their total experience is filtered through symbolic screens. What people perceive and how they judge their perceptions are determined by the meanings of the symbols they have come to understand in their interactions with others. Objects are not merely objects, because people always see them in terms of how they are named or symbolized. Thus our understanding of things—our link with the environment—is achieved by communication.

In different times and cultures such diverse food items as ants, fish eyes, asparagus, and buffalo tongue have been symbolized as delicacies.

Just watch parents try to get a child to eat something new or different. They go to exceptional lengths to symbolize the food as tasty, desirable, socially acceptable—the *in* thing.

Facilitating Thought. The fact that humans are symbol-using beings is what enables them to think. People live in a world of actual things and events, but they also live in a thought world. Human beings are able to think their actions through. They can form concepts, plan, evaluate, and create. The philosopher René Descartes wrote that the singular power of human beings is that they think:

> I am, I exist—that is certain; but how long do I exist? For as long as I think. . . . But what then am I? A thinking being. What is a thinking being? It is a being which doubts, which understands, which conceives, which affirms, which denies, which wills, which rejects, which imagines also, and which perceives.[11]

Cognitive psychologists have studied human thought in some detail.[12] Although the process of thinking is not entirely understood, it seems clear that people understand the world in terms of certain categories. Where do these categories come from? Some may derive from a common human experience across cultures, but most are cultural and learned, developed through communication.

Regulating Behavior. How people act, feel, and think is influenced by their communication with others. Children's behavior is largely directed by others. When children behave in accordance with the values and norms of society, they take these values and norms into themselves and gradually come to regulate their own behavior. Finally, when they learn the ways in which social regulation occurs, they become able to influence others.

This is not meant to imply that people always do what they are told; nor do all people behave in the same way. But people do behave in accordance with the meanings and symbols learned in their reference groups. Whatever order and stability exist in society are functions of the "rules" that arise in social interaction. Leslie White put it this way:

Without speech we would have no political, economic, ecclesiastic, or military organization; no codes of ethics; no laws, no science, theology, or literature; no games or music. . . . Rituals and ceremonial paraphernalia would be meaningless without articulate speech. . . . In short, without symbolic communication in some form, we would have no culture.[13]

There is a dark side to the regulative function of communication. The rules and meanings that come to seem normal and right promote the interests of certain groups over other groups. For example, it seems absolutely fair to stand in line to get tickets to a show. This rule, commonly used to regulate certain crowd behavior, has longstanding validity in our society. But when you think about it, some people are privileged by this rule. Those who have time to get there earlier and stand in line longer will get tickets. Those who have access to transportation will get to the line more easily than those who do not. People who are physically fit can stand in lines more easily than people who are disabled.[14] No rule allows the interests of all groups to be met equally, and people do need to realize that the regulative function of communication is not neutral and value free.

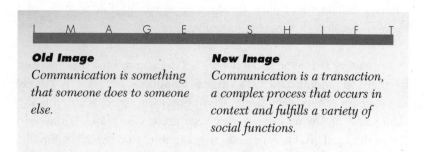

I M A G E   S H I F T

Old Image
Communication is something that someone does to someone else.

New Image
Communication is a transaction, a complex process that occurs in context and fulfills a variety of social functions.

Having set the stage for understanding communication and improving competence, we can now become more specific. The remainder of Part I discusses five basic elements common to all communication: coding, meaning, thinking, information, and persuasion. Some of this material may seem too abstract at first, but we think you will quickly see that these core concepts have important practical applications. As you read, we hope that you will supply examples from your own life to supplement our examples. We are certain that an understanding of these core concepts will serve you well in a variety of communication situations.

In Part II we deal with practical communication settings, including dyadic, group, public, and mass communication. Using our transactional perspective, we point out the commonalities and differences among these contexts. These chapters include practical information to guide your communication with others.

SUMMARY

Communication is a vital binding force in social life, and successful participation demands competent communication. People can become better communicators by using theory, analysis, and practice to enhance their understanding, sensitivity, skill, and responsibility. Communication can be examined from a variety of perspectives. In this chapter we outlined four. The behavioristic perspective stresses response and effect. The transmissional perspective stresses transmission and sequence. The interactional perspective stresses mutual response. Our preferred perspective is transactional, which conceives of communication as a complex process of related events occurring in context.

2 Basic Elements: Language and Nonverbal Communication

I n Dyirbal, an Australian aboriginal language, all objects of experience are classified into one of four groups: (1) human males and animals; (2) human females, water, fire, and fighting; (3) nonflesh food; and (4) everything else.[1] The Dyirbal speaker must precede every noun with its correct classifier. This may seem like a curious way to organize a language, yet every language is in fact a group of codes that classify experience.

Coding, in the form of verbal language and nonverbal signs, is the raw material of communication. Human languages and other codes are rich in variation and meaning, and we adjust and adapt our verbal and nonverbal signals as we move from one setting to another. One of the most important themes of this book is the need to be sensitive to the signs, symbols, and codes of our own and other cultural groups and to take variations in meaning into account when we communicate with others.

THE CODING PROCESS

People communicate by creating **messages** composed of **signs**.[2] The process of using signs to create and understand messages is called **coding**. This word probably brings to mind military intelligence and secret exchanges. Actually, that specialized use of coding is a good illustration of what happens more casually in everyday communication. People **encode** messages by using a commonly understood code, enabling others to **decode** and understand the message. This process, normally taken for granted, comes to your attention when you encounter someone who does not use your familiar code of English. If you have not had this experience, try to get directions from a stranger in a non-English speaking country.

In this chapter we will discuss the nature of the coding process. Then we will move to the two broad types of codes used in human communication: verbal and nonverbal codes. Above all it is important to keep in mind that messages consist of a rich variety of interrelated signs that in actual practice cannot be separated.

Communication codes are so subtle and pervasive that humans cannot escape them. Symbols and codes are part of the very fabric of human life, as noted by Gerard Egan:

One does not listen with just his ears: he listens with his eyes and with his sense of touch, he listens by becoming aware of the feelings and emotions that arise within himself because of his contact with others . . . he listens with his mind, his heart, and his imagination. He listens to the words of others, but he also listens to the messages that are buried in the words or encoded in all the cues that surround the words . . . he listens to the voice, the demeanor, the vocabulary, and the gestures of the other . . . or to the context, the verbal messages, the linguistic patterns, and the bodily movements of the other. He listens to the sounds and to the silences.[3]

In short, "you cannot not communicate."[4] Now let us begin to unravel this tangled ball of string, the coding process.

Signs, Symbols, and Discourse: The Elements of Coding

People proceed through life constantly reacting to stimuli. **Stimuli** consist of all the events in one's body and in the environment that can be sensed—seen, heard, felt, tasted, or smelled. You awake in the morning and hear the patter of feet in the hallway, the shower running. When you push the covers back, you feel a rush of cool air over your warm skin and detect a little ache in your left shoulder. You turn on the light but must quickly shut your eyes again to avoid the brightness. At this moment you are uncomfortably aware of the flood of sensation.

Certain stimuli come to have special importance as signs. **Signs** are stimuli that are used to represent or signify something other than themselves. The pain in the man's shoulder when he gets up in the morning may be nothing more than a passing discomfort, but if he says, "Lousy bed!" he has probably taken the pain as a sign of a too-soft mattress. We human beings have a huge capacity for using signs, and we operate with signs most of the time. We react to some signs automatically without thought, like stopping at a red light, but the most important signs for communication are more complex.

Symbols are special signs that bring concepts to mind. Symbols are therefore special tools of thought and communication. We ponder them, manipulate them, and respond to them in complex and often unpredictable ways. For human beings, reality is mediated through symbols. How a person sees an object, event, or condition is literally shaped by the way in which that person has symbolized it.

Eating can serve as an example. Most animals use food simply to satisfy hunger, but we human beings ritualize eating by treating it symbolically. We enjoy the aesthetic value of a meal and the social aura of eating. For most people, eating is much more than simply abating hunger.

Everyone recognizes that this symbol indicates special arrangements for people in wheelchairs—in this case a reserved parking space.

Commonly understood significant symbols are especially important in transacting meanings during the process of communication. **Discourse** consists of sets of interrelated signs used by communicators to exchange messages. A speech is discourse; so is a memo. Discourse may be complex and long or simple and fleeting.[5]

At this point it is important to realize that there is never just a single message passed from one person to another, for no two communicators will ever tune into exactly the same cues. So, for example, if you were talking to a friend, at least two messages would exist—the one you intended and the one your friend received.

Take the example of an instructor who returned to her office exasperated. A student had confronted her in the hallway, accusing her of putting him down in class. "I don't know what I did," she later confided honestly to a friend. Apparently the student had picked up on a certain behavior of the instructor—her tone of voice, perhaps—and took it as a message.

This idea of multiple messages will become very important later in the book when we seek to explain why communication sometimes fails.

Planned, Spontaneous, and Unintentional Coding

Coding can occur on a number of levels. Sometimes people use codes quite purposefully, to express an idea to another person or audience. This is **planned coding**. You use planned coding whenever you know you want to say something, verbally or nonverbally, and you find the right symbols with which to do so. You see a friend and wave. You get a letter from your dad and sit down to write back. You have a speech assignment coming up and you begin to plan.

But communication is not limited to planned coding. Sometimes we express feelings with **spontaneous coding**. This kind of communication is conscious but unplanned. When you see your daughter come in the front door with your new grandson, you beam with delight. Or you are angry with your roommate and walk to the other side of the room. Or your spouse gives you a birthday present, and when you open it you say, "Wow!"

In each of these examples you are very much aware of a feeling, and you let it be known. Often, however, people become aware of feelings through another person's unconscious actions. This happens when other people "read" our behaviors as indicators of some state: they interpret eye contact as attentiveness, blushing as embarrassment, or trembling hands as nervousness. This is called **symptomatic coding** because receivers take certain signs as symptoms of something else. Just as a physician becomes informed of a heart condition by listening with a stethoscope, and a meteorologist predicts rain from a combination of atmospheric developments, you look for symptoms in other people. Such communication is unplanned and unconscious, and it is often mistaken. When you frown, for example, your co-worker might read the expression—correctly or incorrectly—as disapproval.

Virtually all communication scholars agree that planned and spontaneous coding that is interpreted by at least one other person constitutes communication, but there is quite a controversy about whether symptomatic coding is communication or not.[6] The problem arises because it is often impossible to tell the difference between spontaneous and symptomatic coding. Whether or not it is technically communication, symptomatic coding certainly should be considered in a basic communication course.

Body movement serves as a nonverbal code.

Communication and Metacommunication

Every communication occurs on two simultaneous levels.[7] On one level we provide direct information to another person about whatever we are discussing. This is the **content level** of the transaction. It is normally coded verbally by the use of language, although nonverbal signs may also be used to support or expand upon the verbal message. Less obvious is the **metalevel**, where we "comment" upon or provide information about the transaction itself. On the metalevel, we structure our relationship, reveal our perceptions of one another, guide or regulate our conversation, and provide a host of other relational cues. **Metacommunication** may be verbal, but more often it is nonverbal, subtle, and located out of immediate awareness.

Consider the following example. A father and daughter are together in the park. The little girl falls and scrapes her arm. The father says, "Don't worry; Daddy's coming." On the content level, the message is simple: "Here I come." But a number of metalevel messages might be observed in his tone of voice, facial expression, or bodily movement. On the relationship level he might be saying, "You klutzy kid!" or "I'm annoyed because I was doing something else" or "You're dependent; I'm dominant" or "That happened to me once, and I can feel the pain, too."

This notion of two levels of communication reinforces an important fact about symbolic interaction: We can symbolize symbols, talk about talk, comment on communication. And we do this all the time. Watch people in public and note how they comment nonverbally on their communication behavior.

Metacommunication takes a variety of interesting forms. We are all intuitively aware of the importance of *creating impressions*. Because we perceive selectively, impressions create a screen through which we filter subsequent data about another person. If an impression tells us that the other person is, say, sloppy, carefree, or diligent, we will see this trait more readily when the person next exhibits it. In preparing for a job interview, a first date, or a first meeting with a loved one's family, it is a good idea to carefully plan how the various nonverbal codes will enhance the first impression you make. Similarly, students who participate in class early in the term and who do well on the first assignments often receive better grades than do students who create unfavorable first impressions with their instructors.

Communicating emotions is one of the primary functions of nonverbal codes, especially through facial expression and voice. At a recent card party one young woman was feeling pretty low, and her poor play only contributed to her depression. Several times during the evening her partner said, "Oh, come on; smile, partner." But try though she did, she simply could not stop communicating her negative feelings through the nonverbal codes. Although facial expression communicates much, people's general posture, hand motions, and other body movements create a total context that raises the accuracy with which communicators judge others' emotional state. Eye behavior also contributes to this process, but for practical purposes it is the total physical context, of which the face and eyes are only a part, that is important.

Codes are used also to *communicate the nature of the interpersonal relationship*. We can communicate such feelings as attraction and liking. Indeed, we seem to have a greater degree of nonverbal contact with people to whom we are positively attracted than with those who leave us cold. Lovers who can't take their eyes (or keep their hands) off each other are extreme examples of this. Moreover, we may touch or look more at people toward whom we have negative feelings than those toward whom we are indifferent. We may stare people down, just to make them feel uncomfortable. In any case, a high level of nonverbal interaction usually indicates a heightened level of involvement between two people, which is usually positive but on occasion may reflect animosity.

We can also *communicate credibility, status, and role*. For example, in some social situations high-status people gaze less than lower-status people do. The use of space frequently communicates the nature of an interpersonal relationship in terms of status and role. Thus, the best office space is usually reserved for high-status people in an organization, and preferred seating at a public event is frequently reserved for VIPs.

Various codes also can serve to *regulate interaction*. Regulators are nonverbal cues that adjust or maintain the communication flow among people. Many of us learned as children in school to wait our turn to speak and perhaps even to raise our hand when we wanted to say something. As we matured and moved into less formal situations, we learned more subtle ways to regulate the flow of conversation. Sometimes, without realizing it (but frequently by intention), we send nonverbal signals that say, "Yes, get on with it," "I am interested; keep going," or "Hey, can't I get a word in edgewise?"

Nonverbal codes can function to *augment the verbal code*. They can *repeat* what is said verbally, *substitute* for a word or phrase, *complement* what is being said, *emphasize* the verbal message, or *contradict* the verbal message. You probably know people who would not be able to talk if you held their hands still. They may also punctuate their conversation with active head movements or may add emphasis by slapping their knees or banging their fists on the table. In such cases the integration of verbal and nonverbal codes produces emphasis, redundancy, or repetition.

Having explored the coding process in some detail, let us now turn our attention to the two broad types of codes: verbal and nonverbal.

VERBAL CODING: LANGUAGE

One of our most important assets as human beings is the ability to use language. We have the physical equipment for producing a wide range of finely discriminated speech sounds, and we are able to combine these sounds into novel sentences, each with a unique meaning. Our ability to use language is shaped by both nature and nurture. We are born with a large cerebral cortex, ripe for learning speech. All spoken languages have certain natural features, and the processes of generating and understanding speech are universal human phenomena. At the same time, we grow up in a language community, and the speech we learn within a culture greatly affects our definition of reality.

Language is primarily a speech process. In its natural form, language is produced as particular sounds are combined into increasingly complex units of meaning, from sound to word to sentence. Writing is just an elaborate method of recording what originates in speech.

Originally grammar was seen as a list of prescriptions that speakers and writers should use to produce "proper" sentences. Today the subject is approached differently. We now understand **grammar** to be the important mental process through which the speakers of a language generate and understand sentences. The members of a culture naturally acquire their language's rules of grammar.

Humans are born into language-using cultures. Our reality is mediated by symbols, and we learn the meanings of the objects and conditions around us by interacting symbolically within our social groups. In short, our relation to the world is closely connected to language. The anthropologist Edward Sapir wrote:

> The fact of the matter is that the "real world" is to a large extent unconsciously built up on the language habits of the group.... We see

and hear and otherwise experience what we do because the language habits of our community predispose certain choices of interpretation."[8]

Are people forced to think and behave in certain ways because of their language, or are cultural patterns of thought and behavior reflected in language? This is a chicken-and-egg question. But obviously the relationship between thought and language is such that each affects the other. Clearly, various cultures do think and behave differently, and a culture's patterns definitely relate to its language.

As certain things become more important in the life of a culture, more words are used to allow finer discrimination. English has only a few words for horse, but Arabic contains many terms denoting fine differences. Eskimos have several words for snow, enabling them to think about and discriminate it more elaborately. The Trobrianders, a South Seas culture, have a large number of words denoting various types and qualities of yams, an important dietary staple.[9]

People tend to think that language is objective and has a one-to-one correspondence with reality. But reality is actually defined in terms of the language used in the culture. There are important differences between the reality of one culture and that of another. People need to be very careful in assuming that their linguistic categories are universally accepted, and they need to be conscious of the subtle ways in which words affect perceptions and thoughts.

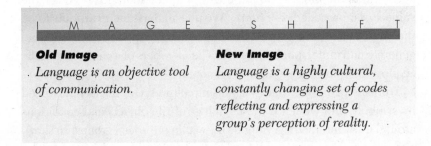

IMAGE SHIFT

Old Image
Language is an objective tool of communication.

New Image
Language is a highly cultural, constantly changing set of codes reflecting and expressing a group's perception of reality.

NONVERBAL CODING

Most Japanese, including those dealing with the public in the larger cities of Japan, cannot speak English, and few Americans can speak Japanese. While traveling in Japan, one of the authors and his wife used translation cards with simple requests on one side and a Japanese translation on the other. They were also helped by nonverbal codes. One morning they attempted to order a breakfast of ham and eggs nonverbally. After much gesticulation, they finally received an egg sandwich. Not too bad. Asking directions was easier: the travelers could point to their tickets or an address, and the respondent could indicate the right direction. Sometimes a Japanese would escort them to the correct train or other destination. Thus, despite their inability to communicate verbally, and the inevitable cultural differences in nonverbal codes, the travelers were able to function quite well using nonverbal communication.

This section discusses nonverbal communication in some detail. You have probably encountered the term before and know intuitively what it is. If the term is unfamiliar to you, perhaps you have heard the synonym *body language*. No definition of nonverbal communication is universally accepted, because verbal and nonverbal coding are so difficult to separate. The best way to understand the distinction is to examine some of the codes commonly studied as "nonverbal," which we will do in this section.[10]

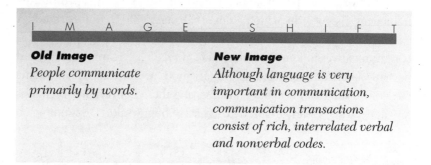

I   M   A   G   E   S   H   I   F   T

Old Image
People communicate primarily by words.

New Image
Although language is very important in communication, communication transactions consist of rich, interrelated verbal and nonverbal codes.

Nonverbal codes are deeply rooted in culture. Different cultures have different expectations or norms for nonverbal behavior. As you move from one cultural setting to another, you will notice that people may have some very different notions from yours regarding how close you should stand when talking to someone. You will also find different notions of time. Some cultures would consider it an insult not to be prompt for an appointment, while others would consider it good manners to be an hour late. Cultures also differ in the way they interpret such cues as distance, touching, and odors. A complimentary gesture in one culture may be obscene in another, and vocal inflections elicit all sorts of different meanings in different cultural settings. A student of ours, Shannon Speier, produced a videotape entitled "Body Talk," in which she had members of various cultures demonstrate gestures that have different meanings in their respective cultures. She found, for example, a variety of obscene gestures, and she found too that certain obscene gestures in one culture can be polite greetings in another.

In Japan, Greece, Ireland, Jordan, Germany, Morocco, and elsewhere, however, some nonverbal coding cuts across cultures and can in fact be extremely useful in multicultural communication contexts. Such facial expressions as the eyebrow lift, smile, or frown will be understood in most cultures. Certain descriptive gestures can also be used effectively across many cultures.

As in the case of verbal codes, nonverbal communication is also significantly influenced by contextual factors. A pat on the back may be interpreted differently depending on whether it follows the achievement of a difficult task or a tragic event in a person's life. The same gesture may be perceived as friendly when coming from a friendly source or derogatory when coming from an unfriendly one. Furthermore, the psychological state of the receiver profoundly influences the way in which nonverbal cues will be interpreted. A gesture or facial expression that may be both appropriate and communicative in one social situation may be inappropriate and perhaps a barrier to communication in another. For example, students sometimes smile or even laugh in class, and these nonverbal expressions are not always clearly related to what is being said. Depending on

Gestures and visual aids can help bridge language barriers.

how a teacher feels that day, or on past events with those students in that class, the teacher sometimes wonders if they are laughing with him or at him.

Although nonverbal codes can be patterned in several ways, we have chosen to divide them into five major categories: (1) the use of bodily activity, (2) the use of voice, (3) the use of objects, (4) the use of space, and (5) the use of time.

The Body

Physical behavior of the body can produce visual cues that can be categorized in a number of ways. For practical purposes, we will break down performance codes into body movement, facial expressions, and physical appearance.

Body Movement. As a means of coding communicative messages, body activity (**kinesics**) is more varied and adaptable than we may realize at first. Human beings may be able to produce as many as seven hundred thousand different physical signs, with perhaps as many as five thousand hand gestures.[11] Several years ago one of the authors participated in an archeological excavation in Petra, Jordan, and was responsible for supervising several young Bedouin men as they shoveled dirt and moved some huge stones that had fallen from large stone arches. How does someone who speaks only English give directions to a crew that speaks only Arabic? And how do crew members respond? The would-be communicators used expansive gestures, shoulder shrugs, and head nods, counted on their fingers, painted pictures in the air, and mimed actions. It wasn't a perfect system, but it worked.

Facial Expression. Scholars have long been interested how facial expression affects human communication. Facial expression refers to movements or combinations of movements of the face that elicit meanings. A friendly smile can brighten one's day; another's tears can touch one's heart.

Most research has focused on the relationship between facial expression and the communication of emotional states. As a consequence, facial expression is frequently referred to in the literature as **affect display**, or display of emotion.

Body movement serves as a nonverbal code.

Prior exposure to a person's face has a significant influence on the way other people evaluate his or her emotional states. In a sense, prior exposure serves us as an "anchor" or a basis of comparison for judging another person's affective condition. A person who is typically bright and smiling can seem fairly glum with the same half-smile that would make a somber person appear ecstatic.

The context in which an affect display occurs also influences the attribution of meaning. Since most expressions of emotions represent combinations, or blends, of various feelings, the context helps people evaluate the facial code more accurately. The presence of another person, the background or scene, even the entire body posture of the person being observed can also influence the overall transaction.

In addition to prior exposure and context, sensitivity to expressions affects judgment of them. Particular types of people tend to be more effective judges of facial expression than others, and some people seem to react more discriminatingly to facial expressions. As a result of a variety of learning experiences, these people seem to be especially aware of facial cues to the emotions others are experiencing.

Eye Behavior. An important means of interpreting facial expression is by observing *eye behavior*. Most people are vaguely aware that the eyes are a particularly communicative part of the anatomy. A wink may be an invitation or at least a positive reaction, and a narrowing of both eyes into a squint may express anger or at least rejection. Some people communicate a general warmth by a twinkle in their eyes (or coolness by a lack of it). Most people tend to mistrust a person whose eyes appear to be too shifty, or who won't look them in the eye. The general amount and length of mutual gaze may not only be a reflection of a positive communication transaction but may contribute to it.

Like much nonverbal communication behavior, eye contact is culture bound. In certain cultures within the United States, direct eye contact can imply politeness and assertiveness. In other cultures, such as Japan, it can be interpreted as intrusive and rude in many contexts.

Physical Appearance. Our culture places a high value on physical attractiveness. Even at an early age, children seem to gravitate toward playmates who are attractive. In extreme situations, children ridicule those who are deformed or handicapped, and adults frequently avoid or reject them.

People tend to render quick initial judgments about other people's personalities on the basis of stereotypes related to body shape and size. As a general rule, people who are round, fat, and apparently soft (endomorphic) are assumed by typical observers to be contented, affable, generous, soft tempered, and so on. On the other hand, people who are tall, thin, and apparently fragile (ectomorphic) are thought to be anxious, meticulous, cool, and sensitive, as well as several other similar characteristics. None of these initial impressions may be correct, but the tendency to make such hasty judgments persists.

Finally, body odor seems to be an increasing preoccupation among Americans. Deodorant, soap, and fragrance manufacturers bombard us with advertisements that intensify our consciousness of this sensory mode. Have you ever been concentrating on some activity only to have an odor break into your consciousness and remind you of a person, place, or experience long forgotten? Like words, odors can symbolize certain messages for us—can elicit meanings and images from previous associations. The meaning and significance of body odor vary widely across cultures. As a rule Americans and Japanese seem to abhor the normal odor of the human body. Japanese eliminate it by extensive and luxurious bathing; Americans both bathe it away and spend considerable money to mask it with perfume and other artificial scents. In contrast, people from Mediterranean countries place a much higher attraction value on the natural odors of the body.

Voice

Most of us have had the experience of receiving a relatively severe reprimand couched in such gentle tones that we were able to continue to feel good about ourselves, despite the fact that something we did had been criticized. We may have also received mild criticism in a tone of voice so decisive or intense that it was unnecessarily (and perhaps unintentionally) destructive. In short, how people say something is as important as what they say. In fact, how something is said can modify what is said so significantly that it actually constitutes a message itself. Consider the following simple sentence:

> *I* like her.
> I *like* her.
> I like *her*.

Merely by stressing a different word, the speaker can change the entire meaning.

The human voice is a remarkable instrument that can be used to share meaning far beyond the potential of particular words. This code, frequently referred to as **paralanguage**, is usually defined as vocal cues other than words themselves that accompany spoken language. Vocal cues have both transmissional ingredients and pattern (transactional) properties (see Figure 2.1).

Transmissional Ingredients. The transmissional ingredients of vocal cues include the variable characteristics of the voice and articulation. Voice can vary in *pitch* (high or low), *rate* (speed), *volume* (loudness), and *quality* (uniqueness).

Figure 2.1
Elements of
paralanguage.

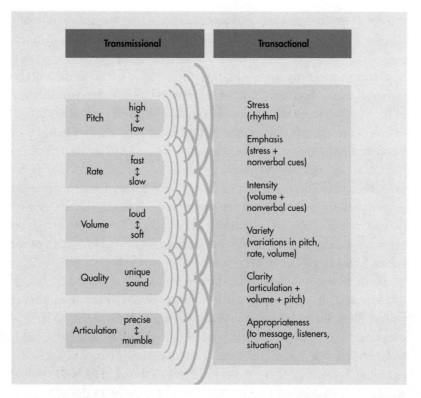

Articulation is the manner in which a person forms the sounds of speech. People with poor articulation—who mumble or slur their speech—can have difficulties in any communication context. Fortunately, articulation is particularly susceptible to improvement through guided practice. The tongue, lips, teeth, and palate can be trained to work in coordination to produce clear, precise speech sounds. For example, if a person has trouble clearly forming *s* or *t* sounds, rapid repetition of the word *statistics* can give the articulators the necessary practice to properly form those sounds. If a person has difficulty being understood or if his or her articulation tends to draw attention to itself, consultation with a speech therapist can provide the necessary professional guidance for practicing articulate speech.

Some people are concerned about cultural accents or regional dialects. We take the position that if one's speech is clearly understandable and conforms to an acceptable local norm, no effort should be made to change it. Notice how clear and acceptable are the articulation of Holly Hunter and Sean Connery, even though the accents are quite distinct.

Transactional Properties. Although the variable characteristics of the voice and articulation may constitute isolated vocal cues, their contribution to the vocal code usually occurs in combination with each other.

Emphasis is achieved by integrating vocal stress with gestures or facial expressions. For instance, an increase in volume combined with a reduction in rate, an emphatic gesture, and an appropriate facial expression will add emphasis to a word or phrase. One of the most common contributors to emphasis is a reduction in rate. In his declaration of war message in 1941, President Franklin Roosevelt achieved remarkable emphasis by combining a slow rate of speaking with other variable characteristics of his voice.

Another important characteristic of vocal cues is *intensity*. Although often associated with an increase in volume, it is really an interaction of volume with the other variable characteristics of the voice, as well as with other nonverbal cues. You can speak with intensity without shouting.

Greater intensity is frequently associated with public speaking contexts. If you listen to recordings of some of the most effective public speakers in recent history (Ronald Reagan, Martin Luther King Jr., Barbara Jordan), you will note that one characteristic that stands out most strikingly is the intensity with which they communicate their ideas. They appear to really care about what they are advocating. A person can use intensity to communicate care in interpersonal communication contexts as well.

One of the most fundamental characteristics of the voice is *variety*. Variety contributes to the variables of emphasis and intensity. If you have been talking vehemently, rapidly reducing your volume and rate to an intelligible whisper may result in greater emphasis. In addition, vocal variety seems to have communicative value by itself.

Also essential to effective communication is *clarity* of vocal cues. Although some writers have argued in favor of ambiguity in the verbal code in certain contexts, few argue that the vocal signal should not be clear. Most people have had the experience of not hearing what another person has said because that person spoke too softly or failed to articulate clearly. Perhaps you have even had the experience of sitting in a club where the music and conversation were so loud that all you could pick up from your conversation partners was the moving of their lips. On the other hand, good articulation and volume can compensate for some intervening noise. In any event, communication suffers when the signal is not clearly transmitted.

The final pattern characteristic of vocal cues is *appropriateness*. That is to say, your vocal cues should be appropriate to your own status and role, the expectations of your listeners, and the context or occasion. Loud talk at a somber occasion, careless articulation or mispronunciation when the listener expects better, or harsh vocal quality when the situation calls for a soothing message can all create difficulties.

Objects

When archaeologists dig for historical artifacts, they are searching for objects that reveal information about an ancient civilization's lifestyle and values as well as something about its interpersonal relationships. Similarly, **artifactual codes** are modern information-bearing objects.

A person's artifacts serve two general communicative functions. First, they create, with varying degrees of accuracy, a general image of the individual. We tend to make all sorts of judgments about people's character, personality values, and lifestyle on the basis of our observation of their use of dress, jewelry, and other objects. Furthermore, these artifacts can be used to code more specific messages. People can say to others, "You are important to me," "I am successful," "I am unavailable," "Being with me is fun," or a plethora of other meanings just by the way they display artifacts.

Perhaps the artifact most extensively used by individuals to code messages is *clothing*. Considerable research supports the notion that clothing is a significant factor in our initial judgment of strangers.

While vacationing some time ago, a college professor dressed down to very casual clothes and went blackberry picking with his children on the edge of the third hole of a golf course. The professor's hair was rather long, and he had neglected to shave that morning. He had been picking blackberries for only a few minutes when a resident of a luxurious home bordering the golf course came by and ordered the group off his "property," concluding, "You hippies go pick your own berries." The next day, dressed in sporting attire and playing golf near

Clothing and other artifacts code nonverbal messages.

the same place with his dignified-looking father, the "hippie" received a friendly wave from the same man.

Gifts can be another important means of communication. Before one of the authors visited Japan, he was warned to take several gifts. Almost everyone he met presented him with a gift, and the Japanese were immensely pleased when he was thoughtful enough to reciprocate, however modestly.

Although gift giving is somewhat less significant in the United States than in Japanese culture, the code is nonetheless an important one.

Have you ever given a peace offering to someone when you wanted to smooth over an argument? As with other nonverbal codes, the meaning of a gift can vary with the context, receiver, sender, and other components of the communication process. A dozen red roses to a friend of the opposite sex might facilitate not only your interpersonal communication but other aspects of your relationship as well. The same red roses to a friend of the same sex might have very different meanings attached to them. Depending on the context, a greeting card or a box of candy may communicate "I'm sorry," "I love you," "Can we get to know each other better?" "Congratulations," or "I care about you."

Decor, or the artifacts used to decorate a space, also has communication value. How often have you entered a room and experienced an immediate feeling of formality, comfort, success, confusion, warmth, or poverty? The style and arrangement of the furniture can create a mood and facilitate conversation. In addition, decor may create not only a communication context but a message itself. Almost every home and office communicates the interests, vocation, and even the temperament of the inhabitant.

In an even broader sense, a community, culture, or nation can also have artifacts that generate shared meanings. These are appropriately called *community artifacts*. Particular cities immediately come to mind when you see a picture of the Golden Gate Bridge, the Eiffel Tower, the Leaning Tower of Pisa, the Space Needle, or the Empire State Building. A huge twenty-by-forty-foot American flag erected adjacent to a freeway became a catalyzing symbol for a large group of conservative citizens in a small northern California town during the Persian Gulf War.

Religious communities also have their artifactual codes. In the years when Christians were suffering severe persecution, for example, members often communicated their identity by drawing either a cross or a fish in the dust of the road. Every religion has a variety of artifacts that carry great meaning for its community of believers.

Even business communities today communicate through the artifactual code. Most large corporations have a logo. Who cannot recognize a Mercedes Benz by its hood ornament or a Metro-Goldwyn-Mayer movie by the head of the roaring lion? And today much concern has been expressed about the graffiti of gangs in U.S. cities. As the Bloods and Crips mark their territory with very specific signs painted on walls and fences, certain concerned citizen groups paint over them to erase the evidence of gang activity in their neighborhoods.

Space

People can communicate through the manner with which they manipulate space. When communicators touch each other, when they choose to keep their distance or move closer to each other, and when they stake out territories, they communicate a variety of messages.

Touching. Ashley Montagu has stressed the importance of physical contact in the development of a normal human psyche. Furthermore, he has advocated that in the development of loving relationships, behaving as though one loves (that is, touching) is a way of learning to love.[12]

Touching is not only important to a sense of well-being but also serves as a significant code for communicating messages. Touching behavior and the meanings it helps people share vary, depending on the body part used in touching, the method of touching, the intensity of the touch, the receiver's perception of the communicator's intent, and the environmental and cultural context.

Meanings can differ with the location and type of touching. Slapping, shaking, and pinching could elicit a variety of meanings, depending on the context, but most people would consider being stroked more positive than being punched, and being embraced more positive than being kicked. The meaning of touch also varies considerably with intensity—or strength, length, and frequency.

The perceived intent of the touching person can also make a communicative difference. Although one would have to be a mind reader to determine the actual intent of a person's touch, people inevitably draw inferences about such intent. If a stranger brushes past you or accidentally touches you in public, you tend to ignore it. But if the same person seemed to touch you intentionally, you might react or perhaps overreact either positively or negatively. In familiar relationships various types of casual pats, pinches, strokes, and kisses may elicit very different kinds of responses, depending on whether the person touched perceives them as gestures of support, liking, acceptance, or seduction.

Personal Space. **Personal space** refers to the area around a person's body—the invisible, but very real, psychological buffer zone that people

carry around them. This space is like an expandable bubble, and it gets larger or smaller from one situation to another. In intimate settings, it may shrink all the way down to the skin, but in more formal situations it may expand way out to the edge of the room. When there is plenty of

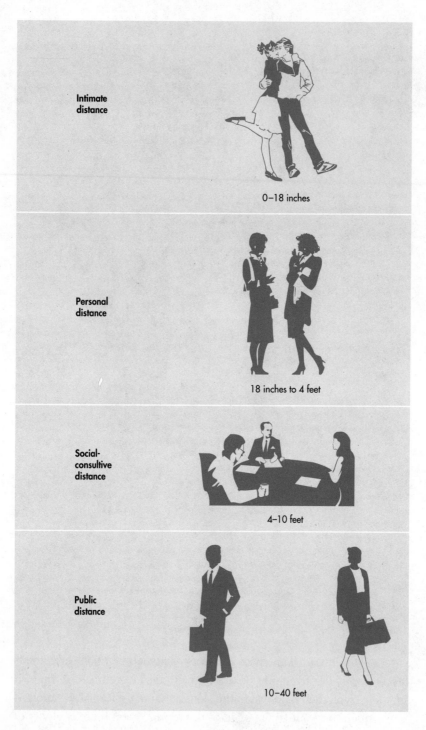

Intimate distance

0–18 inches

Personal distance

18 inches to 4 feet

Social-consultive distance

4–10 feet

Public distance

10–40 feet

Figure 2.2
Categories of personal space.

space, as in a large, empty hall, this bubble around the body may expand considerably, but in tiny, crowded places such as elevators, it will contract down to a fraction of an inch. The bubble usually extends farther in front of a person than behind, because people are more sensitive about approaches from the front than about those from the back.

Edward Hall has classified personal space into four categories: (1) intimate, (2) personal, (3) social-consultive, and (4) public.[13] Although these categories seem to be somewhat arbitrary divisions of a spectrum of distances, human communication behavior does appear to revolve around these or analogous distances (see Figure 2.2).

Hall has found that different cultures have widely different tolerances for personal distance. Within Anglo-American culture, for example, **intimate distance** is about zero to eighteen inches.

Personal distance in Anglo-American culture varies from eighteen inches to four feet. It includes that area in which two people barely have elbow room (but will not touch accidentally) and the distance over which one can just touch the other by reaching out. Personal distance is that at which most casual conversation and less formal interviews occur.

Within **social-consultive distance** in Anglo-American culture, people are situated approximately four to ten feet apart. It is bounded on one extreme by ultimate personal distance and, at the other, represents a space across which people are able to pass an object back and forth if they both stretch to do so. This is the distance at which most group communication occurs—small business meetings, committee meetings, and the like. Eight to nine feet also seems to be the distance at which two people must recognize each other's presence in a group, passing in a hall, or on the street.

Finally the **public distance** in Anglo-American culture ranges from ten feet to thirty or forty feet. It is the distance at which two communicators cannot touch each other or pass an object back and forth but can hear each other easily. Generally it is the distance at which most public meetings are conducted. Greetings can be exchanged, but the content of those greetings cannot be concealed from anyone who wishes to eavesdrop.

Measurements of intimate, personal, social, and public space vary considerably with different cultures. Substantial evidence suggests that in American, German, and Japanese cultures, for example, extended distance is more tolerable than in Italian or Arab cultures. That is to say, an American might judge a room full of people to be crowded, whereas an Arab might judge the same room to be spacious.

Territoriality. A special case of personal space, **territoriality** is the marking of one's ownership or possession of a space. Notice the clamor for reserved seat tickets to such events as the Super Bowl, a Grateful Dead concert, the World Series, or the NCAA basketball finals.

Our territory can change in various ways. In the case of the backyard of a private home, the territory is relatively long-term, but saving a seat in the cafeteria by putting a purse or coat on it reserves only a temporary occupancy. Territoriality can also change geographically, as when you are standing in line for movie tickets and someone cuts in front of you.

Territoriality is used as a spatial code in communication as an indication of openness (or lack thereof). If we are free or open with our territory, we may communicate acceptance, friendliness, or the idea that we are pushovers. If we are very protective of our territory, we may communicate an attitude of exclusiveness, hostility, indifference, or toughness. With the increase of crime in cities in the past several years, gated communities have become popular. These places resemble medieval castles: entire housing developments are

Even in public places such as airports, people stake out their temporary territories.

surrounded by high walls and have gated entries with guards. The message is clear: Keep out!

Time

A final nonverbal code is the temporal code. This code can be defined as the manipulation of time to formulate messages. What do you think when people show up an hour late for no apparent reason? You may feel that they are at best insensitive and at worst indifferent about your friendship. Conversely, one couple drove hundreds of miles to visit a friend but waited in their car for a half hour because they arrived before the agreed-upon time.

As in the case of dress, people transmit how important they consider a communication event, as well as certain personality characteristics, by the way they use time. Most Americans would not dream of being late (whatever that might mean in our culture) to a job interview or a meeting with the corporation president, but a certain amount of leeway might be acceptable in arriving for a very casual get-together with close friends.

As noted earlier in this chapter, different cultures have different senses of time. What might be considered insultingly late to a Dane might seem punctual to a Puerto Rican. Indeed, some cultures might not consider the concept of lateness insulting at all.

Thus, like all other aspects of coding, the use of temporal codes is highly cultural. For example, most cultures originating in Europe, such as the Anglo-American, think of time like a line, from past to present to future. Ursula Le Guin explains that our way of understanding time is not universally shared:

> We know where the future is. It's in front of us. Right? It lies before us—a great future lies before us—we stride forward confidently into it, every commencement, every election year. And we know where the past is. Behind us, right? So that we have to turn around to see it, and that interrupts our progress ever forward into the future, so we don't really much like to do it.
>
> It seems that the Quechua-speaking peoples of the Andes see all this rather differently. They figure that because the past is what you know, you can see it—it's in front of you, under your nose. This is a

mode of perception rather than action, of awareness rather than progress. Since they're quite as logical as we are, they say that the future lies behind—behind your back, over your shoulder. The future is what you *can't* see, unless you turn around and kind of snatch a glimpse. And then sometimes you wish you hadn't, because you've glimpsed what's sneaking up on you from behind. . . . So, as we drag the Andean peoples into our world of progress, pollution, soap operas, and satellites, they are coming in backwards—looking over their shoulders to find out where they're going.[14]

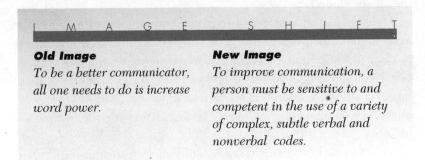

I   M   A   G   E   S   H   I   F   T

Old Image
To be a better communicator, all one needs to do is increase word power.

New Image
To improve communication, a person must be sensitive to and competent in the use of a variety of complex, subtle verbal and nonverbal codes.

PROBLEMS OF CODING

So far in this chapter we have been discussing the effective use of verbal and nonverbal coding. But what happens when communication is ineffective? People are very quick to label problems between societies or people as "communication problems." Although this approach is usually simplistic, we do think that miscommunication contributes significantly to many personal and societal problems. Let us examine some ways in which the misuse of coding contributes to problems in communication.

Inexpressiveness

Several years ago one of the authors was pruning shrubs in his backyard with less-than-gratifying results. As he snipped away awkwardly, an elderly neighbor who was a consummate gardener dropped by for a chat. She stood nearby with her arms crossed and then with a slight smile on her face said, "If my gardener pruned my shrubs like that, I'd fire him." The novice gardener broke into laughter, for he knew she meant well. After that, the relationship between these neighbors was always open and cordial, partly because they could speak their minds and seldom had to guess what the other was thinking. In contrast, many people are inexpressive, forcing others to guess their meaning. All too often, the guesses are wrong.

Inexpressiveness is the inability or unwillingness to code messages adequately to share meanings that need to be shared. It is evidenced in both verbal and nonverbal complexes. Some people are quiet; others are chatterboxes. Some people talk easily in small groups but say little in large groups and almost nothing in public meetings. We suspect that such differences are related to anxiety or to a perceived threat in the situation. In short, people behave according to the adage "What you don't say can't hurt you."

But inexpressiveness can harm all parties to communication, and it can harm relationships as well. How many parents and children neglect to say that they love each other? How many parents cannot find the words to communicate adequate sex information to their children— sometimes with disastrous results? Although the negative effects of inexpressiveness may be much more subtle and less immediate than the adverse effects of expressing ourselves, they are nonetheless serious.

The same is true of nonverbal codes. It is easy to guess the thoughts and feelings of some people; their posture, facial expressions, and body movements reflect what is on their minds. Other people are more difficult to read because their nonverbal codes are inexpressive. This form of inexpressiveness can also lead to misinterpretation and misunderstanding.

However, sheer quantity of expressiveness is not the desired goal. At times a poker face is the most appropriate response and in some situations may even constitute a message. Sometimes people can say too much. You need to be willing and able to express yourself in all the verbal and nonverbal codes whenever the communication situation calls for it and be able to restrain your coding when appropriate. Flexibility and appropriate use of coding are the keys to avoiding miscommunication.

Furthermore, it is important to remember that all communicators are both coding and decoding almost continuously. As you listen to another person's verbal message, you are usually coding a nonverbal message of your own. Miscommunication results either when people fail to express their response to a communicator or when they express an irrelevant or contradictory message. This happens every day. Your friend looks over your shoulder at someone else while you are talking; a small boy shrugs off his mother's touch; a student reads the newspaper or sleeps while the instructor is lecturing. Unless these messages are intended, the miscommunication can lead to impaired relationships. By being conscious of insufficient or inappropriate use of verbal and nonverbal codes, people can reduce miscommunication.

There are significant individual and cultural differences in the degree to which people rely on verbal versus nonverbal coding. Some cultures tend to require much explicit verbal explanation; others rely more on what is happening in the context.[15] **High-context cultures** like the Japanese use cues in the environment to determine what is happening and how to behave. Members of high context cultures are guided much more by who a person is than by what a person says. They decide what to do more on the basis of where they are than on what people tell them to do.

Low-context cultures like the Anglo-American require more verbal information to figure situations out. They are suspicious of intuition and "hidden" cues. Rather, they want to talk things out, get things clear, and make sure they understand what other people are trying to say.

The amount of verbal and nonverbal expressiveness required, then, is largely relative, depending upon the culture and participants. The amount of verbal and nonverbal expressiveness required depends upon the rules being used in the situation, and good communicators learn to adapt to these rules.

Cultural and Contextual Blinders

Low- and high-context cultures illustrate the importance of culture and context in communication. Another factor contributing to miscommunication, then, is the tendency to ignore the communication context—especially the cultural context. When American tourists dress and talk in a Japanese Buddhist monastery the way they would dress and talk on a southern California beach, they are saying, "We are insensitive." If you joke in a sarcastic manner with strangers or even acquaintances the way you do with friends, you are likely to be misunderstood, and feelings may be hurt. If you use street language at a formal gathering, you may be considered rude or crass.

Different cultures, subcultures, and even people have very different concepts of time, space, and abstract concepts like success, happiness, and so on. An achievement-oriented North American might find it difficult to get on the same wavelength as a Latin American who believes that "It is better to live richly than to die rich." The violent clashes of cultures in Northern Ireland, South Africa, Bosnia, and the Middle East are extreme examples of how communication difficulties arise daily when people do not recognize the cultural and contextual differences that lead to miscommunication.

During the 1980s sexual harassment received more and more publicity. Clarence Thomas's Supreme Court confirmation hearings in 1991 made the topic even hotter. Sexual harassment is basically a problem of contextual insensitivity. It usually arises when a superior or peer, usually a man, uses verbal and nonverbal signs with another person, usually a woman, that are inappropriate for the setting. It is certainly natural and acceptable for people to express attraction toward one another in social situations, but to do so in professional settings is no longer acceptable in American society. For this reason inappropriate touching, sexual remarks, and persistent unwanted social attention are not acceptable in the workplace.

Insensitivity to the Coding Complex

Earlier we spoke of inexpressiveness as the restriction of the number and variety of cues a communicator generates. Similarly, communication can be less than maximally efficient if communicators are insensitive to the various coding complexes. It has been said, somewhat facetiously, that there are always ten percent who "don't get the message." Some people are generally more sensitive than others to particular codes. When you talk with someone who simply does not pay attention you probably want to shout, "Listen to me!" Although such instances can result from various distractions, it seems that some people are simply insensitive to the communication around them.

Perhaps more common but less noticed is the situation in which a person is sensitive to some communication codes but insensitive to others. For example, a child who is raised by parents who say what they

Eye contact is an important nonverbal regulator of communication.

think and feel may not need to develop great sensitivity to nonverbal codes. In passing through life's significant experiences—a loved one's death, marriage or divorce, having children, accomplishing something unique—people become sensitized to the communication cues in a variety of codes that emerge in those particular situations and subsequently become more attuned to communicating with others who have shared these experiences.

Finally, problems arise from being sensitive to various codes at inappropriate times. One history professor repeatedly takes off and puts on his glasses while lecturing. This tends to distract students from the verbal message, for they must try to ignore the nonverbal behavior and attend to the lecture. Not all students can do so, however. One student actually counted the number of times the professor took off and replaced his glasses. By attending to an inappropriate coding complex, this student learned less history than the rest of the class.

Inflexibility

Some people think that language should never change and that alterations in language signal the degradation of society. But history proves that language does change; it changes naturally and constantly.

There is nothing wrong with searching for better ways of saying things. To argue that new phrases or new uses for old terms are illegitimate is to deny human nature.

Some people also think that one form of a language is superior to another, and, of course, it is usually the form they speak. Linguistic variation is a fact, and it provides richness to life. Unfortunately, people do tend to be prejudiced against certain dialects or accents and favor other ones. We think that the best way to overcome this form of ignorance is to help people better understand the nature of language itself. It is true that certain forms of a language are more appropriate in particular settings, and you should learn to switch codes as necessary to fit into a business setting, a family setting, a street setting, or any other situation in which you must communicate and relate to others. So the "proper" English you learn in college is important for many of the professional situations you will encounter, but you should not abandon other forms of English you may have learned as a child, at home and with friends.

Many people these days clutter their talk with the ungrammatical use of *like* and *be like*, often seasoned with lots of *you-knows*. You hear this type of talk all over: "Like, you know, I was like all, 'How can you do this to me?'" This kind of colloquial talk is perfectly appropriate, and even expected, among friends, but it makes you look like a nitwit in professional circles. We have found in our teaching that students quickly rid themselves of these expressions once they become aware of the need to do so.

Recently there has been much criticism of so-called politically correct language. You may think it stupid to change the name of "manhole cover" to "streethole cover," but such gender terms really can affect and reflect the sex of the worker you imagine to be under the street. You might think it odd to refer to certain citizens as African-American, but for many Black Americans whose historical ancestry is important to them, the new label says something they could not express with *Black* or *Negro*. Although *handicapped person* may sound perfectly acceptable to most people, it reflects great insensitivity to individuals who have specific impairments but are fully capable in other ways. Everybody is rightfully concerned about labels. People who are quick to criticize others' labels become quite defensive about their own.

In short, linguistic inflexibility breeds prejudice and arrogance, and it focuses attention on how people say things rather than on what they mean. It belies the importance of the constructive nature of language and the ways in which a person's language can tell you something about who the speaker is and what he or she considers important. Inflexibility with coding is ethnocentric and denies the experience of a variety of groups and cultures different from one's own.

Misreading Codes

Most communication codes, both verbal and nonverbal, are imprecise. Unlike a military code, in which a direct correspondence can be made between the signal and its meaning, ordinary language can be interpreted in a variety of ways. Nonverbal codes can be even more ambiguous. Communication always requires interpretation, and people frequently misunderstand each other's meanings and intentions.

One of our students told of an incident in which a male American college student was tutoring a female Japanese student in the United States. At one point, to express his approval for a correct answer, he gave his student an innocent little hug around the shoulders. She rushed in tears from the room because such touching means something entirely different in her culture.

Another student, who is white, said that he had seen African American students at his high school using a particular hand gesture that he mistook for a friendly greeting. While riding on the bus, he tried the gesture out on a group of African American youths standing at a bus stop, and they responded angrily by throwing bottles at the bus. He later found out that he had used a gang sign, which the boys took as an insult.

You cannot always avoid misunderstandings, but by greater sensitivity to the multiple meanings of words and signs, you can become more cautious and tentative in your interpretations.

SUMMARY

This chapter has discussed the coding process in terms of communication and metacommunication; signs, symbols, and messages; the nature of codes; verbal and nonverbal coding; and the problems of coding and decoding.

Verbal coding, or the use of language, involves the interaction of nature and nurture. Although people seem to be born with a knack for acquiring language, specific language behaviors are shaped by specific cultures.

Nonverbal coding is more important than many people realize, for it is deeply rooted in the culture and context of the communication situation. Nonverbal codes include performance codes of body movements, facial expressions, and physical appearances, and vocal codes that combine the variable characteristics of the voice to achieve properties of emphasis, intensity, variety, clarity, and appropriateness. Artifacts shared by individuals, groups, and larger communities also can be used to code messages. Other useful nonverbal codes are touching and manipulation of space and time.

Problems of coding and decoding can result from inexpressiveness, cultural and contextual blinders, and insensitivity to the coding complex. This chapter should have made you more aware of the great variety of coding complexes. By developing your sensitivity to the various codes, you can apply them more appropriately and more flexibly.

3 Basic Elements: Meaning and Thinking

Willa Cather, in a well-known and beautiful piece of historical fiction, tells the story of the Catholic missions of New Mexico in the late nineteenth century. Cather's story, *Death Comes for the Archbishop*, revolves around the life of a fictional character, Jean Marie Latour, who began his career in New Mexico ignominiously lost in the Southwest trying to find his way to Santa Fe. Forty years later he had become the highly beloved archbishop of that region. (The story is based on the life of Archbishop Lamy, the first Archbishop of Santa Fe.)

Latour dreamed of building a great cathedral, and late in his life, after years of fund-raising and planning, the project was complete. The St. Francis Cathedral, just off the Santa Fe plaza, remains a major landmark, an active church, and a popular tourist attraction.

For the fictional Latour and generations of actual Catholics in New Mexico, the cathedral has been more than a building. It is an important symbol. Cather wrote about Latour's return to the cathedral just before his death in 1889:

> The next morning Father Latour wakened with a grateful sense of nearness to his Cathedral—which would also be his tomb. He felt safe under its shadow; like a boat come back to harbour, lying under its own sea-wall. He was in his old study; the Sisters had sent a little iron bed from the school for him, and their finest linen and blankets. He felt a great content at being here, where he had come as a young man and where he had done his work.[1]

In Chapter 2 we saw that the key to the relationship between mind and world is the symbol. In this chapter we will probe the intricate relationship of person, symbol, and world. The generic term for this relationship is **meaning**. Later in the chapter we will discuss some ways in which people manipulate meanings through thinking.

Human beings live in a world of events and objects, like Latour's cathedral, but we never experience this world directly. It is filtered through symbols and meanings. As we proceed through life, our symbolic images of the world develop, grow, and change. Each new experience adds to this backdrop of meanings, which in turn affects how we perceive each new situation. As the philosopher John Dewey wrote,

"This active and eager background lies in wait and engages whatever comes its way so as to absorb it into its own being."[2]

THE NATURE OF MEANING

What is your meaning of the word *paper*? What is your image when you hear this word? Do you see something to write on, to start a fire with, to throw in the air as confetti, to indicate a legal agreement, to read the news in, or to wrap a fish with? The word *paper* may bring to mind all these images and more, but one thing is certain: people's images for a given word are personal and varied.

In brief, *meaning is the conception brought to the mind by a symbol.* It is determined by an intricate interaction among at least five elements of communication: the message, the communicators, the communicators' purposes, the communication channel, and the situation within which the communication takes place. These determinants are diagrammed in Figure 3.1.

Figure 3.1
The five elements that interact with experience to produce meaning in communication.

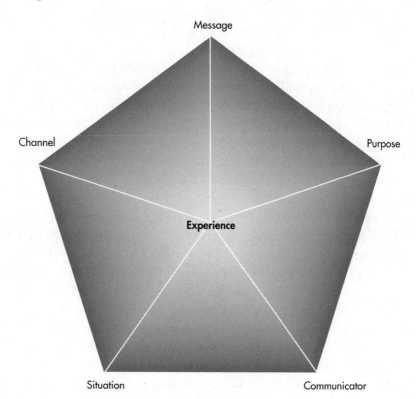

In the center of the figure is experience, which accrues as you encounter the five elements again and again in your life. Your experience with messages, purposes, communicators, situations, and channels creates a host of meanings that enable you to make sense out of the situations you encounter. Let us now examine each of these six determinants in more detail.

The Message

A **message** is a symbol or organized set of symbols used to express meaning. A message is designed to affect communicators' perceptions and responses, and people's meanings are definitely influenced by the messages they have sent and received in their lifetimes.

Several years ago one of the authors began showing dogs. Before that time, his conception of dogs was rather simple. He recognized a few breeds, but could not make subtle distinctions within them; all German shepherds, for example, looked pretty much alike. After years of raising and training basset hounds and traveling to many dog shows, however, he learned an increasing vocabulary of words to describe dogs. As a result, his conception of dogs became more complex, and he was able to see things in dogs he had never seen before.

Of course, people have different conceptions for the same symbol, and consequently messages will affect different people in different ways. Two communicators' conceptions may be similar, but they will never be the exactly the same, and sometimes they will be drastically different. The meanings assigned to a message differ because symbols are abstract and because connotations are very personal.

Symbols Are Abstract. Imagine a familiar object in all its infinite detail. No matter how astute your observations, no matter how powerful your microscope, you can never see everything in the object. It simply cannot be done. You are forced to leave something out. This process of leaving out details is called **abstraction**. When you say the word *fruit*, for example, consider how much you have not said.

Symbols vary in abstraction. Some words are highly abstract and leave out much detail; others are more precise. Thus *animal* is more abstract than *dog*, which is more abstract than *basset*. Messages can be made more precise by careful use of language, but people can never eliminate uncertainty completely. The phrase "small, tan, floppy basset puppy" tells you quite a bit, but there is still considerable latitude for individual interpretation.

Since any message is abstract to some extent, it can elicit a variety of conceptions in listeners, depending on which details are brought to mind. Because people have different experiences with the object or situation being symbolized, they will fill in details differently. Indeed, at dog shows, for example, different judges have quite different meanings for winner. Some judges focus on the dogs' heads, others on their fronts, and others on their leg structure or movement.

One of the most widely known "laws" of behavior is that people perceive only part of any object or situation. Any situation will generate a number of stimuli. What you take into account is influenced by several factors, including your expectations. Because each person's background and experience are unique, each is susceptible to taking certain aspects of a situation into account while ignoring others. Psychologists refer to this phenomenon as **selective perception**. Many holdup victims are unable to give a good description of the robber because all they could see at the time was a big black gun.

You may have seen in a science museum the fascinating Ames trapezoidal illusion. It involves a rotating "window" that appears to wave back and forth even though a mirror above the object shows it to

Meanings vary with the people involved in each situation and exchange.

be turning in a complete circle. A small ball attached to the edge of the window appears to detach and float around in front of the moving object, and a bar running through the middle of the window appears to bend up and down.

There are a number of reasons for this bizarre distortion, including the neural make-up of the human brain. But cultural susceptibilities also seem to come into play. The object is actually a trapezoid, but people are so accustomed to seeing windows as rectangles that they "see" this window as a rectangle in perspective.

Connotations Are Personal. Another reason why people respond differently to a message has to do with connotation. Symbols elicit both connotations and denotations. A **denotation** is the relatively objective, agreed-upon referent of a symbol, but the **connotation** is much more subjective. It involves personal, emotional associations. For example, *Mercedes* "denotes" a certain brand of automobile, but it could also "connote" wealth, beauty, ostentation, envy, pretense, and other things.

Consider the following terms that share a single denotation: *die, pass away, expire, perish, succumb, go to be with God, drop dead, depart.* Each of these terms will elicit a different personal response because each has a different connotation. Communicators are usually sensitive to connotation, which is why they may weigh their words carefully in important situations. A doctor would not say, "I'm sorry, but your husband just kicked the bucket."

People's meanings for a word or other symbol vary. This is one reason why miscommunication occurs. You cannot simply pass your thoughts to another person by giving a message. This notion is the greatest misconception of the transmissional perspective of communication. Unfortunately, people too often labor under the **fallacy of monousage**—the idea that any word or symbol has a single meaning that people agree upon.[3] This could not be further from the truth.

Since a message can be taken to express a variety of meanings, the speaker's intended meaning is not the only way in which a message can be understood. A message can influence people's thoughts and actions in a variety of unintended ways. It can be useful and informative, therefore, to point out some of the alternative "readings" of a message.

The communication scholar Sut Jhally, for example, has produced a startling and dramatic video entitled "Dreamworlds," in which he shows that although the producers of rock videos do not intend to do so, they contribute to an adolescent male fantasy in which women are objectified sex objects.[4] He shows how this fantasy can and does promote violence against women in society at large. The video shows that what you see in a message may not be the meaning intended and that both meanings are legitimate.

The Purpose

A second determinant of meaning is the communicator's intentions. Whenever you ask, "What did he mean by that?" or "Why did she say that?" you are inquiring about purpose. A person sends a message in order to accomplish something. If your roommate tells you she is thirsty, she may be trying to get you to bring a glass of water, to let you know why she is leaving the room, or just to inform you about her physiological state. If your friend says, "I don't feel like going out tonight," you might feel hurt, thinking you did something wrong, when he was just trying to tell you that he is really busy.

You communicate for a wide variety of reasons. You make requests, promises, and demands. You express embarrassment, give accounts, and make declarations. You say vows, announce resolutions, and provide comfort. In each of these cases, the content of your message expresses only part of the meaning. Full meaning must take into account your purpose in making the statement—what you are trying to accomplish when you say what you do.

The Communicators

The meaning in a communication situation is also affected by your perception of the participants. How often have you heard, "It is not what is said but who says it"?

Several aspects of a communicator can influence meaning. We have already discussed the importance of the communicator's purpose. Another major factor is trust among people in a variety of communication contexts—a topic addressed in more detail in Chapter 4. The way people perceive the other person's similarity or dissimilarity from themselves also affects the meaning generated from what is said.

Meaning can vary when we encounter people from cultures different from our own.

The role of the communicator can be seen around election time, when voters examine the candidates. One of the authors once worked in the congressional campaign of a local candidate. The candidate had, over the years, built an image of trust among his constituents by competently holding positions of authority in government and in a law firm. He had enhanced his image of integrity by being involved in church activities. He identified with the majority of his constituency by sharing their dominant beliefs, attitudes, and values, yet he was dissimilar from most of his constituents in his superior competence and experience. Perhaps even his boyish good looks contributed to the support given by his constituents. The author was not surprised when he won.

Suffice it to say here that the reputation of, or the experiences that people have had (or not had) with, another communicator will go far to influence the meanings generated in a given situation.

The Situation

Another determinant of meaning is the social and physical situation in which the communication occurs. The physical surroundings of the communication event can have a major influence on how a message is read. Most people, for example, are acutely aware of the importance of the atmosphere when they are seeking romance. Low lights, soft music, flowers, and a beautifully set table for two can strongly influence how your date will respond to your "message."

The social situation may be the single most important constraint on the meaning people derive from communication. The social situation consists of communicators' beliefs, attitudes, and especially values. What is their history or background, and what traditions do they revere? What recent experiences or current events have influenced their thinking?

Notice how carefully trial lawyers attend to the situation. In capital offenses they probe prospective jurors about their views on capital punishment; their relationship to the defendant; their sex, age, and race; and finally what they have heard or read about the crime. When crimes have received extensive publicity, defense lawyers often request a change of venue (location) because the location where the crime was committed does not permit choosing an "impartial" jury.

The Channel

Your meaning is also influenced by the channel in which the communication occurs. Whether a message comes by telephone, computer network, face-to-face, on the radio, on television, in film, or through print media will affect your response.

As an audible channel, for example, radio is limited by the absence of visual images, yet it allows receivers to become more involved by creating images for themselves. Books, on the other hand, rely entirely on the written word—and sometimes artwork and photographs—to relay meaning. As mixed channels, movies and television provide more visual and audible information than either radio or printed material. This mixture does influence meaning, as we show in Chapter 9.

Once when visiting Athens, one of the authors was awakened in his hotel in the middle of the night by a telephone call from the front desk. A relative from the United States was trying to reach him, he was told, and would call back later. Needless to say, the author lay awake all night wondering who had died, since a phone call in the middle of the night in a foreign country could mean nothing but disaster. His worry and sadness turned to anger when he learned the next day that a sister had called about a trivial matter and had forgotten about the time difference. As this example shows, the channel in which the message is sent very much affects the meaning of that message.

Experience: The Crux of Meaning

When you encounter communication, how do you respond to it? What meanings come into your mind to help you understand it? The answers to these questions will be different for each person. The experiences you have had over a lifetime provide you with a set of resources for interpreting and responding to messages. Except in the simplest situations, you will not be limited to a single reading of a message because most texts are rife with possible meanings. At the same time, however, you will not be free to read a message in any way you wish. The factors outlined up to this point in the chapter constrain what you can see and do.

The philosopher Hans Georg Gadamer says that there is an interaction between the message and your experience, each affecting the other.[5] Your experience allows you to interpret the message, but the message in turn stretches your experience. This is why we put experience at the center of meaning in Figure 3.1.

Your meaning for a symbol or message consists in large measure of your expectation for how you will use or relate to it. How does the symbol fit into your life? If you have ever told a friend that material you were studying was not very "meaningful," you probably meant that you could not see its potential use in your own life.

This symbol-experience link is two-way. Symbols elicit behavior toward the referent, thereby affecting experience; likewise, experience in a situation influences future behavior, thereby changing meanings. A colleague of ours once made an intriguing study of the prisoners in a county jail.[6] He found that prisoners' meanings for various symbols were influenced by the potential of the referent for helping or hindering their lives in prison.

One of the most interesting examples was the "toilet telephone," a plumbing communication system by which the prisoners were able to send messages throughout the jail. Since water conducts sound well, the prisoners could pass messages by talking into the toilet bowl. Before officials discovered what was going on, they were mystified by the fact that prison visitors were always expected at every point along the tour, even before the news of their arrival could travel along customary channels. Thus the prisoners' meaning for the word *toilet* included this unusual experience.

Meanings are always a product of social interaction. Our meanings for symbols and objects are learned by communication. The film *Paris Is Burning* is a fascinating documentary about the Black gay male culture in New York City, in which cross-dressing and transsexualism are common. When you watch the actions depicted in the film and listen to the interviews with members of this culture, you come to realize how important the symbols, messages, language, and meanings are for the identity of this group and how these meanings are established through communication within the group. Some of the group's practices have even spread to other groups, as in the case of vogue dancing, which originated in the gay balls of New York City.

Because of the role of communication in the establishment of meaning, meaning is highly cultural. Broadly defined, a culture is a large grouping of people who share similar beliefs, values, and norms. One characteristic of a culture is that its members usually share a common language, both verbal and nonverbal. Thus, urban African-Americans speak English, but they may be distinguished from other cultural groups because they share a variant of the language rich with shared experiential meanings. One person's meaning for a symbol may be different from another person's because they come from different cultures. Culture shock occurs when people find themselves suddenly in the middle of a new set of experiential meanings.

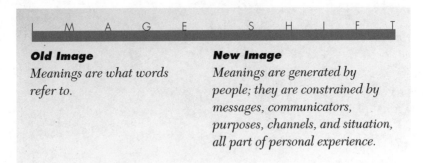

I M A G E   S H I F T

Old Image
Meanings are what words refer to.

New Image
Meanings are generated by people; they are constrained by messages, communicators, purposes, channels, and situation, all part of personal experience.

Working with the Bedouins on an archeological excavation produced a type of culture shock for one of the authors. The workers seemed to move so slowly that he felt as if he were watching a film in slow motion. He immediately conceptualized the Bedouins as at best lazy and at worst antagonistic to the project. But after six weeks in the blazing

Jordanian sun, the author was amazed at the amount of work they had accomplished by pacing themselves; his meanings for them had come to include smart, productive, and capable.

Thinking can be hard work.

THE NATURE OF THINKING

In the previous section, we found that people encounter the world of objects, situations, and experiences through a symbolic filter of meanings. Human beings have the ability to manipulate their meanings, arranging and rearranging their personal worlds. This process is what we normally mean by thinking. Thinking is part and parcel of communication. People can transact meanings with messages only because of their ability to manipulate symbols—to think. Thinking is a multifaceted gem, offering a wide repertoire of thought forms to human beings in their quest to understand and deal with the world.

Two types of thinking, illustrated in Figure 3.2, are covered in this chapter. First, people think to interpret: They figure out their perceptions by conceptualizing and reasoning. Second, people think to solve problems; that is, they test their environment, hypothesize solutions to problems, and act to change situations.

Thinking to Interpret

Human beings are constantly trying to make sense of things. Confronted with a confusing mass of objects, we put them together, take them

Figure 3.2
Human thinking.

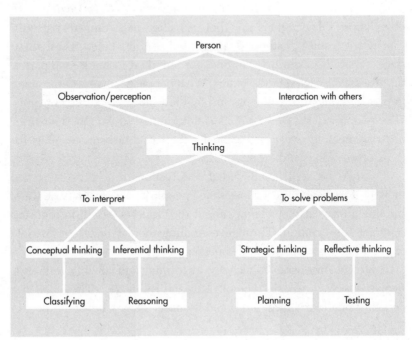

apart, rearrange them, and try to figure out what we cannot observe directly. Watch any preschool child. The early years, which constitute the most intense learning period of life, epitomize interpretive thinking. Young children move from one object to another—putting various things together, asking endless questions, and struggling to make sense of it all. But all people, regardless of age, seek to interpret what they perceive.

Interpretation involves four kinds of thinking: conceptual, inferential, analogic, and narrative. Conceptual thinking is a process of grouping and labeling; inferential thinking is a process of drawing conclusions on the basis of observations; analogic thinking is a process of making comparisons; and narrative thinking is the sequencing of events into a story.

Conceptual Thinking. People never experience the world directly. They always symbolize what they experience, and they interpret their experience through meanings. They do this by conceptual thinking. A **concept** is a group of things that are distinguished by common qualities.

Conceptual thinking is a three-stage process. It begins with observation. Observations are then classified according to patterns. Finally, the resulting categories are symbolized, or labeled. These three stages do not necessarily occur one after another; instead, each part of the process is affected by the others. What people observe is determined in part by their prior concepts and by their labels for those concepts. How people classify observations is determined in part by their prior observations and experiences and by their established meanings for those observations and experiences.

It should be kept in mind that observations are both direct and indirect. Firsthand observations shape people's concepts in basic ways, but much of what they "know" about the world is based on reported (indirect) observation. Through communication with others, people expand their observations and concepts.

There is an inseparable link between forming and labeling a concept. People observe a certain type of plant and call it *tree*. They look at a certain type of structure and name it *house*. They label some people *men* and others *women*. The point is that language enables people to conceptualize.

There is nothing "true" or "right" about any concept. The same set of things can be conceptualized in many different ways. The main question is whether the concept is useful for a given person in a particular situation. For example, you might normally conceptualize a key as a means of opening a door, but if you were under attack you might think of it as a weapon.

Everyday life provides many examples of the use of concepts. You try to guess your opponent's hand in a card game on the basis of what is in your own hand and what has been played. A physician diagnoses an illness on the basis of symptoms and test results. A detective solves a crime by observing various clues.

Inferential Thinking: Inductive and Deductive. The initial stage of observation can be considered an important starting point for all interpretive thinking. Ultimately, what people think is based on what they observe. Observations—both firsthand and reported—might therefore be thought of as data for interpretive thinking. Reasoning from data to reach conclusions is called **inferential thinking**.

Most people need to perceive themselves as reasonable, as communicating with others on a reasonable basis. Their conversations are punctuated with phrases like "It just stands to reason" and "Let's look at this logically." The study of the reasoning process began with a concern for formal rules. So philosophers would examine statements like

If all *B*'s are *A*'s
And all *C*'s are *B*'s,
Then all *C*'s must also be *A*'s.

Put in more concrete terms,

If all counties lie within states
And all states lie within the nation,
Then all counties must lie within the nation.

It soon becomes apparent, however, that, in order to conform to the formal rules of logic, statements either must deal with certainty (or near certainty) or must be so restrictive that they rarely occur in the real world. For that reason we will disregard formal logic and will define **reasoning** in communication contexts as the mental process whereby one draws conclusions about lesser-known events on the basis of events that are better known.

Scholars have traditionally identified two major types of reasoning: inductive and deductive. **Inductive reasoning** proceeds from specific data to broader or less probable generalizations. For example, you touch a red element on the stove, and it burns you. Later you touch a piece of red metal in a campfire, and it also burns you. After several such experiences (usually not too many), you form a conclusion: "Metals that are red are also hot and will burn."

People draw conclusions inductively from various combinations of evidence. A specific experience combined either directly or vicariously with corroborative statements from a trusted source may lead people to the same conclusion they would reach through several direct experiences.

Perhaps the most familiar and in some ways the most precise form of induction occurs in medical research. Thousands of laboratory animals are fed or inoculated with a substance to be tested. Based on those thousands of specific tests, generalizations are drawn about how the substance affects the health of animals.

Franklin Roosevelt was using inductive reasoning in a public communication context when he said,

> Yesterday the Japanese government also launched an attack against Malaya. Last night Japanese forces attacked Hong Kong. Last night Japanese forces attacked Guam. Last night the Japanese attacked Wake Island. This morning the Japanese attacked Midway Island. Japan has, therefore, undertaken a surprise offensive extending throughout the Pacific area.[7]

Deductive reasoning proceeds from generalizations (usually called premises) to conclusions about specific cases. The classic form of deduction is the *syllogism*, of which the following is an equally classic example:

All humans are mortal. (major premise)
You are human. (minor premise)
Therefore, you are mortal. (conclusion)

Of greater usefulness is a form of reasoning Aristotle called the **enthymeme**. Early logicians considered this a "probable syllogism." Three characteristics distinguish the enthymeme from the formal syllogism and thus make it more useful in analyzing conceptual thinking in human communication.

The first characteristic of the enthymeme is that at least one part is missing. Here is an example:

Look at the smoke coming from that chimney.
(Implied: Where there's smoke, there's fire.)
(Implied: There is a fire in the fireplace.)

Second, the enthymeme deals with probabilities rather than certainties. An example is,

Since it usually snows by Thanksgiving, it is likely to snow by Thanksgiving this year.

Third, and perhaps most important, the enthymeme involves transactional participation by both speaker and listener, for the listener actively supplies at least one part of the reasoning process. Consider this exchange.

Michele: Do you think it will snow by Thanksgiving?
Denise: Well, it usually does.

In general, most deductive reasoning is preceded by inductive reasoning; that is, the major generalizations from which people reason deductively have been arrived at inductively. Assume, for example, that the Russians and the Japanese have been asked repeatedly, especially by the United States, to stop whaling. Assume further that the two countries have continuously resisted such pressure. You might well

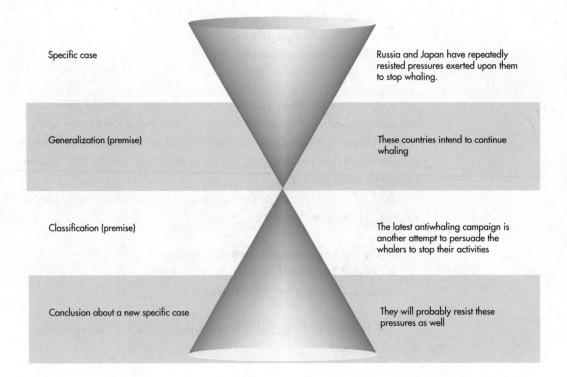

Specific case — Russia and Japan have repeatedly resisted pressures exerted upon them to stop whaling.

Generalization (premise) — These countries intend to continue whaling

Classification (premise) — The latest antiwhaling campaign is another attempt to persuade the whalers to stop their activities

Conclusion about a new specific case — They will probably resist these pressures as well

Figure 3.3
Induction and deduction

conclude inductively that the countries intend to continue whaling. Next, by reasoning deductively, you might think that the Russians and the Japanese will continue to resist pressures to stop whaling. This relationship between inductive and deductive reasoning is represented in Figure 3.3. Note that in this figure we have reasoned inductively from many specific data (instances in the form of statistics) to form a single generalization; then we have reasoned deductively to arrive again at specific instances.

In communication transactions people very "reasonably" may draw opposite conclusions, either because of inaccurate or insufficient data or because they simply are using different data or generalizations. Furthermore, one communicator may have access to data that are withheld from another.

Although traditional approaches to the analysis of interpretive thinking illuminate some of the processes at work in communication contexts, they do not explain them all. For instance, suppose a communicator reasons from the specific to the specific by saying, "Since the Russians and the Japanese have continuously resisted pressures to stop whaling, they probably will not respond to the latest antiwhaling campaign." Traditional approaches to inductive and deductive reasoning cannot deal effectively with this type of discourse. Let us turn, therefore, to a contemporary approach that is more useful in understanding conceptual thinking as it applies to human communication.

Inferential Thinking: The Toulmin Model. Stephen Toulmin in *The Uses of Argument* describes a model of reasoning that not only emphasizes the relationship between specific evidence or data and the conclusions one draws from them but also accounts for reasoning from specific to specific and other forms observed in communication contexts.[8] The essence of the **Toulmin model** is the relationship between the **claims** people make and the **data** on which those claims are based. This relationship can be represented as follows:

$$\text{data} \longrightarrow \text{claim}$$

Toulmin maintains that the data and claim are connected by the **warrant**, or the reason why the claim follows logically from the data. The model then becomes:

$$\text{data} \longrightarrow \text{claim}$$
$$|$$
$$\text{warrant}$$

Consider again our hypothetical claim, "The Russians and the Japanese probably will not respond to the latest antiwhaling campaign." The data are instances of our experiences over the long history of whaling. The warrant, which is usually unstated, might be, "National economic practices are relatively fixed and hard to change." Since the warrant is unstated (and is often obscure even to the person using it), we consider its usefulness in communication contexts to be less significant than the basic data-claim relationship.

Toulmin advances two other concepts in his reasoning model that we do consider significant: the **qualifier** and the **reservation**. The qualifier is simply a statement of the degree of probability inherent in the claim. Just as a meteorologist cites the percentage of probability that it will rain tomorrow, so most people qualify their conclusions with words like "remotely possible," "possible," "fairly probable," "highly probable," or "virtually certain." Sometimes people even ask, "Who really knows?" The reservation is a recognition of possible extenuating circumstances or exceptional contexts in which the claim may not apply. Toulmin's model of reasoning now looks like this:

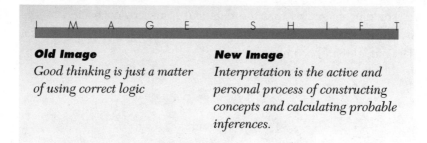

Thus, in a human communication context we might say, "Since the Russians and the Japanese have continuously resisted pressures to stop whaling [data], they probably [qualifier] will not respond to the latest antiwhaling campaign [claim], unless they can be shown the economic advantages of stopping [reservation]."

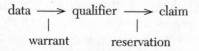

Old Image
Good thinking is just a matter of using correct logic

New Image
Interpretation is the active and personal process of constructing concepts and calculating probable inferences.

Analogic Thinking. **Analogic thinking** is closely related to conceptual thinking because it relies on making connections. People often interpret events by looking for ways in which certain things are like other things with which they are familiar. Analogic thinking is commonly used in communication, as people express themselves by making comparisons.[9]

Your minister tells you that life is like a stream that begins as a trickle and ends in the roar of a river after many tributaries come together along the way. You tell a friend that you can't find a suit that will fit because you are shaped like a pear. A professor worries about her students, saying that she sometimes feels like the Pied Piper.

Everyday language is filled with analogic content. *History* in English, *Geschichte* in German, and *histoire* in French are based on the root meaning "story." An intelligent person is "bright." When you get a "shot," the nurse "sticks" you with a needle. When someone is accused of doing something wrong, he or she is "fingered," and someone who is not taken seriously is said to be a "joke."

Analogic thinking is a natural and effective form of interpretation because human's ability to understand new things is always limited by that which they already know. So when you encounter something new, you are bound to ask yourself, "What is this like?"

Narrative Thinking. Storytelling may be one of the few cultural universals. All peoples, it seems, value stories in one way or another. And stories are one of the ways in which people interpret events.[10] People often seem to understand experiences in terms of their plots,

Our experiential meanings begin coming to us early in life.

characters, and situations. You don't have to listen to a conversation very long before someone ends up telling a story. When you explain something to another person, you will often find yourself explaining it in narrative form.

Most people are attracted to a good story, which is why public speakers often make use of stories. Sporting events come off like a story; television sitcoms and dramas are very popular; and millions of viewers listen intently to talk-show guests telling their stories. In short, narrative is one of our most common methods of interpretation.

Thinking to Solve Problems

Have you ever stopped to consider what makes a problem? You might be familiar with the following situation. Two roommates are having an argument.

> *George:* What a slob you are! Haven't you ever heard of a drawer? I can't even get to my bed without stepping all over your things.

> *Tom:* Well, at least I'm normal rather than compulsive like you. Why don't you just relax instead of getting all uptight whenever a pencil gets left on the table?

For George the lack of tidiness is a problem, for Tom it is not.

This vignette illustrates something important about problem solving: there is no such thing as an objective problem. A problem exists for a person whenever that person perceives a discrepancy between what is and what he or she thinks should be. But people have different wants, needs, and values, and so they will not always see the same situation as a problem to be solved.

In 1963 American intelligence agents detected a buildup of Soviet offensive nuclear missiles in Cuba. Over a thirteen-day period, President John F. Kennedy and his advisers developed and successfully implemented a plan to have the Russians remove the weapons. Throughout this period, they constantly monitored the political and international environment and made plans to deal with developing situations. The problem-solving involved in this situation was immense. For example, simply to monitor the activity around the missile sites in

Cuba required a carefully designed plan to step up U-2 (surveillance) flights over that country.

In solving a problem, the order in which people attack its elements is all-important. Years ago, the philosopher John Dewey made the point that good problem solving follows certain stages.[11] First, he said, some perplexity or difficulty demands attention. Usually people have an immediate idea about how to deal with the problem. Sometimes that initial idea works, but when it does not, **reflective thinking** must begin. In the next stage, called **intellectualization**, two processes emerge. First we define more exactly the problem at hand. Good problem solving cannot proceed until the vague difficulty has been broken down into some manageable, clearly understood problem. Often the problem actually consists of a number of subproblems. The second part of intellectualization involves analysis, or the search for information about the problem—its causes and its effects.

The next stage of problem solving involves hypothesis. Now we posit possible solutions to the problem. Then, through reasoning, we think through, refine, and elaborate on the preferred solution. Finally, the hypothesized solution is put into effect and tested. Our tests may lead us to develop and test new hypotheses or solutions. This process is diagrammed in Figure 3.4.

Suppose, for example, that your car were stolen. What would you do after it became clear that the police were unable to apprehend the thief and get it back for you? This is a classic problem-solving situation. According to this model, you would first define the problem. A car theft could create a number of types of problems. Perhaps you would decide that the most critical one is getting transportation to work and school. You would undoubtedly analyze the situation, considering, for example, the distance between your home, work, and school. Then, you would assess the options—buy a new car, borrow a car, take a bus, use a taxi,

Figure 3.4
Dewey's approach to reflective thinking.

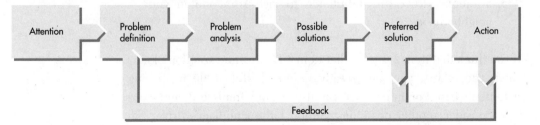

ride a bike, or hitchhike. You would weigh these, eliminate impossible or undesirable ones, and make a tentative decision. Then you would try it out and perhaps discover new problems resulting from your choice.

This situation involves the basic elements of problem solving that are used by all people in their daily activities. Whether a problem is small (like choosing what to wear in the morning) or large (like changing a difficult childhood behavior), people sense the problem, define it, test the situation, analyze, create plans, and retest. The wonder is that people can do this in their heads—all because of their ability to use symbols.

COMMUNICATION PROBLEMS: MEANING AND THINKING

It should be clear that communication problems can arise in any situation because of the way people think and handle meaning. Such communication difficulties generally relate to how people observe or perceive the environment and how they attribute meaning or draw inferences from their observations.[12]

Inference-Observation Problems

Suppose you are driving home one evening and you see an ambulance parked in front of your neighbor's house. Answer the following questions by saying "true," "false," or "don't know":

1. Someone is ill at your neighbor's house.
2. There is a vehicle with ambulance markings parked in front of your neighbor's house.
3. Someone related to the medical profession is visiting one of your neighbors.
4. There are no vehicles on the street in front of your neighbor's house.
5. Someone drove an ambulance to visit someone in your neighborhood.

If you think that item 2 is true, that item 4 is false, and you don't know about the others, you are already rather skillful at distinguishing statements based on inferences. But if you think items 1, 3, and 5 are true, consider another possibility. Suppose the ambulance driver ran out of gas while returning to the garage after an emergency. The ambulance may simply be parked in front of your friend's house while the driver walks to the nearest service station. Clearly, the odd-numbered statements are based on inferences; you cannot say with a high degree of confidence whether they are true or false.

Does that mean you should never make statements based on inference? If so, you would think very little and would talk less. But communication problems arise when people either make or receive statements of inference as though they were statements based on observation. This problem is commonly called **inference-observation confusion**.

Problems also arise even when people know that a statement is based on inference—if the statement's degree of probability is grossly misinterpreted. Sometimes inferences of very low probability are represented or interpreted as having very high probability. Perhaps the most familiar example of this situation is unwarranted credibility given to gossip.

Of course other inference-observation problems can also occur. You can base inferences on inadequate data. You can make poor use of analogy by employing false comparisons. You can reason erroneously from one claim to another. You can fall victim to a number of fallacies. We do not discuss these types of problems here, although they are developed in somewhat more detail in Chapter 9.

Inferential thinking is often done jointly with other people through communication. In communicating with others, you sometimes exchange information in the form of observations (or the reported observations of others). You may use this information as the basis for inferences, and often people will reason together and try out different inferences based on shared observations. Sometimes, you share an inference with another person, and they accept it, reject it, or ignore it. The warrants of your arguments may be accepted or questioned, and others may add qualifiers and reservations to your reasoning.

The process of linking observations and inferences, then, is often accomplished with other people through communication. That communication can be improved by clearly understanding the difference between an observation and an inference and by knowing the mental process by which they are linked.

Allness

Another communication problem occurs when people assume either that they have observed all there is to observe or that they have said all that can be said about a subject. General semanticists call this phenomenon **allness**. Have you ever tried to communicate with someone who knows it all? The frustration is nicely summarized in the statement "People who think they know it all are particularly annoying to those of us who do!"

In some cases allness results from a lack of awareness of selective perception and the multiple factors of meaning. Obviously, not all sensory stimuli in the environment can be processed. People need to be selective in order to survive; besides, there is really no way anyone can observe everything. This condition is both normal and desirable, as long as people remain aware of the limitation and do not assume that their meanings are complete. To most people a mosquito is just a mosquito, but certain entomologists have devoted years to the observation of several dozen species, and even they will never know all there is to know about mosquitoes.

Allness also results when people assume they can say all there is to say about a subject. As we pointed out earlier, words are abstractions. Whenever people communicate, they leave out more than they say. A person who says the word *pencil* has limited the possible shared meanings considerably but still could talk for hours and not say everything that might be said about this familiar object. Nor should communicators become immobilized by the awareness that words are abstractions and do not say all there is to say. Rather, people can improve communication by keeping the idea of allness constantly before them.

Stereotyping is a special type of allness. The problem of stereotyping involves labeling and treating people according to general similarities rather than individual differences. For example, professors are labeled "absent-minded"; young people are assumed to be "naive"; and Orientals may be seen as "bright and clever." Stereotyping is an outgrowth of selective perception. Since people cannot process all available stimuli, they categorize and abstract on the basis of general types. This is often necessary, and it is not always bad as long as people remember that they are doing it. But communication problems occur when they label a person and then respond to the label or stereotype instead of to the

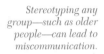

Stereotyping any group—such as older people—can lead to miscommunication.

person. Thus many people stereotype older people as being weak, forgetful, helpless, unhealthy, and unattractive. To the contrary, many older people are vocationally active, in good health, self-sufficient, skillful at a variety of crafts and hobbies, and exceptionally intelligent. Similar misconceptions abound regarding racial and sexual stereotypes. When people forget that they are stereotyping and respond to some label rather than to the person or the message, communication problems arise.

Another problem with stereotyping is that it can follow the Pygmalion effect, becoming a self-fulfilling prophecy. That is, people tend to become what other people expect of them. Thus, if people expect older people to become a burden on society, or if a teacher expects a student to be "slow," these situations may very well happen. People live up to or down to what others expect of them—and to what they expect of themselves.

Bypassing

The phenomenon of **bypassing** occurs when communicators attribute different meanings to the same message or word within a message, when they behave as though meanings reside in words and messages rather than in people. Bypassing also occurs when people behave as though words or messages can be interpreted in only one way. Bypassing can be avoided if people keep in mind two simple principles. First, everyone knows but tends to forget that a single word can have a number of representational meanings. Consider the possible meanings of the word *strike:*

I had a strike! (A trout hit my lure.)
Strike one! (The batter missed.)
The miners are on strike. (They are not working.)
Strike the tent. (Take it down.)
It strikes me that . . . (I think that . . .)

Second, many words can have the same or similar meanings. *Roget's Superthesaurus* (1995) contains 609 pages of synonyms and antonyms. A casual examination produced these synonyms for the noun *vigor*: *power, force; boldness, intellectual force; spirit; punch* (slang); *point; piquancy; raciness; verve, ardor, enthusiasm, glow, fire, warmth; gravity; weight*. Of course these words do not mean the same thing, nor will any one of them elicit the same meaning from different people in different contexts. Yet they all can elicit similar meanings, even though each adds nuances unique to the situation.

Misunderstanding Intentions

Although bypassing does occur and can cause amusing and sometimes tragic consequences, most people manage to understand the content of messages pretty well. Much more common, in our opinion, is misunderstanding the intentions of another person's message. You may understand the words perfectly well but misconstrue what the communicator wanted to accomplish by uttering those words. Your brother says, "I could use your help with the car," and you cancel a longstanding date because you take his polite request as a demand. You tell a friend you cannot go to the movies, and he leaves angry because he mistook your honest statement about being busy as a personal rejection. A professor asks you in class for your opinion, and you feel picked on because you don't realize that he selected you because of his respect for your work.

People often misattribute motives to friends, family members, and associates. What is intended as a perfectly benign comment may be taken as a hostile one. An honest question is sometimes heard as unfriendly criticism. Advice is seen as domination. A complaint is falsely taken as a request for help, or a request for help is taken as a complaint.

How you respond to another person depends upon what you think he or she is trying to do in the message. If you think a request is being made, you will probably grant or deny it. If you think a promise is being made, you will remember it as such. If you think criticism is being delivered, you may show hurt feelings.

Too often, especially in important situations at home and at work, people do not discuss their messages enough. They assume that because the words are clear, the intentions are likewise clear. We recommend that you explore others' intentions before reacting strongly to their messages.

Inadequate Problem Solving

We do not have the space here to thoroughly develop this significant category of problems, but the subject is covered more completely in Chapter 7. Here we will merely say that problems can occur at any stage of the problem-solving process. The problem can be poorly defined, or it can be incompletely analyzed. Individuals and groups can lack the creativity to produce a number of possible solutions, or the consequences of the alternatives may be inadequately explored.[13]

SUMMARY

The rich symbolic world of the human mind revolves around meaning and thinking. Meaning is generated by people as the message, communicator, purpose, channel, and situation all interact with their past and present experiences. Meaning is affected by the abstract and personal nature of symbols and messages. The people involved in the transaction affect the meaning that is generated, as do their intentions. Shared trust, similarity, dissimilarity, and perceived attractiveness can affect the meaning people generate. The physical and psychological context constrain the meanings that people generate, as do a variety of verbal and nonverbal channels of communication.

An individual's symbolic world is made up largely of thinking processes. Thinking functions first as part of interpretation. Interpretive thinking involves concept formation, concept utilization, and reasoning. In thinking to solve problems, people monitor situations, define problems, hypothesize solutions, and act to reduce or eliminate undesirable situations.

A number of communication problems can arise that are related to meaning and thinking. Inference-observation problems result from not understanding the difference between what has been seen directly and what has been concluded through reasoning. Allness is the failure to recognize the abstractness of symbols and the complex nature of meaning. It leads to overinclusive statements and unfounded confidence in them. Bypassing is a misunderstanding between communicators that arises because of insensitivity to the personal nature of meaning and a subsequent failure to adapt to the other person. Misunderstanding intentions can be a serious source of difficulty in communication. Finally, problem solving can lead to a host of difficulties.

4 Basic Elements: Information and Persuasion

As you begin this chapter, reflect a moment about your immediate sensations. What are you aware of inside and outside your body? Think about what is coming through each of your senses. What do you see? What do you hear? What do you taste, smell, and feel? If you were able to go beyond the range of your senses, what would you perceive in the next room? Outside? In the next town? Across the country? Around the world?

Now think about what you believe about people and things. How do you behave toward others? What are your attitudes and values? Your sentiments? If you were to put all these things together in a personal book—an impossible task—you would be describing your image of the world.

Your **image** is your personal universe of space, time, interpersonal relations, nature, and feelings.[1] Your image is a fluid whole that changes from moment to moment as various new stimuli enter or leave your awareness, and from year to year as a result of new experiences. It is important to recognize that messages in communication affect your image. What you are told by others—what you hear, see, and read—always affects your personal world, your image.

Messages affect the image in two general ways. First, messages *clarify* your image by providing information. Second, messages *change* your image by altering how you feel, think, and behave. This effect of change is called persuasion. These two effects—information and persuasion—go hand in hand.

I   M   A   G   E   S   H   I   F   T

Old Image
Information and persuasion are fundamentally different. Information adds to one's knowledge; persuasion changes one's mind.

New Image
Information and persuasion are not fundamentally different. All messages have the potential of altering one's reality. The term information is used to emphasize aspects of the message that clarify; persuasion is used to emphasize aspects of the message that change.

THE USES AND PROCESSING OF INFORMATION

During all their waking hours people are bombarded by stimuli from the environment. They ignore most of this stimulation but use a good deal of it to orient themselves to their surroundings and to help themselves function in other ways. In Chapter 3 we saw how people symbolize and thereby assign meanings to perceived events. Once a person has perceived and interpreted an object, event, or situation, that stimulus becomes information.

Information as a Means of Reducing Uncertainty

Any stimulus has informational potential. The stimulus can be used in some way to help a person interpret or understand what is going on. Imagine waking up in some strange place. First, you would study your surroundings, no doubt looking for clues about where you were. In other words, you would want to reduce uncertainty about your situation.[2] There is no limit to the number of cues you might use to reduce uncertainty in any situation, and any two people will take different cues into account. Since people's images are all different, a given message may carry vastly different amounts of **information** for different people.

Now imagine waking up in a very familiar place, where there is little uncertainty. The more certain you are about the situation, the more redundant additional information about that situation will be. Although people generally think of **redundancy** as useless repetition, it is an important positive element in communication. For example, a weather forecaster uses a variety of indicators in making predictions. Sometimes these indicators are additive, but usually there is some redundancy. Besides telling about an approaching storm, a television weather reporter may show radar and satellite pictures, use various visual aids, give barometer readings, and provide temperature changes. Viewers get the message: prepare for bad weather. If humans were perfect information-processing beings, redundancy would be unnecessary. But we need a certain amount of redundancy to maximize the benefits of information.

Redundancy has four important functions. First, it counteracts noise, which is any disturbance that inhibits reception or understanding. Have you ever missed a portion of a news broadcast and then listened attentively to the rest of the program in hopes of picking up clues about what you missed? Or have you missed something someone said because of slurred words but gotten the gist of it from context? Redundancy makes this possible.

Second, redundancy reduces ambiguity. Because people have various meanings for any given word, ambiguity is common. When messages are repeated, alternate words and forms may be used that will clarify the intended meaning.

Third, redundancy promotes learning. It is one thing to hear and understand; it is quite another to integrate and remember. Only a few gifted people can remember most of what they see and hear. The rest of us do not have that advantage and must rely on concentration and repetition.

Finally, redundancy reinforces attitudes, beliefs, and values. All people need stability in their lives. Although we enjoy adventure and change, ultimately we need to have some things we can count on, and redundancy is one of the ways in which we get this sense of security from communication.

Besides redundancy, there are a number of other ways in which information reduces uncertainty. Every decision people make is affected in one way or another by information. By reducing uncertainty, information acts on this choice-making process in three major ways. First, information may change our perception of the effectiveness of a given alternative. People make decisions in order to attain goals. If we are led to believe that one alternative is more likely to help us reach our goal, that information will affect our choice.

Consider a young woman who is trying to decide which of two companies to work for. If high income is her goal and she believes that the first company will pay more, she will lean in that direction. But perhaps she will discover that in the long run her chances for advancement—and ultimately more money—are greater in the second company. She may quickly change her mind.

Second, information may provide skills, competence, or knowledge that enable people to use an alternative more effectively. This helps them learn how to make a given choice operate better in achieving their goal. The job seeker may be shown how to manipulate the system in the first company in a way that increases her chances for advancement. The scale may thus be tipped toward the first company once again.

Finally, information actually may change people's goals. When this happens, an alternative that was originally appealing may no longer be effective in meeting the new goals. For example, our job applicant may find out that the economic benefits in both companies hinge on much overtime work. Now she may decide that her income desires are unrealistically high, and she may look instead for a company that has reasonable working hours.

So far we have discussed the ways in which people use information to reduce uncertainty and the desirable effects of doing so. But is it always desirable? Apparently not.

People do not always desire to reduce uncertainty in their relations with others. Sometimes people do not want to know everything because knowing entails the responsibility of acting in certain ways. Parents of teenagers often do not want to know everything their children are doing because of the mental burden of having to figure out how to respond. People also use uncertainty to guard self-esteem. Sometimes we would prefer not to know everybody's opinion of everything we do. And people use uncertainty to avoid conflict. Sometimes it is better to let things lie than to tackle them with both arms, and if our differences with other people are not always clear, we can avoid the hassle of having to deal with them. Realistically speaking, communicators do need respite from the vagaries of life, and maintaining a bit of uncertainty is one way in which to achieve some relief. In fact, communicating with **equivocation** is a common practice and not always bad.

Equivocating means waffling or remaining unclear in one's message. How do you respond when someone asks your opinion of a hideous piece of art? You equivocate with something like, "I've never seen that medium used in such a novel way." Notice how equivocation allows you to meet more than one goal at once. You can state an opinion while also protecting the other person's feelings.

It seems that equivocation is a good strategy for an **avoidance-avoidance situation**, a situation in which you are faced with two or more alternatives that are equally undesirable. In the above example, you can either be honest and hurt the person's feelings or lie and be dishonest. You don't want to face the unpleasant consequences of either of these choices, so you equivocate.

Uncertainty, then, can be an important ingredient in the communication process. Most of the time, uncertainty is an uncomfortable state of affairs, and people seek information to reduce it. Often, however, uncertainty fulfills definite functions and is promoted through equivocation. Now let us turn our attention to how information is processed.

Information can provide skills, competence, and knowledge that reduce uncertainty.

Information Processing

People understand information coming from the environment within the framework of their own cognitive systems. The **cognitive system** is a complex organization of beliefs and memories that provide order for people's worlds. Things relate to one another because of the associations made within the mind, and the cognitive system is the pattern of associations people hold in memory.

Thinking, as discussed in the previous chapter, is made possible by the operations of the cognitive system. The cognitive system consists of two parts: structures and processes.[3] **Knowledge structures** are the patterns of information organization, or the ways in which pieces of information fit together in your mind. If you are an experienced cook, for example, certain foods and ingredients are associated with cooking methods and implements.

Cognitive processes are the mechanisms or operations required to manage and use information. There are essentially seven. **Focusing** involves attending to the details of information, as when you read a recipe and think about what will be required to prepare a dish. **Integration** is making connections, as when you realize that cream of tartar is necessary to help egg whites congeal when being beaten. **Inference** is the process of filling in missing details on the basis of what you do know. You might, for example, realize that you will need a lot of "headroom" in your oven if you are preparing a dish with a lot of eggs that will rise. **Storage** means putting things into memory, and **retrieval** means pulling them out again; together these processes enable you to recall whether you have cream of tartar in your cupboard or whether you will have to add it to your shopping list. The next cognitive process is **selection**, or choosing appropriate behaviors in an operation. For example, in making a meringue, you will have to remember the proper method, which could involve a whisk, copper bowl, or perhaps a mixer.

The final element of information processing is **implementing**, or carrying through with an action. Once you understand the recipe and establish plans for preparing the dish, you will actually carry out the process.

To an experienced cook, these processes of focusing, integrating, inferring, storing, retrieving, selecting, and implementing come easily because the cognitive structures make each piece of information immediately relevant. The same person, however, might have more trouble in the realms of auto mechanics, mountain climbing, giving a speech, or diving for abalone.

When you are confronted with new information, you will seek to make it relevant within some knowledge structure you already have, or you will ignore it. Information is considered to have **relevancy** when it is immediately understandable and useful within some easily accessed part of the listener's knowledge. Most mundane information exchanged in ordinary communication is relevant in this way, but not always. And people often confront situations when they are pretty sure that information is not relevant.

When you listen to someone talking, your mind is really quite busy integrating the speaker's comments. While your ears are listening, your mind is searching for a "context" in which to interpret what is being said. Since it would be nearly impossible for you to search everything you know, you will use some smaller part of your cognitive system as the context with which to interpret what the other person is saying. This is like searching your cupboard for whatever spices are available as opposed to making a trip to the supermarket. Just as a cook may not have just the right seasonings, the listener may not select just the right context. And this is how misunderstanding occurs.

Speakers know that their listeners must come up with a context for understanding what is being said and therefore help the listener to do so. Teachers, for example, face this problem every day and attempt to communicate in a way that helps students integrate new knowledge into what is already known. In actual practice communicators work together, back and forth, until relevance is found.

Obviously, processing information so that communicators understand one another requires a certain amount of cognitive **flexibility**. A person with high flexibility can assign a number of meanings or interpretations to a message or sign. A person with low flexibility is rigid in assigning meanings. High flexibility, then, means greater ability to find relevance in information. Flexibility also involves moving away from simple good-bad judgments about things. The more possibilities a person sees in a piece of information, the less apt he or she will be to make a simple, and potentially incorrect, judgment.

This consequence was made clear to one of the authors when a young woman came into his office to pick up her registration packet. She was listed as a speech communication major, but the professor had not seen her before. She rejected his attempts to provide academic counseling, and his first impression was that she was a "pseudomajor" who was using the department simply to get registration materials. But his ability to help this student was enhanced when he considered other possible explanations for her strange behavior. Perhaps she was confused and uncertain about what to major in. Perhaps she was reticent, a shy communicator. Maybe she was afraid the professor would force her to take speech classes. Once he considered these possibilities and overcame his initial negative judgment, he was able to talk openly with the student about her program. Only by being flexible was the professor able to communicate with this young woman. As a result, he helped her to see that her interests pointed in a different direction. Flexibility thus led to improved communication.

Information Load and Capacity

The ability to process information—to understand, integrate, remember, and find relevance—is affected greatly by the amount of information received in a given period of time—the **information load**. Sometimes

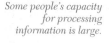

Some people's capacity for processing information is large.

you may feel understimulated and bored. At such times you are probably underloaded; you would like more information. At other times you may feel pressured, harried, or overstimulated; then you are probably overloaded. Everyone needs a certain amount of sensory input to remain interested, but too much information leads to confusion, fatigue, reduced critical thinking, inflexibility, and anxiety.

Think about how people design their homes, offices, and other spaces to provide greater or lesser degrees of information load. When people need greater stimulation, they seek a place with a high load of information. But when they are tired or need a break, they seek a place with a low information load. A student we know recently redecorated his room to offer variable loads of stimulation. The room serves as bedroom, sitting room, and study. When the lights are dimmed and soft music plays on the stereo, the information load is light; the setting is comfortable after a hard day's work. At other times—with full lights and lively music, some books on the desk, and visitors present—the information load increases greatly.

Related to the idea of information load is the concept of **information capacity**. Load involves the amount and diversity of information reaching a person; capacity is that person's ability to handle the information. At some point, an individual's capacity will be reached, and additional stimulation simply will not be processed. Capacity varies over the course of a day. Some people think more clearly and are better able to deal with information early in the day; others reach their peaks later. Capacity is also affected by fatigue, mood, and other emotional and physical factors.

People differ in their ability to screen out information. Some people—**screeners**—can control their capacity by tuning out unwanted stimulation. Others—**nonscreeners**—cannot. Some students can read a difficult book or write a paper in the middle of a living room with the television or radio blaring and children running through the house. Screeners like this are much less likely to experience overload. Nonscreeners, on the other hand, need a low-load environment in order to process information efficiently.

The concepts of information load and capacity are extremely important in everyday communication. A common fault of beginning speakers, for example, is to present more information in an eight-minute speech than the audience can process in that time. Speakers can do much to organize and develop their messages in a way that considers the listener's load and capacity. We will look at such practical concerns later in this chapter and in our discussion of public communication (Chapters 8 and 9).

In this section we have covered the basic nature of information and some of the factors involved in processing information. Of course, the cognitive system is not static, and information affects how people think. In the following section we investigate some of the ways in which thinking and behavior can change.

PERSUASION AS CHANGE

It has been said that nothing is as permanent as change. Consider the grandfather of one of the authors. As a young man he joined the rush for land when the Oklahoma territory was opened. During his lifetime he saw the development of electric appliances and the invention of the automobile, radio, and television. He lived through the Spanish-American War, two world wars, and the Korean conflict. Although he had been born before the Wright Brothers flew the first plane, shortly before his death he flew by commercial aircraft from one coast to the other in just a few hours.

Change is a constant in everyone's life. The world is changing at an exponential rate, and to live fully requires adapting to that change. In this section we will discuss how people change and how communication functions in the process.

Basic Definitions and Concepts

The role of communication in change is often referred to as persuasion. Early theorists defined **persuasion** as the attempt to influence the thoughts, feelings, and actions of the receiver. This transmissional definition has two disadvantages: it has a manipulative focus, and it does not distinguish persuasion from other forms of human influence such as physical force, coercion, or signal responses. For us, persuasion is better understood as a transaction with several characteristics: It is interpersonal—accomplished between people. Persuasion is accomplished by messages, not physical force. The communicators must perceive a choice. To the degree that communicators do not perceive a choice, the transaction is coercion. Also, persuasion is the effect intended by the communicators; it is not accidental or incidental.

Many people's general concept of persuasion is misleading, for they see it as a means of one person manipulating others to do or think what he or she wants. Even when persuasive communication is thought to be for the receiver's "own good," it still usually centers on the transmitter, which can lead to various communicative difficulties discussed later in the chapter. Furthermore, this view runs contrary to our discussion of ethical responsibility in communication (see Chapter 1).

Messages meant to persuade can appear in unlikely places.

If, as we have argued, change is both desirable and necessary for a fully human existence, then persuasive communication becomes an instrument whereby two or more individuals together determine the most desirable form that changes should take.

In a recent treatise on the subject of presentational speaking, Sonja Foss and Karen Foss discuss persuasion as "transformation" in these terms:

> Any change that results from presentational speaking is not forced on the audience. Your efforts are directed at enabling transformation— making it possible for those who are interested—not imposing it on those who are not. The speaker's invitation is an offering, an opening, an availability—not an insistence. Some in the audience may choose to accept this invitation; others will not. Your communication may appear to change thinking and behavior, but you do not and cannot change others. Such changes are the results of decisions by listeners who choose to hear others or to learn from others. Transformation

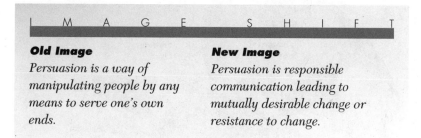

IMAGE SHIFT

Old Image
Persuasion is a way of manipulating people by any means to serve one's own ends.

New Image
Persuasion is responsible communication leading to mutually desirable change or resistance to change.

occurs only through the process of self-change generated by interaction with other perspectives.

Beliefs, Attitudes, and Values

It is difficult to discuss persuasion without coming to terms with beliefs, attitudes, and values.[4] Although they are sometimes used interchangeably, we prefer to discriminate among these terms, for the concepts are important to understanding persuasive communication.

It has been traditional to treat a **belief** as an accepted datum about the world that can be expressed by completing the statement "I believe . . ." For example, you might say (or think): "I believe

the sun will rise tomorrow."
the continent of Australia lies below the equator."
there is a God."
college professors have gone to school a long time."

Attitudes are clusters of beliefs about a particular object, person, topic, or situation that predispose a person to act in a certain way. For example, if you believe that capital punishment deters crime, is not discriminatory, and is sanctioned by the Bible, then you would probably hold a favorable attitude toward capital punishment and even vote for a candidate who favors it.

This does not mean that you can predict a person's behavior on the basis of an attitude. As we will see below, beliefs and attitudes are part

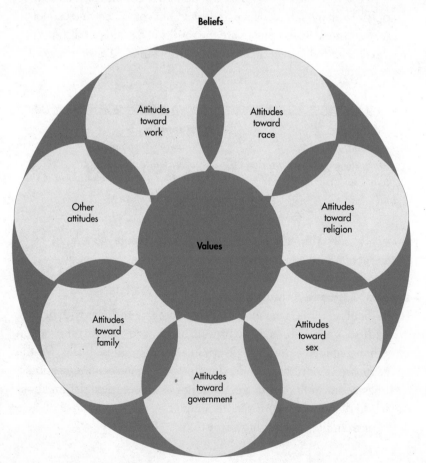

Beliefs

Figure 4.1
Interrelationship of beliefs, attitudes, and values.

of a larger cognitive system, and the larger system has much more control over behavior than does any single part of it.

Values are centrally held beliefs that provide standards for behavior or goals toward which behavior is directed. Being central to the belief system, they have a basic influence on how people behave. They constitute "life guides" and therefore are difficult to change. Because they are so fundamental, values are relatively few in number. Examples of values are peace, security, freedom, and responsibility.

Beliefs make up people's most common images about the world and number perhaps in the millions. Attitudes are clusters of beliefs, numbering probably in the thousands, whereas values are individual beliefs of central importance to a person, numbering but a few dozen. All values and attitudes are also beliefs; in addition, they may overlap. This relationship among beliefs, attitudes, and values is represented in Figure 4.1.

How do attitudes, values, and other beliefs interact to influence behavior? As we suggested earlier, not every attitude results in an identifiable behavior. But every attitude includes the tendency toward certain behavior.

Research has demonstrated that the relationship between an individual's behavior and his or her attitudes, values, and beliefs is not

The attitudes and behavior learned in war-torn countries is vastly different from what children learn in peaceful places.

simple, and it is far from absolute. Indeed, only rarely does a belief result directly in a particular behavior. Why, if an attitude is a predisposition to respond in a particular way, does the behavior not follow? The answer may be found in a statement heard often: "It is not that I value this less, but that I value that more." Clearly, many attitudes, values, and other beliefs operate simultaneously and frequently conflict with one another.

For example, if you are competing with someone from a different ethnic group for a job, your favorable attitude toward that group and your value of equality may conflict with your value of ambition. Something has to give. Furthermore, most theorists agree that attitudes, values, and other beliefs form a hierarchy of importance for each individual. This hierarchy differs for each individual, and it changes over time. Viewing attitudes, values, and other beliefs as vectors of varying strengths pushing or pulling on an individual, we see a situation of movement, or change, in the individual. The movement, or change, is the sum total of these conflicting or complementary vectors of varying strengths; they push and pull the individual in an internal tug of war (Figure 4.2).

Furthermore, individuals' behavior depends in large measure on the situation in which they find themselves. Attitudes, beliefs, and values are resources people use when they make decisions about how to act or

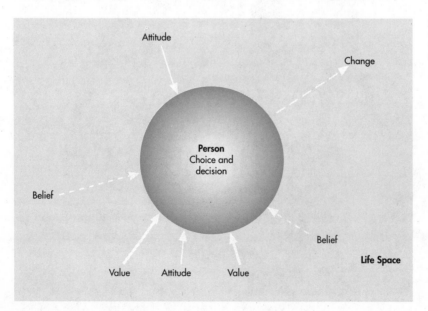

Figure 4.2
Relationships of beliefs, attitudes, and values with behavior.

what to do. Rarely is anyone stuck with just one kind of response. In essence, you have a repertoire of behaviors appropriate in a given situation and are faced with the problem of choosing how to respond.

Suppose, for example, that two of your friends decide to run against one another for a school office. Each of them asks for your support. What will you do? This is a decision that is virtually impossible to predict in advance. In essence, you will draw on your resources and do your best to respond effectively, which could include supporting both or neither.

How People Change

Earlier we suggested that persuasion is the process of changing one's image through communication. Now that we have described the nature of the image in terms of attitudes, beliefs, and values, let us take a closer look at the process of change. Several major factors are involved, including learning, tension reduction, changes in perception and reception, information processing, and source credibility.

Learning is change resulting from new information, rewards, and punishments received from the environment.[5] Some things are learned by direct experience, but much of what we learn comes from communication. People learn to make new associations through the messages they receive. Language itself is full of associations that affect learning throughout life. As children acquire language, they learn how things can be associated with one another.

People also reward and punish one another through communication. Like Pavlov's dog, which learned to salivate at the sound of a bell associated with food, human beings come to respond favorably to compliments and statements of regard, and they can respond unfavorably to criticism and statements of disrespect. Indeed, our sense of self is influenced by social interaction more than anything else. This too is a kind of learning.

Later in the chapter we discuss some of the ways in which learned information is integrated into the cognitive system.

Tension Reduction. One sales manager for an investment company maintains that he can more effectively persuade people to purchase an investment program if he can identify their "dominant want"—not their most basic need but their most fundamental desire or dissatisfaction. To illustrate this, he tells the story of a woman who seemed so self-satisfied that none of the salespeople in the office could interest her in an investment program. On deeper questioning, however, he discovered that although she had no particular desires for herself, she pitied a relative who had suffered many setbacks and difficulties. The salesman then was able to sell her an investment program that would help her relative.

Over the years people involved with change in human beings have dealt either intuitively or intentionally with the phenomenon of tension reduction. In explaining how people's images change, early psychologists referred to need (tension) while persuasion theorists focused on remedy (tension reduction).

The rhetorician Kenneth Burke called the state of tension **division** and referred to the state of tension reduction as **identification**. He also described this relationship as involving guilt (tension) and redemption (tension reduction). The religious overtones of Burke's terminology remind us of traditional Christianity's emphasis on sin (tension) and grace, or forgiveness (tension reduction).

As these examples show, observers for centuries have recognized the role of what we will call tension reduction in the process of human change. (Persuasion theorists have described this phenomenon in more specific and elaborate terms.)[6] Explanations of change based on tension reduction can be categorized into two groups: those focusing on internal sources of tension, and those focusing on external ones.

Explanations of human change based on tension resulting from internal sources have been referred to as drive-motive theories. **Drives** are conceived as internal, physiological states of tension. They can be either primary (innate) or secondary (acquired). Primary drives are rooted in the functions common to all animals, such as the need for food and water, the need to eliminate waste, the need to reproduce, the need to grow, the need to move, and ultimately the need for self-preservation or preservation of the species. But what causes some people to satisfy their hunger drive (tension) by eating hot chili, while others eat cold yogurt? As one colleague commented when he refused a tongue sandwich, "I'd never eat something that came out of the mouth of a cow. Pass the eggs, please."

Figure 4.3
Maslow's hierarchy of needs.

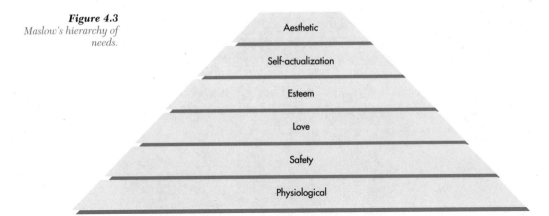

Abraham Maslow originated what may be the most sophisticated theory of change based on the assumption of innate needs. Besides the traditional "deprivation" needs relating to physiology, safety, and love or belonging, Maslow included three positive, humanistic needs: self-esteem, self-actualization, and aesthetics. **Self-actualization** is the degree to which people fulfill their highest potential and develop and use all their capabilities. It may be manifested through public service and altruism as well as by achieving superiority in some other aspect of life.

Another important part of Maslow's system is the hierarchical nature of needs. In a sense, people must satisfy their more basic needs before fulfilling the less basic. This **hierarchy of needs** can be represented as a pyramid, as shown in Figure 4.3.

Although we tend to agree with Maslow's general hierarchy, we take exception to its strict application. We have observed people whose basic needs for safety, love, and self-esteem may have been threatened in one aspect of their lives—say, family or career—but who still seem to be self-actualizing in other aspects of their lives. A crack may develop in some of life's aspects, while the remainder of the pyramid remains intact (see Figure 4.4). In any case, we think Maslow's theory of image change is useful.

Several explanations of human change deal not with internal drive states but with tension arising from external inconsistencies that people perceive in the environment. All such cognitive consistency theories operate on the assumption that a person is less likely to change behavior

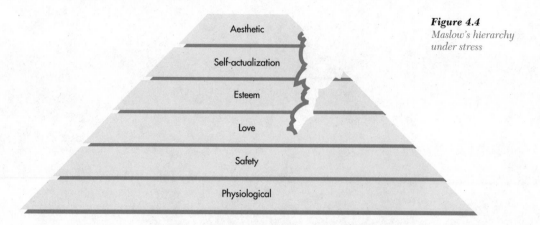

Figure 4.4
Maslow's hierarchy
under stress

if his or her cognitions of the outside world are consistent, not only among themselves but also within the individual's mind set. However, if a person's cognitions of the world are inconsistent with others' cognitions or with the individual's own image of the world, tension will build and the propensity to change the existing image will increase.

Take the example of Alex. When he was in high school back in the 1950s, his parents (whom he loved and respected) did not allow him to smoke cigarettes. After moving away from home, he was encouraged by a close friend to take up smoking. Tension developed. Should he defy his parents or his friend? Under peer pressure and wanting to act "adult," Alex decided to repudiate his parents' advice and try smoking. Tension was reduced somewhat, and Alex reduced the tension even further by downplaying his parents' wisdom. After he became thoroughly addicted and was smoking two packs a day, the surgeon general's report on cigarette smoking was released, stating that it is injurious to health. Tension again mounted. This time Alex reduced it through rationalization and by switching to low-tar cigarettes. Finally, at age forty-nine, he suffered a mild heart attack, and the doctor warned him to stop smoking at once. The tension skyrocketed, and at last he made a change: he quit smoking.

Incongruous cognitions of the external world can take various forms. First, people may receive incongruous messages or arguments. Most attitudes can be supported by valid arguments on either side. For instance, one group argues, "All guns should be banned; they promote violence in our society," while an opposing group argues, "The banning of guns violates the basic constitutional right of all Americans to bear arms." Second, people can perceive inconsistencies between a message and its source, as when a valued friend supports a cause that you despise. Should you think less of the friend or despise the cause less, or some of both? Third, people may perceive discrepancies among sources. In this case a valued source advocates something contrary to your image, while a disliked source supports your position. Whom should you believe?

So far we have been discussing tension reduction before or during the change process. But tension can also arise after a decision to change has been made. This usually involves a discrepancy between a new behavior and formerly held attitudes. That is, people believe one thing but do another. Such tension is usually called **dissonance**, and it can be handled in several ways. People may:

1. Derogate or depreciate the source.
2. Decide that the discrepancy is not very important or rationalize it in some other way.
3. Seek social support or supportive evidence for their viewpoint or action.
4. Misperceive the source's position.
5. Compartmentalize (ignore or forget that the cognitions are discrepant).
6. Attempt to convince the source (if available) of his or her error.
7. Modify their attitudes, beliefs, or values.[7]

Most observers of human behavior have concluded that people desire stability and consistency. When discrepancies are perceived, a "strain toward symmetry" occurs in any one or a combination of the above ways; as a result, change frequently takes place in one's personal image.

Changes in Perception. Would you characterize yourself as a liberal or a conservative? Because the study of communication almost inevitably involves discussion of social issues, we authors are regularly characterized by some students as being "fairly liberal." Friends in the business community usually push that to "extremely liberal," while many colleagues might say "fairly conservative." Actually, we characterize ourselves as "slightly left of center"; indeed, the longer we associate with the more "liberal" university community, the more liberal we seem to feel when interacting with other friends outside the university.

One widespread way of explaining how people change their beliefs, attitudes, and values is by describing how they define, or "place," themselves with respect to messages they receive. Usually referred to as social judgment theory, this approach describes human change as an interaction between people's judgment of where they stand with respect to messages and their ego involvement with the topic.[8] **Ego involvement** is the degree to which a belief, attitude, or value is central to a person's "being"; it has to do with issues, objects, or situations that the person considers vital to existence.

Several aspects of the social judgment process have important implications for how people change their belief systems and behavior. First, there is the process of comparing the position advocated in the message with what they perceive their own position to be. Their own position—or the locus of beliefs, attitudes, and values that they tend to favor—is called their **anchor.** Perhaps someone has judged a friend's behavior as being silly and foolish when you think it was perfectly normal. If so, you are comparing the behavior with an anchor that is different from the other person's.

Another aspect of judgment of messages is the notion that instead of having a single attitude about an object or situation, people have a range of related attitudes, values, and other beliefs that they more or less accept or reject. For this reason people seldom have the opportunity to vote for a political candidate who shares their exact position on all issues; rather, they tend to accept a range of views from a candidate who represents their general political outlook.

In the process of judging and responding to stimuli, people tend to distort the message in interesting ways. Their anchor can bend their judgment of the stimulus. For example, if you put one hand into a bowl of ice water and the other hand into a bowl of hot water and then plunge both hands into lukewarm water, it will not feel the same to each hand. The lukewarm water will seem warmer to the cold hand and colder to the hot hand. Similarly, if your political views are very conservative, a moderate viewpoint will seem liberal; but if you are ultraliberal, the same middle-of-the-road attitude will seem conservative.

Furthermore, if a message falls within people's range of acceptance, they will not only **assimilate** it into their belief systems but will also judge it as being closer to their anchors than it actually may be. And if a message falls outside their range of acceptance, they will not only reject it but will also perceive it as being more at odds with their position than it actually may be, a process called contrast.

Finally, people tend to make finer discriminations among various positions close to their anchors, and more gross discriminations among messages far from their anchors. As a conservative commentator once put it, "There are dozens of different kinds of conservatives, but there's not a dime's worth of difference between liberals, socialists, and communists." One could imagine a liberal murmuring back, "A conservative is a conservative is a conservative."

The heart of a social judgment explanation of change is the interaction between ego involvement and a person's judgment of social issues and situations. In general, the greater the ego involvement, the larger will be the range of rejection and the smaller the range of noncommitment. This has two effects on judgment and behavior. First, the greater the ego involvement, the more resistant one becomes to change. Perhaps you have known someone who held tenaciously to what you considered a strange and relatively unimportant view. For that person, however, the subject may have been highly ego involving, thus making him more resistant to change. Second, the greater the ego involvement, the more polarized one's position becomes. That is, people have a normal range of acceptance and a large range of rejection, and the range of noncommitment approaches zero. This is the situation when a person charges, "If you're not for me, you must be against me."

Another class of perception explanations of change has been termed **attribution** theories.[9] Early theorists such as Fritz Heider maintained that people behave as "naive social scientists" in an attempt to diagnose the behavior of other people as well as themselves. On the basis of observed behavior, people attribute to other people (or themselves) certain intentions, motives, beliefs, or attitudes that serve to explain or rationalize the observed behavior.

Sometimes people attribute behavior to the situation and sometimes to personal dispositions. **Situational attributions** rationalize people's behavior on the basis of things they cannot control, like being late for class because of a flat tire. **Dispositional attributions** explain people's behavior on the basis of things they can control, like being late for class because of sleeping in.

There seems to be a strong tendency in our society to use attributions to explain one's own and others' behavior. For example, imagine that your parents send you a check each month to cover your expenses. (Wouldn't that be nice?) What would happen if you failed to get the check one month? You would immediately try to figure out why. Perhaps you would use a situational attribution and conclude that your parents were so busy they forgot or that the Post Office delayed delivery. Or you might use a dispositional attribution and conclude, "Egad! They are cutting me off."

There is a funny thing about attributions. People tend to blame other people for things the others did wrong (dispositional attributions) but blame the situation for things they themselves did wrong (situational attributions). If your friend failed a test, you might conclude that he didn't study hard enough, a dispositional attribution, but if you failed the test, you would be more likely to conclude that the test was unclear and too hard, a situational attribution. Regardless, attributions can be either favorable or unfavorable, and the trust we feel toward others is definitely affected by the kinds of attributions we make.

One of the most significant contributions of the attribution approach is that it helps explain self-attributions. The way people attribute to themselves certain beliefs, attitudes, values, motives, and emotions on the basis of what is going on around them and their response to a situation. Attributing one's own behavior to dispositional factors can have a powerful change affect. If you infer that your behavior is related to things you can control, you may change other aspects of your cognitive system to reflect this behavior.

Here are some predictions based on the above idea:

1. The less you are able to rationalize your behavior on the basis of the situation, the more you will make adjustments in your cognitive system. The less you can say, "I had to do it," the more you must say, "I did what I believed in."

2. If your actions result in desirable consequences, you will make necessary adjustments in the cognitive system in order to take credit for those consequences. When something good happens to you, you are likely to say to yourself, "Well, I certainly have the right attitude."

3. The more you repeat a behavior in different situations, the more likely you are to attribute this behavior to your own good ways of thinking, and you will adjust your ways of thinking as necessary to justify the action. You will reason, "Since I keep doing that, it must be the right thing to do, and I must have correct attitudes."

Two techniques of persuasion are based in part on the above predictions. The first technique is what has been called **foot-in-the-door**. Compliance with a small initial request can result in a change in your cognitive system, which then leaves you open to larger requests. For example, one of the authors once loaned his second car to a relative "until I can buy a new one." What the author thought would be a one- or two-day inconvenience stretched into two months. This required changes in the author's attitudes toward himself, his relatives, and the meaning of "family."

Proattitudinal advocacy is a second technique that is well explained by attribution theory. Proattitudinal advocacy is defined as advocating publicly any argument that falls within a person's latitude of acceptance but that is discrepant from one's anchor. Making a public statement serves to strengthen a person's position, make action more likely, and make the person more resistant to change. Common examples of proattitudinal advocacy are found in testimonials given at business, religious, and other types of meetings.

Information Processing. One way of explaining how people change is to look at the way they process and integrate new information into their cognitive system and the way that information affects subsequent behavior. Imagine that you are cooking up a pot of vegetable soup. You combine some broth, onion, carrots, celery, and other ingredients. You taste the soup and decide it needs more onion. After adding more onion, you taste it again and decide it tastes too much like onion. You add more of the other ingredients, an herb, a potato, some pasta. Each time you add another ingredient the complex taste combination changes.

An attitude is like this vegetable soup. It is made up of a complex mixture of beliefs about an object. Each time new information is added to the pot (the cognitive system) the attitudes within the system change.

Martin Fishbein and Icek Ajzen have attempted to quantify the process whereby new information affects existing attitudes.[10] They first assume that people assign two probabilities to new information bearing on a belief: value and weight. The **value** of the belief is the degree to which a person evaluates the new information positively or negatively. Thus, when an environmentalist hears a proposal that toxic wastes be stored near her home, she may anticipate a degradation of the environment and evaluate that as a minus seven (-7) on a scale of ten. A local businessperson, on the other hand, may anticipate increased sales and evaluate the same information a plus nine (+9).

The **weight** a person places on the new information is the probability she or he assigns to its being accurate or actually happening. The impact the new belief has on one's attitude is determined by multiplying the value times the weight of the information. Thus, if the environmentalist thought the probability of environmental degradation actually happening was a plus eight (+8), the total impact on her attitude toward the storage proposal would be a negative fifty-six ($-7 \times +8 = -56$). If the businessperson was somewhat skeptical that his business would improve and assigned a plus two (+2), his attitude would be affected by a plus eighteen ($+9 \times +2 = +18$).

This relationship is represented mathematically as:

$$\text{Belief} = \text{value} \times \text{weight, or } B = vw$$

Few attitudes are composed of a single belief, however. The environmentalist or businessperson may also have beliefs about cost, an increase in population, jobs, health, national security, and various other matters related to toxic wastes. Thus, the mathematical formula for a single attitude might be:

$$A = (v_1 w_1) + (v_2 w_2) + (v_3 w_3) + (v_4 w_4), \text{ or}$$

Attitude toward toxic waste disposal = belief about environment plus belief about business plus belief about cost plus belief about . . . , etc.

In reduced form, then, the formula for an attitude looks like this:

$$A_o = S\,w_i v_i,$$

where A_o = attitude toward object; S = sum of; w_i = weight; and v_i = value. As you can see, each new piece of information can change the total mix of the attitude just as the addition of any ingredient will change the flavor of your vegetable soup. Thus, attitudes can be changed by new information that changes the weight or value of a belief or adds a new, relevant belief to the mix.

Fishbein and Ajzen have suggested that, instead of trying to predict behavior directly from an isolated attitude, it might be better to consider a person's *intent* to perform a certain behavior. Instead of attempting to measure your general attitude toward recycling newspapers, we should try to assess your intent to do so. Your intention to perform a behavior is determined by your attitude and by the social norms that you consider important.

A person's intent to behave in a particular way is called the **subjective norm**. The subjective norm is the person's judgment of the expectations or beliefs of significant others about the behavior in question. The individual asks, "What would my parents (or friend or religious leader) think of this behavior?" Subjective norms are a composite of the beliefs an individual attributes to significant others and his or her motivation to comply with those beliefs. The formula for the subjective norm could be expressed:

Subjective norm = normative beliefs × motivation to comply

Expressed as a mathematical formula it would be:

$$SN = NB \times MC$$

When the formula for subjective norms is combined with the previous formula for determining attitudes, the formula for a person's intent to perform a particular behavior becomes:

Behavioral intent = attitudes + subjective norms, or

$$BI = (A)w + (SN)w$$

In English, your intent to do something is determined by your attitude and the opinion of other people in your life. Your attitude and others' opinions are weighted. Sometimes attitudes are more important, and sometimes others' opinions are more important. Will you recycle your newspapers? The answer depends on your attitude toward recycling and how important that attitude is to you and on the opinions of your friends and family and the importance of that opinion to you.

For our purposes the mathematical formulas are less important than an understanding of the importance of attitude and the beliefs of significant others in the process of personal change. Motivation to conform to subjective norms has not been found to contribute significantly to change.

The theory of reasoned action is an intuitively appealing explanation for how information affects attitudes and behavior. Another popular approach is the **elaboration likelihood** model (ELM) advanced by Richard Petty and John Cacioppo.[11] The essence of the ELM is the idea that change is a function of the degree to which people become involved in the communication process and therefore "elaborate" on the incoming message of new information. The ELM is based on the assumption that people want to have what appears to them as "correct" attitudes or beliefs but that it is not possible for people to carefully evaluate every bit of information with which they are bombarded each day. Therefore people evaluate, or "elaborate," messages selectively.

According to Petty and Cacioppo, in order to become actively involved in processing new information, people must be both *able* and *motivated*. If you are watching an ad on television that you couldn't care less about, you will not become involved in thinking or elaborating about the issues in the message. Furthermore, if you hear a message that you don't understand, you will not be able to analyze it carefully.

If you are both able and motivated toward the issues in the message, the ELM posits that you will become involved and process the message through the **central route** in your cognitive system. The central route employs the relevant beliefs and attitudes in an active way. When you use central processing, you are more critical and therefore not likely to change, but if change does occur, it will be both persistent and stable over time. In addition, new attitudes and beliefs will be relatively resistant to change in the future.

According the ELM, if people lack either the ability or motivation to actively process a message through the issue-oriented central route, they process it through the easier **peripheral route**. The peripheral route consists of the personal relationships, emotions, and other marginal cues that require little active thought to process. Although beliefs and attitudes can be changed more easily by the nonanalytic peripheral route, such change will be less enduring, less accessible, less resistant to subsequent change, and less predictive of later behavior.

Unfortunately, the ELM overlooks the possibility that people might actively think about how their relationships affect their behavior, and it completely ignores the role of values in persuasion. Nonetheless, the ELM is a very useful way of looking at people as proactive agents in the persuasion process.

Source Credibility and the Trust Bond. Aristotle argued that there are three main kinds of persuasive appeals: logos (logical appeals), pathos (emotional appeals), and ethos (personal appeals). He further argued that personal appeals are the most influential and are derived from the somewhat invariant factors of good sense, good character, and good will. More recent rhetoricians have referred to competence, integrity, and good will as the factors or dimensions of ethos—something that today we would call credibility.

Modern scholars have devoted considerable research to identifying the factors of what they call, still in somewhat transmissional terms, source credibility. A receiver's perception and judgment of other people is, of course, an element in all theories of change, but we have chosen to discuss it separately because of its significance in communication and because a large body of research is devoted to it. A review of this extensive literature reveals some interesting findings.[12]

Generally speaking, the characteristics of personal influence have been found to be situational rather than invariant. Such factors as dynamism, poise, and sociability have emerged occasionally. A majority of studies have found evidence for a characteristic that we would call competence but that also is referred to as qualification, authoritativeness, reasonableness, and so forth. The dimension of personal influence that emerges in most studies of credibility is what we will call integrity. This dimension has also been referred to by researchers as character, safety, morality, and trustworthiness.

Whether based on "competence" or "integrity" or some combination of dimensions, we think source credibility ultimately arises from mutual

Trust contributes to interpersonal influences.

trust between communicators or among a group of communicators. This **trust bond** is one of the most fundamental variables in human change and in communication generally.

Most people are familiar with the power of the trust bond, which can be illustrated by an incident reported by a professor. A student in a public speaking class once strode to the podium, placed a small pair of shoes with red stains on them in front of the listeners, and said, "This is all I have to remember my sister by." There followed a strong persuasive appeal for safe driving. The clear suggestion was that the speaker had lost a sister in an automobile accident. After class, when the instructor expressed regrets about the tragedy, the student replied, "Don't worry about it; I never had a sister." Besides the serious ethical implications of this incident, it had specific repercussions. Several classmates overheard the exchange, and when the student next made a persuasive appeal, the entire class knew about the incident. They responded derisively and sat unmoved by the student's most skillful attempts at persuasion.

Similarly, when trust is destroyed in a marriage, communication between wife and husband becomes difficult, and the marriage itself is jeopardized. Whether in business, the classroom, social settings, government, or the home, the trust bond facilitates—indeed, makes possible—communication and change.

Communication theorists usually discuss the development of trust in terms of methods extrinsic or intrinsic to messages. Trust can be developed by manipulating variables within the communication context but outside the message itself. These variables usually involve prior experiences with other communicators, endorsements by others, or contextual evidence of trustworthiness. Let us elaborate on these three means.

The most direct and effective way to develop a trust bond is through extended personal experience. In all communication situations people must consider not only the short-term effects of their communication but also the long-term effects. It may take years to develop the trust bond needed for a successful business, marriage, or political career, and such a bond may be destroyed in a matter of moments.

Building trust through prior experience is not always possible, however. People with a budding political career, a newly opened business, or a blind date may need someone to vouch for them until they can establish credibility. In a sense, they borrow trust from another person or organization who endorses their candidacy, product, or personal integrity. Every salesperson knows that a referral by a trusted friend is the best introduction to a new client. When any persuasive campaign moves into a new territory, the endorsement of a familiar and trusted name (either individual or organizational) will accelerate the establishment of the trust bond.

Finally, trust can be developed by providing contextual evidence of credibility. Virtually any association with another credible source— which can be established or suggested by the contextual variables within which communication takes place—can enhance the trust bond. During political campaigns, some churches invite candidates to speak to members of the congregation. Although the church is not endorsing the candidate, the fact that voters remember the candidate in association with the church may contribute to their trust in the candidate.

Variables within the message itself can also help build trust. These variables can be coded either verbally or nonverbally. Intrinsic methods of building trust basically involve building personal identifications with other communicators, which can take the form of shared experiences, self-disclosure, or context and language variables within the message.

One of the reasons Rush Limbaugh is so popular is that he expresses articulately and passionately a point of view shared by many conservatives. Regardless of what you yourself may think of him,

Limbaugh's daily talk radio program resonates with the feelings of many people who do not have the skill to express their ideas as clearly as he. His language is simple and forceful, and he speaks with great confidence. That is why Rush fans respond with a simple "ditto."

We have seen that people change as a result of learning, tension from both internal and external stimuli, interaction between cognitions and ego involvement, and finally mutual trust. Now let us see why people often resist change.

Why People Resist Change

In the previous sections we have argued from the assumption that change is a pervasive and necessary process and a mutually desirable result of the communication transaction. But what if you consider change to be undesirable? What if you want to keep yourself or another person from changing a behavior? Consider the incumbent politician who has won the past few elections handily. What he or she wants to do is keep supporters from changing their voting behavior and defecting to an opposing candidate. Similarly, most parents spend years instilling values into their children, and they want their children to maintain these values and the associated attitudes and behaviors. Thus, incumbents and parents have a vested interest in knowing which variables enhance or induce resistance to change. Meanwhile, communicators who want to persuade people to change need to know what causes resistance so they can try to remove the barriers to their goal.

Variables That Affect Resistance. In general, the process of inducing resistance to persuasion involves messages that seek to reduce susceptibility to persuasive communication. Such messages are designed to strengthen a person's resistance to counterarguments and future persuasive attempts. Resistance factors have been grouped into two broad classes: (1) those that produce resistance to change without regard for specific topics or sources and (2) those that produce resistance to change in specific situations or on specific subjects.

Certain personality variables and psychological states seem to influence resistance to persuasion and are not related to particular topics. Instead, these characteristics of a communicator's psychological makeup cause the person to be generally more or less persuadable.

These characteristics include level of self-esteem, anxiety level, and degree of hostility.

Early research seemed to show that people with high *self-esteem* were less persuadable than people with low self-esteem. Later theorists have recognized a curvilinear relationship between self-esteem and persuadability: people with very high or very low self-esteem are less susceptible to persuasive appeals than are people with moderate self-esteem.

Anxiety level also appears to be associated with resistance to change. However, the relationship between anxiety and change is complex. As in the case of self-esteem, anxiety and change seem to have a curvilinear relationship. That is, people with very high or very low anxiety seem resistant to change, whereas people with moderate anxiety seem to be the most persuadable.

Hostility is another personal characteristic related to change. In general, it has been found that hostility increases people's resistance to change. Interestingly, however, hostility makes people less resistant to persuasive messages that advocate harsh or violent actions.

Although self-esteem, anxiety, and hostility have been found to be related to change, a word of caution is in order. The relationship in each case is complex and hence not absolutely predictable. Furthermore, attempts to manipulate such characteristics as anxiety and hostility in fellow human beings may be risky at best and downright unethical at worst. Finally, the enhancement of self-esteem in order to induce resistance to change probably would require an extended interpersonal relationship.

There are also other ways to induce a generalized resistance to change that do not require personality alterations. They include linking, commitment, reduced inconsistency, and inoculation.

The term **linking** is used to describe the phenomenon of connecting a belief, attitude, value, or action to related beliefs or attitudes, to accepted values or goals, and to significant individuals or groups. It is much easier to tear a single page of a book or break a thin wire than it is to tear a telephone book or break a giant cable. Similarly, if beliefs have centrality and interrelatedness, they should be more resistant to change. On the other hand, if one of the anchored or linked beliefs is attacked successfully, all associated beliefs tend to become more vulnerable.

This "multiplier effect" can cause the beliefs in a system to fall like dominoes. We have all known people who felt completely dejected because of a minor disappointment in only one part of their lives. Similarly, many people have "lost their faith" when one religious belief was shattered.

Enhancing the **commitment** of communicators is one of the most effective ways of inducing resistance to persuasion. Generally speaking, an increase in commitment to a belief, attitude, or value increases resistance to subsequent appeals to change. It has been suggested that commitment can be enhanced by strengthening a private belief, securing a public endorsement of a belief, securing a behavioral

People who become active in political campaigns are highly resistant to the persuasive messages of opponents.

commitment, or revealing an external commitment to a belief. In the case of an incumbent politician, the commitment of supporters can be intensified if they speak out in public in favor of the candidate, contribute money, or work on the campaign. While these behaviors may not win any converts, they do wonders in ensuring the commitment of existing supporters.

Not only can resistance to change be induced generally, but people can be made resistant to persuasive appeals relating to particular topics. For example, if people can be encouraged to change in order to reduce cognitive dissonance, then the *reduction of cognitive inconsistency* should induce resistance to change. The more satisfied constituents are with their current situation, the less likely they are to change their voting behavior. As most politicians learn, it is difficult to defeat an incumbent during peace and prosperity.

One of the most fascinating concepts related to resistance to change has come to be known as **inoculation theory**.[13] Just as a physician inoculates a patient with a harmless dosage of a virus in order to build up the patient's natural resistance, so a communicator can "inoculate" another person with information and arguments that will counteract anticipated appeals to change.

Arguments designed to inoculate can either support the established position or anticipate refutational arguments with appropriate answers or counterarguments. In the case of supportive inoculation, parents who don't want their children to use drugs may take their kids on an enjoyable outing and then say, "You don't need drugs to have a good time." The refutational argument might be, "Your friends may tell you that drugs have no physical side effects, but they don't mention that you could have a fatal car accident while you're high or that you can become seriously addicted."

Communicator Involvement. The most consistent findings of research that has examined resistance to change relate to communicator involvement. Generally speaking, the more involved people are in the communication process, the more enduring will be their beliefs, and hence the more resistant the people will be to change. Involvement can be increased through role playing, counterattitudinal advocacy, and overt feedback.

We are all familiar with *role playing*; some have claimed that we play roles throughout our lives. But here we are referring to a more formal form of role playing, in which people consciously assume particular roles in a preconceived dramatic situation. The technique of role playing has been used extensively in therapy and in training programs to improve interpersonal relationships, group problem solving, and family communication. If a school conducts a workshop to improve relations among administrators, teachers, students, and parents, members of these groups are commonly asked to exchange roles and act out scenes of common problems. Presumably, this exercise enables participants to see the other point of view more clearly. In any case, role playing tends to increase both attitude change and resistance to subsequent persuasive appeals.

Counterattitudinal advocacy is a special kind of role playing in which a person generates arguments publicly in opposition to prior beliefs. Generally, counterattitudinal advocacy enhances both attitude change and resistance to subsequent change. As many political strategists know, if a voter has taken a public position in favor of a candidate or initiative, he or she will have difficulty changing back at voting time.

Finally, communicator involvement and hence resistance to subsequent change is enhanced by *overt feedback* from one or another communicator. In both public and private contexts, overt feedback can increase people's involvement. Parents may ask a child, "When do you plan to get home?" Or a car salesperson may encourage the customer to verbalize why the particular car meets his or her needs. In both cases, the overt feedback increases the communicator's involvement. The child is likely to get home on time, and the customer will be more satisfied with the purchase. In public contexts, a salute to the flag or the singing of the national anthem or other songs may enhance commitment to one's country. Part of Jesse Jackson's appeal is his encouragement of overt feedback from his audiences. Overt feedback has long been encouraged as a way of monitoring the accuracy of message reception, but researchers are now realizing that it also can have communicative value by inducing resistance to subsequent change.

PROBLEMS OF INFORMATION AND PERSUASION

By considering information and persuasion, two fundamental elements of speech communication, you should now have a better idea of how messages affect images. Here we will consider some common problems related to information and persuasion. There are, of course, more potential problems in these areas than we can cover in a few pages, but if you can become more sensitive to the most common pitfalls, you will be well on your way to becoming a better communicator.

Information Load and Capacity

Human beings have a finite capacity for processing information. People simply cannot handle all available information in a particular time period. Yet many communicators seem to assume that they can: "Get this report ready by tomorrow!" "There will be an exam on the first two hundred pages tomorrow in class." "Hi, I'm bringing the gang over for a little party in about an hour."

Many members of organizations complain about the enormous amount of information they are expected to process. The term "information explosion" is trite but true. For example, every day the authors are stuck with the job of sorting, scanning, and processing our mail. Typically, we divide it into three piles: discard, hold, and use. (It's interesting how the middle pile seems to build up over the year. By June we move much of the "hold" pile to the circular file—the wastebasket.) When you add mail to phone calls, meetings, interoffice memos, and other daily input, you can imagine the kinds of information overload college professors can be subject to.

Many employees now enjoy the benefits of voice message service (VMS) on their telephones. This is a great innovation unless you forget to check your messages regularly. If you have ever used VMS, you know the sinking feeling when you pick up the phone and hear, "Welcome to VMS. You have twenty-three messages." Or worse, you log into your E-mail and face fifty-seven new messages.

When originating messages, communicators need to be sensitive to problems of overload. Good communicators adapt to the situation by considering the capacities and obligations of other communicators. You should never be surprised if the information that you consider crucial is ignored or unnoticed by other communicators. In fact, it is sometimes beneficial to use multiple channels. In some college departments, printed announcements are often supplemented by oral announcements. Remember that redundancy is an important part of sending and receiving messages.

Message originators can also help by organizing their information usefully. Message organization is an important part of good communication, and we will explore some practical guidelines concerning this in Chapter 9.

The important thing to remember in dealing with problems of channel capacity and load is to know your own needs for information and to be sensitive to what other people should know. Ask yourself, "What do I need to learn from this?" And think to yourself, "What is most important for my listener or reader to understand in this situation?"

A related problem is that people sometimes are underloaded. Human beings need a certain amount of stimulation for personal growth; boredom is no fun. For that reason they tend to be uncomfortable when they want and need information but none is forthcoming. In such situations, the stimulation load is low, and people want to learn all they can. A good message or set of messages contains an optimal amount of information: enough for the problem at hand but not too much to process.

Timing

An eleven-year-old charged into her father's study and blared out, "How can I earn some money, Dad?" Her father replied, "I don't know. I'm very busy right now and don't have time to think about it." A few moments of silence passed. "But I really need some money. Could I wash the car?" Again the parent replied, "I'm sorry, but I'm in the middle of this project and can't talk." More silence. "Maybe I could cook dinner tonight." That was the last straw: "Please! I've got to concentrate on this. Ask me later." Then, with a slam of the door, the girl screeched, "Well, see if I ever come to you for advice again!"

Children are often insensitive to the problems and involvements of others. But timing of communication can be a problem in the adult world as well. Human capacity to deal with information changes from moment to moment, and people differ in their abilities to shift attention from one thing to another. Communicators must be aware of such differences. On one occasion a student showed up for a class with an "Add" card she had received by mistake from a secretary. Even though more than a dozen students were ahead of her on the waiting list for the class, she wanted to argue the matter with the instructor in front of the class, despite the fact that the period had begun. Needless to say, the professor was not very receptive.

People can mitigate problems of timing by becoming more sensitive to the demands of the situation. In addition to assessing how much information you or other communicators need, try to be aware of when information is needed—or not needed—and when it is best to seek information you would like to have.

Appropriateness of Information

Besides being aware of timing, you should consider the appropriateness of giving or seeking specific information. For several years a friend of the authors has been planting a garden on a vacant lot that is part of a neighbor's yard. The neighbor was always delighted to have the garden, but our friend has often thought it would be nice to own the lot herself. Recently the neighbor died, and our friend began to wonder about the disposition of the neighbor's property. But it seemed inappropriate to inquire about the property immediately after the neighbor's death. After enough time had passed, our friend made her inquiry and was able to buy the parcel.

When seeking or providing information, it is best to consider a number of situational factors. What is the other person's state of mind? Are you ready to get or give this information? Is this the right place to exchange the information? Are others present who should or should not participate in the exchange of the information? We are not suggesting that you be deceptive or secretive, but good communicators are adaptive; they are sensitive to timing and appropriateness in their transactions with others.

Adequacy of Information

Adequacy is a catchall word. One could ask, "Adequate in what sense?" Recall that information is useful to the extent that it reduces uncertainty in the image. Thus we can ask, "Is the information adequate for clarifying or adding to the communicator's image of the situation?" Three elements of adequacy are important: quantity, focus, and validity.

First, we need to question whether information is adequate in *quantity*. Quantity is not the same as load. *Load* refers to the amount of information relative to channel capacity, whereas quantity refers to the amount of information relative to what is needed or desired. If you feel you do not have enough information to solve a particular problem, you are questioning the adequacy of the information at hand. Of course, you can get too much information, as students sometimes feel. "Ask a professor what time it is," said one student, "and she will give you the history of the clock."

Information adequacy also depends on appropriate *focus*. Does the information relate directly to the situation or problem at hand? Information is not adequate if it does not tell you what you want to know. People often run into this problem when seeking information in building-supply stores. It can be frustrating to present a plumbing or electrical problem to a salesperson and get all kinds of information about nuts, bolts, connectors, and pipes but nothing that really answers the main question.

Finally, adequacy can be evaluated from the standpoint of *validity*, which is the accuracy or credibility of information. Perhaps the reason you are suspicious of many commercial advertisements is that you question the validity of their information. Is it really true that this detergent gets clothes cleaner than that detergent, or that this pain reliever eliminates your headache faster than the rival pain reliever?

Mistrust

Perhaps one of the greatest causes of communication problems is mistrust. We would go so far as to say that trust is the foundation of communication: without trust, any communication is in serious trouble. Consider door-to-door sales. Many people establishing a household have bought a product from a door-to-door salesperson only to find out that the claims were exaggerated or distorted. How does that experience affect the possibility of a second sale? Obviously, persuasive communication is destroyed. Although people may choose to tell white lies or use other questionable means of communication, they must continuously weigh the immediate purpose against the long-range effect of weakening or destroying the trust bond. Aside from the ethical and legal implications of insincere communication, serious problems can result from the destruction of trust.

Ego Involvement

Have you ever observed a wife attempting to teach her husband to drive a car, or vice versa? Or a parent teaching a child to swim? With over sixty years of teaching experience between us, the authors still find it difficult to teach our own children much of anything. Yet we both enjoy teaching other people's children. It has been said that a doctor who treats himself or herself has a fool for a physician. Why? Because these professional activities, as well as other forms of communication, require a degree of objectivity that is impaired by excessive ego involvement. Not infrequently—in the family, at work, in organizations—if ego involvement is too great, communication problems can develop.

There is no cure-all for this malady, although several suggestions might help. The first is to increase awareness. If you are approaching a communication situation that could be overly ego involving, you can consciously strive not to overreact; and if you cannot control yourself, you can postpone the situation until a better time.

If communication with a particular person or about a particular topic becomes impossible because of ego involvement, you have two alternatives: avoidance or professional help. Sometimes one can simply choose not to talk about certain ego-involving topics with certain people. This is well and good, if the topic can be avoided. But sometimes one cannot avoid a topic or a person that is ego involving. In such a case, professional help should be sought from a qualified, objective third party. Perhaps fewer marriages would end in divorce if couples had their marital communication checked by a professional as often as they have their teeth checked.

Intolerance for Ambiguity
In our world of uncertainty, information rigidity is a real handicap. Both in information processing and persuasion, you must have a certain amount of flexibility and a willingness to accept a number of possibilities for meaning. Equivocation is common and sometimes salutary, and unintended ambiguity is inevitable.

Good communicators are willing to explore a variety of possible meanings with other communicators. They are willing to accept the eventuality of having other peoples' meanings for the same message differ from their own. And they do not get too upset when what they want does not necessarily come to pass. That's what is meant by living in the world of reality. The common response to overly rigid people with an intolerance for ambiguity is usually something like, "Get a life!"

SUMMARY

Information and persuasion are both aspects of a message that affect the receiver's image. The perception and interpretation of messages constitute information; information reduces uncertainty in our image. Redundancy of information serves to counteract noise, reduce ambiguity, promote learning, and reinforce attitudes, beliefs, and values. Information helps reduce uncertainty by changing perceptions, improving competence, and altering goals.

Communicators do not always seek to reduce uncertainty. Sometimes they communicate equivocally, a typical response in an avoidance-avoidance situation.

Information is always processed through one's cognitive system, which is an organized set of categories and operations in the mind. The cognitive system consists of knowledge structures and cognitive processes. Cognitive processes include focusing, integrating, inferring, storing, retrieving, selecting, and implementing. The goal of communication is to make information relevant to the cognitive system, and senders and receivers work together to achieve relevance. Information processing is also affected by flexibility, information load, and information capacity.

Persuasion can be viewed as change resulting from symbolic interaction. In persuasion, as opposed to coercion, there is a perceived choice on the part of the participants. Persuasive communication is designed to lead to mutually desirable changes. Changes may occur in beliefs, attitudes, values, or behavior.

Learning can change people's belief structures, as can internal tensions or drives. Persuasion also occurs through changes in perception. People's judgment of external messages in relation to their own position (anchor) and ego involvement can influence those perceptual changes, as can various causal attributions. The well-known techniques of foot-in-the-door and proattitudinal advocacy operate in this way.

Another factor of change is information processing. The way new information is integrated and organized into the cognitive system affects the degree and type of change, and how people process information depends in large measure on ability and on motivation, which is affected by ego involvement. Finally, people change their attitudes and behavior on the basis of personal relationships with other communicators—they look for credibility and trust.

Resistance to change can be induced by using strategies that affect a communicator's level of self-esteem, anxiety, or hostility. In addition, resistance is enhanced through linking, commitment, reduced inconsistency, and inoculation. Role-playing, counterattitudinal advocacy, and overt feedback—all means of involvement—are also ways of inducing resistance to change.

Problems in communication can arise from information overload, violation of channel capacity, poor timing, inappropriate seeking of information, inadequate information, mistrust, excessive ego involvement, and intolerance for ambiguity.

Communication Settings

5 Understanding and Improving Interpersonal Communication

I t is dinner time in a typical American home. The teenaged son is talking with his mother about his date for the evening. The father's mind is wandering, and the younger sister is eating quietly. "We may come here after the dance," the son comments casually. "OK," his mother responds, "there are snacks in the refrigerator."

Later that evening, after the sister has gone to bed, mother and father watch the late news on television and then go to bed. As they are drifting off, the front door opens, and the boy and his date enter the house. They get some food from the kitchen and settle down in the living room for a "quiet conversation." Mother and father stir, finding it difficult to sleep: the price of parenthood.

The front door opens again, and a dozen noisy teenagers invade the living room—friends. The noise level rises dramatically as the party gets underway. Father fumes for a while and then suggests, "Why don't we go in there and tell them to hold it down?" Mother replies, "I don't want them to feel unwelcome in our home. Besides, I'd rather have them here than out somewhere getting into trouble." "But don't we have a right to some consideration in our own home?" father asks, his anger rising. "You're overreacting," his wife responds, as she rolls over and pretends to sleep.

Still later, when the party has broken up, an argument develops between mother and father. Accusations and overstatements result in hurt feelings and damaged egos. It takes a week of concentrated effort before turbulent emotions are calmed and family relationships and communication return to normal.

As this example shows, interpersonal communication can profoundly affect people's lives. In this chapter we will discuss some principles that apply to all interpersonal communication and then focus on communication with family and friends and in professional settings.

RULES AND RELATIONSHIPS: A TRANSACTIONAL PERSPECTIVE

From a transactional perspective, interpersonal communication involves dynamic, ongoing interaction within a physical, social, and cultural setting. It is the primary means by which human beings make connections with each other, and it is the process by which social reality is constructed. Interpersonal communication is possible because people have expectations about what certain acts mean and what responses those acts require. Interpersonal communication, in other words, is made possible by rules.

An interpersonal transaction is a rule-governed event. **Rules** are expectations about how people will behave in a relationship. They are guidelines for interaction. Usually communication rules are tacit, or unspoken; they are followed rather automatically, although sometimes people are highly aware of the rules governing a particular situation.

For example, you may or may not be comfortable at parties. It is hard for some people to move about in a crowded room, conversing superficially with one person after another. Others do this easily. In this setting, you may become very conscious of the unspoken rules involved, rules governing how long you are expected to chat with another person, what topics are permitted, how close to stand, when to touch, and how to end a conversation politely. Rule behavior is not this obvious in all settings, but it is almost always in operation.

There are two broad sources of rules in any given context. **External rules** come from outside the immediate relationship; these are social and cultural expectations about how people should behave in general. The most obvious example is how a greeting should be made. **Internal rules** arise from the unique interaction within any given relationship. These are the guidelines worked out by two people or a group of people and are not necessarily shared by society at large. You might, for example, have worked out a special greeting with a particular friend that is different from the usual, "Hi, how are ya."

In general, your behavior around others is governed by a combination of external and internal rules. External rules help you out when you don't know the other person very well, and internal rules govern your behavior around people with whom you have an ongoing relationship. External rules are important because they help define what people have in common with their culture. Internal rules are important because they help define what people have in common with particular other people.

It is important to understand that rules are guidelines for behavior, not laws. They help reduce the ambiguity about how to act with a particular person in a particular situation, but they may or may not be followed. In addition, internal and external rules both change. In fact, one of the best ways to initiate a change in a relationship is to change the rules that have developed in it (internal rules). Tension, conflict, and even breakup in a marriage can be caused by a realignment of the old rules of that relationship.

Similarly, one of the most common methods of social protest is the deliberate violation of behavioral expectations (external rules). The civil rights movement was launched into public awareness when Rosa Parks refused to follow the rule of sitting in the back of the bus, and in Montgomery, Alabama, the rules were changed with the famous bus boycott.

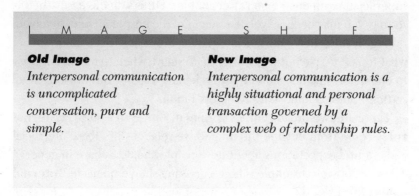

Old Image
Interpersonal communication is uncomplicated conversation, pure and simple.

New Image
Interpersonal communication is a highly situational and personal transaction governed by a complex web of relationship rules.

Let us look now more carefully at the nature of interpersonal relationship. We begin by examining communication patterns.

Communication Patterns in Relationships

Whenever two people have expectations for one another, a relationship exists between them. Sometimes this is a long-term relationship, but often it is short lived. Some relationships, such as marriage, are very important, and others, such as that between customer and store clerk, are less so, but expectations and a pattern of actions are present in either case.

A relationship is defined by this normally subconscious pattern of actions, thoughts, and feelings. For example, one of the most common aspects of supervisor-subordinate relationships in organizations is status. Higher-level members are expected to have more status than those lower in the hierarchy. As a result, subordinates usually pause at the

Most interpersonal communication takes place between dyads— two people.

door of a supervisor's office, awaiting an invitation to enter. This subtle communication behavior and others like it define the dominance-submission relationship.

A relationship, then, is defined by what people do and say; at the same time, what a person does and says is influenced by how a relationship is defined. Pausing for an invitation before entering the door of a supervisor's office both reflects and reinforces the supervisor-subordinate relationship.

The rule structure of a relationship leads to a pattern of interaction that comes to characterize the relationship. Look at your family as an example. Over time, certain patterns of interaction develop and become predictable, and the nature of the family relationship is determined by these patterns of communication.

We learned in Chapter 2 that messages consist of two dimensions— communication and metacommunication. In interpersonal relationships, the first dimension is the **content level** and the second is the **relationship level**. The content message deals with the subject at hand, and the relationship message defines some aspect of the relationship at that moment. When a mother tells her son that he cannot go swimming unless she is present, she is expressing information (the content), but she is also saying something about her authority (the relationship).

Because relationship patterns are being formed with every communication act, relationships are constantly being remade. People's everyday actions toward one another reinforce the existing set of expectations or set up new ones. Sometimes relationships go smoothly because the participants are comfortable with the expectations and act accordingly. At other times relationships are not very smooth because the participants are having a hard time establishing a pattern.

Coordination is a crucial element of the relationship.[1] Relationships can exist in three states—uncoordinated, unhappy coordination, and happy coordination. An uncoordinated state occurs when one or more members feel that their own or other members' responses are inappropriate or confusing, when the rules are unclear, or when others seem to be violating the rules. This state of affairs is relatively common, and it can be a serious communication problem. Almost all close relationships have periods in which the partners have trouble meshing their actions, when rules need to be clarified or renegotiated.

Most people find it hard to live within a confused system for long periods of time, and if the partners in a relationship fail to achieve some semblance of coordination, the relationship may fail. Even good relationships occasionally enter periods of poor coordination. Relationships may be good precisely because the partners are able to live through these periods and accept the changes that they may portend.

Although coordination can be a sign of a successful relationship, it is not necessarily so. Some patterns of interaction are highly coordinated but in a negative way. If the partners in a relationship do not like the pattern, no matter how coordinated it is, the relationship is probably in trouble. An **unwanted repetitive pattern** can be terribly dangerous because it is neither desired nor controllable. The battered spouse syndrome offers a good example of an unwanted repetitive pattern. The rule structure dictates a certain abusive pattern in which one partner batters the other, apologizes, and says it will not happen again; the victim accepts the good intentions of the violent member; and the pattern occurs again and again in a predictable fashion.

Of course, coordination can also produce a very happy state of affairs. If the partners in a relationship are satisfied with the pattern and come to rely on it, the communication is about as successful as it can possibly be. Mutual satisfaction in a relationship is probably a sign that communication needs are being met.

Communication Needs in Relationships

All people need human contact. Interaction is as essential to good health as food. But people vary in the amount and kind of interaction they need, and their needs can be met in a variety of ways. Within a relationship, communication needs are established and met according the rules of the relationship. Here we look at several types of communication needs.

Inclusion, Control, Affection. People have a need for **inclusion** with others. That is, they need to feel part of a group, to be accepted. When a person's need to be included is met, he or she feels worthwhile. Anyone who has moved to a new town or a new school has probably felt the inclusion need acutely.

The second communication need involves **control**. When this need is met at the desired level, a person feels competent and responsible. For example, most people have experienced the frustration of dealing with some bureaucratic situation in which they were unable to get what they wanted and needed. At such a time the need for control is particularly salient.

Finally, people need **affection**, which is expressed in terms of closeness to others. When the affection need is met, a person feels lovable. when someone is rejected by a close friend or lover, the need for affection becomes acute.

Not everyone has an equal need for inclusion, control, and affection, but a moderate need for these responses is healthy and produces growth. The most well adapted and comfortable communicator is someone who is included by others and reciprocates; is willing to take responsibility for control or accepts the guidance of others as appropriate; and both loves and is loved by others.

You now should see why certain couples or friends are more compatible than others. Compatibility is partly a matter of meshing interpersonal needs, or establishing expectations within the relationship that these needs will be addressed in some appropriate form. Two people with strong needs to control probably would have a difficult time getting along, as would two people who had a strong need to be controlled. Similarly, someone with a very strong inclusion need probably would not make it with an independent-minded mate. One reason that certain couples have a hard time establishing a clear and comfortable set of internal rules is that their respective needs are very different.

One cause of the failure to have one's communication needs met is apprehension. Everyone experiences normal apprehension from time to time when communicating with others. Some people, however, display high **communication apprehension** as a trait, fearing almost all communication situations. These people's needs for inclusion, affection, and control go unexpressed and unsatisfied.

We are not talking about simple stage fright or even shyness. Abnormal communication apprehension is a deeper interpersonal problem that occurs not only in public speaking but in interpersonal and group situations as well. It is intense anxiety associated with real or anticipated interaction with others. The problem probably develops in early childhood and is reinforced during later years.

People with extreme apprehension tend to avoid direct communication. Research shows, for example, that fifty to seventy percent of speech students who have this problem have dropped a speech class, even though it was required. Furthermore, people with high anxiety are perceived less positively by others than are people who are not abnormally apprehensive, a fact supported by "virtually all of the related research."[2]

Extreme communication apprehension can be treated successfully through the use of relaxation techniques and other methods. Communication apprehension involves an inability to develop a transactional attitude about communication, a problem that can be overcome. If you think you might have high communication apprehension, we advise you to talk with your speech instructor about the problem.

Face Needs. Human beings seem to have a universal need for respect and validation. Every culture recognizes the importance of personal identity, and people of every culture communicate in ways that respect that identity. This personal identity is called **face**, and we all have the need to have our "face" protected and nurtured. We expect others to meet our face needs, and we try to meet those of other people. One of

Signs like these are a kind of facework. They save the person from outright begging.

the most important functions of interpersonal communication, then, is to meet face needs.

Meeting face needs is called **facework**. **Positive facework** consists of saying things that make others feel good about themselves. We meet positive face needs by compliments, polite address, and acknowledgments of all types. **Negative facework** consists of saying things to avoid hurting another person's feelings. Often in the course of daily events, it is necessary to threaten another person's face by intruding or interfering in some way.

A common example is a request. Whenever you ask other people for something, you risk the possibility that they will feel imposed upon. Bald requests and other impositions can result in making other people feel that you do not respect their time, money, status, or other aspects of their identity. If you were working hard on a project with your door closed and a friend came in to talk, you would feel that this person did not respect your need for work time unless certain negative face needs were met at the same time.

Negative facework consists of apologies, offers, and other acts that acknowledge an intrusion or imposition. Facework is almost always done in face-threatening situations, but it is done very differently depending upon the circumstances. Members of different cultures have different face needs, and they handle their facework in different ways. You may accomplish your facework differently with different people.

Facework, like many aspects of relational communication, is governed by rules. In general, people follow external rules of polite address, polite request, expression of appreciation, use of honored titles, and so on. In specific relationships, people follow internal rules about how these goals should be accomplished. This is why you may do facework differently with your father than with your mother.

There are innumerable ways in which facework can be done. People can present excuses and apologies, express appreciation, acknowledge face threats, deny the intent to harm, tease, or express empathy. Actually, facework can be done in many subtle and clever ways, and human beings tend to be quite adept at accomplishing a variety of goals while simultaneously meeting the face needs of another person.

One of the most common and obvious forms of facework is politeness. People use polite forms to make others feel good about themselves and to avoid hurting or bothering them. But politeness varies, and we are not equally polite with everybody. In general, we tend to be more polite when the risk of a face threat is greater, when the other person has more power than we do, and when there is some social distance between us.

Politeness is not always appreciated. You may occasionally meet someone who rubs you the wrong way because of excessive politeness. People who are fawning, manipulative, insincere, or inappropriate in their politeness can make others feel awkward and even irritated. Again, facework is governed by rules, and violation of those rules can lead to negative relational consequences. Failure to follow rules of politeness—being too polite, not polite enough, or polite in the wrong way—is not always a matter of malice or social stupidity, however, because people raised in different cultural groups often have very different standards of what is appropriate.

Control in Relationships

In the section above, we said that control is a common communication need. But control is more than an individual need. It is a pattern of interaction that develops within a relationship. Control never rests unilaterally with one person because one member of a relationship can never solely determine the control pattern. Control is like a dance: it includes a certain amount of both pushing and pulling.

If you listen to an important conversation between people in an established relationship, you will probably notice one of four things: (1) one person seems to control the conversation; (2) neither individual asserts control; (3) the communicators compete for control; or (4) control is divided rather evenly between them. Who controls a conversation at a particular moment is less important than the overall pattern of control within a relationship over many conversations.

A message that is perceived by the communicators as asserting control is called a **one-up message**. If you needed ingredients for a salad, for example, you might ask your sister to go to the garden and pick some vegetables. This is a one-up message. A message that accepts the control move of another person is a **one-down message**. If your sister agreed to bring you something from the garden, she would be accepting your control at that moment. When there is no clear perception of control in a message, it is **one-across**. After you asked your sister to get some salad vegetables, she might respond ambiguously with something like, "Is it your turn to make the salad?"

These control moves are natural, and the pattern of moves between people over time defines the actual control pattern in the relationship. There are several possibilities. There is **complementary interaction** when a one-up message is greeted by a one-down, or vice versa. You ask your sister to pick some vegetables, and she agrees. Complementary interactions are coordinated. **Symmetrical interaction** occurs when the response to a message is of the same type, as when both speakers are vying for control or both are abdicating it. This would be the case if your sister denied your request. Symmetrical interactions are not very coordinated.

Over time in a relationship, patterns of control develop. Four such patterns are important. In a *rigid complementary relationship*, one person usually takes control and makes decisions, while the other normally allows his or her partner to control the relationship. This is a highly coordinated pattern.

A *flexible complementary relationship* is one in which control flows back and forth between the partners; at one point one partner leads, and at other times, the other person takes control. These relationships are also well coordinated.

A *rigid symmetrical pattern* is one in which the partners constantly struggle for control or one in which neither partner asserts control. Rigid symmetry may involve a lot of fighting or bickering, or it may mean that the couple never gets anything done.

A fourth pattern of control is *flexible symmetry*, in which the couple goes back and forth between struggle for control and withdrawal. Both of these types of symmetrical relationships are good examples of communicators' failure to coordinate.

It is impossible to say which of these patterns is best, but symmetrical relationships, especially rigid ones, are often a sign of difficulty. Many couples, especially those with traditional ideals, find the rigid complementary relationship to be most satisfying; however, the strong value of independence and equality that is so prevalent today leads many couples to adopt the flexible complementary pattern.

Understanding Within Relationships

Understanding involves being in touch with another person's meanings and feelings. When you say something to a friend, will he or she understand your message as you intended it? Understanding is a goal worth achieving, and it can have beneficial effects in relationships. But at the same time, the success of a relationship does not always depend on total understanding. A well-coordinated relationship that is satisfying to the participants, even though they do not completely understand one another's state of mind, should be considered successful.

Still, in middle-class European-American relationships, understanding seems to be a valued measure of the success of close relationships. We will therefore address this concern in detail. In particular, we discuss the role of three contributors—openness, similarity, and trust.

Openness. The degree of understanding in a relationship depends in part on the partners' openness. **Openness** consists of both sensitivity and disclosure. Sensitivity is a person's ability and willingness to perceive the other person accurately. It involves attention to and awareness of the cues presented by the other person. Sensitive communicators listen well and relate what they see and hear to the particular situation.

Openness in inter-personal communication requires sensitivity and self-disclosure.

Openness also involves disclosure. For understanding to occur, communicators must be willing not only to tune into each other's presentation but also to disclose facets of themselves in their own presentations.

Self-disclosure involves revealing things about oneself to another person. Interpersonal understanding can occur only when communicators disclose both factual information and also here-and-now feelings. The statement "I was born in Los Angeles" is one kind of self-disclosure (factual), but emotional statements such as "I'm so mad at you, I could burst!" provide perhaps a more important level of self-disclosure for interpersonal understanding. Chapter 3 explained why people's meanings for messages differ, and self-disclosure is a key for helping others to understand your meanings.

Of course self-disclosure is not simply something a person does or does not do. You can use varying levels and types of disclosure. In general, a high level of self-disclosure involves intentional and copious honest communication that reveals both positive and negative intimate information.

The companion of self-disclosure is **feedback**, which traditionally includes all cues, verbal and nonverbal, given by a "listener" to a

"speaker." From a transactional perspective, both communicators simultaneously send and receive messages, so our definition of *feedback* is expanded to include all cues used by communicators to judge their effects on one another.

Communicators monitor each other and provide messages that say how things are going in the communication. Sometimes feedback is verbal: people use words to tell another person how they are reacting to the message. But much of the time feedback involves nonverbal cues such as facial expressions, body movements, and vocal patterns.

Since good communication is adaptive, people need information from others to make it possible to adjust their messages to others' meanings. Understanding can occur only when communicators constantly adapt to each other's frames of reference, bringing their meanings closer and closer together. The most complete understanding occurs in couples with long-term, close relationships, in which much feedback has been exchanged.

You should see by now that feedback is a form of self-disclosure. In telling someone how you are reacting, you disclose information about yourself—perhaps the most important kind of information for a successful transaction. Feedback serves at least three functions in communication.

First, it helps communicators gauge the degree to which they have understood the meaning the other person intended. A puzzled look, a question, or a simple "I don't get it" may prompt one person to rephrase or explain further. Second, feedback can indicate interest or lack of interest. (Have you ever cut a particular topic short or livened it up a bit because your partner showed signs of losing interest?) Finally, feedback can reflect agreement or disagreement, helping the communicators adjust to each other's state of mind.

Good self-disclosure and feedback are a sign of solidarity. They are most common in relationships with compatible people—people we are attracted to, people we trust. Not all relationships involve this kind of solidarity, however, and people are not always willing to be totally open or transparent.

In actual practice, you have to make judgments about the appropriateness of disclosure in any given situation, asking yourself questions such as the following: What is important for the other person to understand, and what is important for me to understand? What do I need to disclose in order to share this aspect of myself? What must I consider in order to share meanings with the other person in this situation?

As we have seen, understanding can be important, but it is not the only guiding value of a relationship. Relationships meet a variety of goals, and openness may work against some of these. For example, most people want both sharing, which involves openness, and autonomy, which means keeping some things private. When you share personal feelings, you give up some of your separateness and make yourself vulnerable to the judgments of others. On the other hand, when you keep certain feelings to yourself, you give up intimacy and the possibility for support. A good relationship values both intimacy and autonomy, and achieving both is tricky business.

Most people manage a boundary between what is shared and what is kept private.[3] You often think actively about what you are willing to disclose and what you are not, and your decision about what to share and what not to share may or may not match that of your partner. In a relationship, then, this boundary is often negotiated and renegotiated.

Some couples are very open with one another, keeping few secrets. These couples have achieved a high degree of coordination in disclosing feelings and information. Other couples are rather closed and are happy to keep it that way. These couples too are highly coordinated because they share a value for autonomy. Most people, however, are somewhere in between. There are times when you want to reach out and achieve understanding and intimacy. Other times, you may want to protect your private self a bit more.

How do successful couples manage this in-between state of affairs? Coordination is the key. Somehow successful couples manage to mesh cycles of disclosure and autonomy. They have a flexibility that enables them to "dance" with one another and manage their privacy boundaries as a couple. When one person signals the desire to disclose, the other person opens up to that disclosure. Sometimes the invitation to reveal personal information is given indirectly, and a sensitive partner will respond tentatively and take the time necessary to explore the subject gently.

A wide variety of factors contribute to interpersonal attraction.

Similarity. Another factor that can build interpersonal understanding is similarity. Obviously, you will understand someone like yourself more easily than you will understand someone who is different. People enjoy talking with people like themselves, and we tend to be more open with them. After all, they probably can identify with our problems and values. Empathy tends to be higher between similar people, and we are better able to support such people.

Dissimilarity demands extra effort in coming to understand the other person's point of view. It requires greater care in sending and receiving feedback, and eager willingness to be flexible and adaptive. And because we live in a world of diversity, successful communicators are able and willing to put forth the effort to do so.

Although similarity leads to overlapping meanings and thus greater understanding, it does not provide much new stimulation or change. The ideal relationship probably involves both similarity and difference— enough similarity to promote understanding but enough difference to provide stimulation and change.

Trust. Chapter 4 discussed trust as a factor of persuasion. **Trust** is also important to facilitate understanding in interpersonal relationships. Let us look more closely at trust as a concept.

Trust occurs when one person relies on another person and risks something of value to help achieve a goal. If the trusted person fails to carry out the desired action, the trusting person will experience an unpleasant consequence. An extreme example occurs in mountain climbing. One climber relies on others to get to the summit. Much personal risk is involved; if the trusted partners fail in their responsibility, the climbers may not reach the top, and injury or death may result.

Trust in a close relationship means that you can explore feelings and meanings without risking harm. In a trusting relationship, the partners are concerned about each other's well-being, and they share responsibility for the outcome of their transactions. This means that they self-disclose appropriately, provide accurate feedback and complete information, and are sensitive to each other's needs.

This level of trust is hardly universal. Some people are generally more trusting than others; most people are more trusting in some relationships than in others; and trust levels may wax and wane even in a single relationship. Perhaps you have known of cases in which spouses were unfaithful or parents were dishonest with their children. In addition to the ethical and moral implications of these behaviors, subsequent communication was affected by the erosion of trust. One of the reasons that honesty is usually the best policy is that if you get caught in a lie, you will struggle for a long time to rebuild trustworthiness.

A person's natural tendencies may affect how trusting he or she is. One important aspect in this regard is self-esteem. People who like themselves tend to be more confident and have less to lose in a relationship. High self-esteem usually engenders trust in oneself. But if you do not trust yourself, you will probably have trouble trusting others.

Trust is also affected by one's perceptions of the other person. People tend to be more trusting of those who appear competent, dependable, and open. Of course, perceptions at a given moment are affected greatly by the history of the relationship. It is hard to trust someone who has repeatedly given incorrect information, hurtful or dishonest feedback, or false self-disclosure.

The amount of risk perceived in the transaction also affects the trust level. It is easier to trust when the risk is low; a person who has a great deal to lose by disclosing a particular feeling may be less trusting than usual.

Risk involves several elements. The less power one person has over the other, the greater that person's risk. In addition, the greater the chance that the other person might gain from violating one's trust, the greater one's risk.

Finally, trust is affected by the importance of the goal. Generally, the more important the goal, the more one person is likely to trust another, other things being equal.

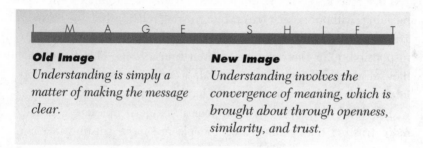

I M A G E S H I F T

Old Image
Understanding is simply a matter of making the message clear.

New Image
Understanding involves the convergence of meaning, which is brought about through openness, similarity, and trust.

INTERPERSONAL CONFLICT

Conflict, resulting from differences in beliefs, values, behaviors, or interests, is a knotty but common aspect of communication. Although conflict often raises difficulties and produces anxiety, it is not necessarily bad. Conflict can produce better ideas. It can facilitate personal growth. It can induce communication. Yet conflict has to be understood, and it has to be managed. Too often people run from conflict when confrontation is just what is needed.

Our chief concern here is the role of communication in conflict situations. Communication enables people in conflict to exchange information about their intentions, strategies, goals, and values. Communication also enables people to cooperate in surveying their alternatives and thus achieve mutually beneficial outcomes.

Sometimes people in conflict avoid direct communication. In silent conflict only sketchy nonverbal messages are exchanged. When extreme, silent conflict involves exchanging information only in the form of "moves," or decisions. Imagine two serious chess players who make move after move without saying a word. Only the moves themselves inform each player of what the opponent may have in mind. There are many other examples: trials without pretrial communication between prosecution and defense; collective bargaining in which only formal offers and counteroffers are made; silent bidding at auctions; and the silent treatment between spouses or roommates.

Often people close off channels of communication unnecessarily. In open conflict full disclosure and discussion are undertaken. Of course, conflict situations range between the extremes of totally open and completely silent.

If it is not possible to communicate directly, it usually is better to show good faith by acting cooperatively. Research has shown that cooperation often stimulates further cooperation. Moves that are independent or nonresponsive to the other person's moves may engender competitiveness, but shifting from a competitive stance to a cooperative one often induces the other party to do the same. Conversely, shifting from cooperation to competition may lead to anger, hostility, and retaliation.

When communication is allowed, it usually takes the form of attempts to influence. Nowhere are power and control more evident than in

Some kinds of interpersonal conflict are more obvious than others.

conflict communication. Further, conflict communication is usually emotional and anxiety-provoking. This is why people close communication channels during conflict. Who wants to be yelled at?

Although emotionality is common in the heat of conflict, it is not inevitable, for conflicting parties can be very reasonable. Often, however, the initial release of tension through emotion and confrontation can be functional, especially in close relationships.

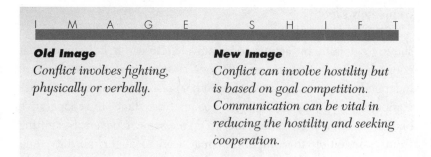

I M A G E   S H I F T

Old Image
Conflict involves fighting, physically or verbally.

New Image
Conflict can involve hostility but is based on goal competition. Communication can be vital in reducing the hostility and seeking cooperation.

Conflict can be handled in a variety of ways. A useful model of "styles" of conflict includes concern for other and concern for self.

Figure 5.1
Conflict styles.
(Adapted with
permission from author
and publishers from:
Kilmann, R. H., and
Thomas, K. W.
Interpersonal Conflict-
handling Behavior as
Reflections of Jungian
Personality Dimen-
sions. *Psychological
Reports a,* 1975, 37,
971-980. © Psychologi-
cal Reports 1975.

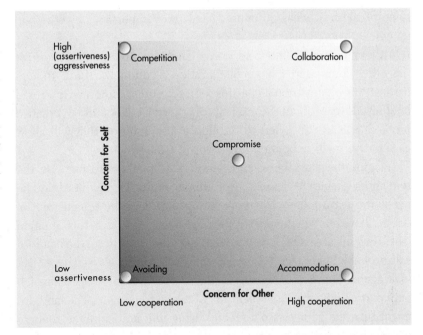

Figure 5-1 shows how these two dimensions are related. When you are highly concerned about meeting your own goals, you are assertive, and when you are less concerned about your goals, you are unassertive. When you are very concerned about the other, you are highly cooperative, but when you are not concerned about the other, you are uncooperative. You can see that low assertiveness and low cooperation lead to **avoiding**, the first style of conflict. High assertiveness and low cooperation lead to **competition**, and high cooperation and low assertiveness lead to **accommodation**. **Collaboration** is the result of high assertiveness and high cooperation, high concern for self and for the other person. Finally, **compromise** falls in the middle.

Each of these modes of handling conflict has its place. Sometimes it is best to avoid conflict, at least temporarily. Accommodation, which is giving in, and competition, which is pushing to win, are also sometimes necessary. Compromising, making trade-offs to meet somewhere in the middle, is an obvious and common solution. Compromise can be a useful and honorable approach, but when you compromise, you may trade off some of your most valued goals. Because in compromise you end up with everyone's second choice, some of the best ideas go unused, and most important objectives go unmet.

Although you may find it necessary from time to time to use one of the other four approaches, collaboration is often the best, though hardest. In collaboration all parties want to protect their own interests, but they also care about the interests of others. Collaboration is creative problem solving, designed to develop a new solution that will allow each party's goals to be met. It is a win-win solution.

Imagine the clash between a landlord who wants to increase the rent and a tenant who cannot afford to pay more. The landlord says he needs the extra money for property upkeep, and the tenant says he doesn't have enough money to pay more. On the surface, this situation looks unresolvable. One must win and the other must lose; the landlord will probably win, and the tenant will have to move elsewhere. But look again. There may be several more creative solutions by which both parties can win. The tenant might take a roommate. The landlord might turn the garage into a second living unit and combine rents to make even more than he wanted in the first place. Perhaps the landlord could be persuaded to hold off on the rent increase for a few months, or the tenant might be induced to begin a gradual increase toward the desired rent. Maybe the tenant would be willing to do some of the upkeep work as in-kind rent. You see, what looks like a win-lose conflict is not always so.

Now let's look at some of the principles of collaborative conflict resolution. First, maintain respect for the other person. Avoid transferring your anxiety, frustration, and anger about the problem to the person involved. There is a strong tendency in conflicts for the parties to make bad attributions, thinking the other person malicious, ignorant, uninformed, unethical, or crazy. Collaboration is impossible when these kinds of opinions are held. It is simply a fact of life that equally well-meaning and intelligent people sometimes come to opposing sides on issues. People have good reasons for their positions, and it is arrogant to think that only your point of view is legitimate. Concentrate on the problem, not on the people.

Second, define a conflict as a problem to be solved, not a case to be won. Too often people see only the clash between positions in a conflict, and their sadly uncreative approach is to muster their arguments to win their side. As the anecdote of the landlord and tenant illustrates, however, conflicts are not always simply a matter of clashing positions. But when you put yourself into a win-lose mode of thinking, you will not be able to collaborate on a creative solution.

Third, move from stating positions to analyzing interests. One way of avoiding a win-lose trap is to get away from looking at the initial positions of the conflicting parties and concentrate on the interests that lie behind these positions. In the landlord-tenant dispute, for example, the landlord's position was to increase the rent, but his interest was to get enough money to keep the property up. The tenant's position was to keep the rent the same, but his interest was to keep from having to move. Once the interests are established, you can look for creative solutions.

Fourth, be creative. Invent proposals that might meet both persons' interests. A husband and wife were once in a struggle over the thermostat. The husband kept turning it down because he was too hot, and the wife kept turning it up because she was too cold. They argued about it a lot until they decided to get creative. The wife found that if she put a heating pad under her feet, she was perfectly comfortable even when the room temperature was lower.

Fifth, discuss criteria for a solution. Instead of wasting a lot of energy and time fighting about positions and interests, use the same amount of time to discuss what a good solution should entail. How will you evaluate and choose the right course of action? Two college students were planning their wedding. The young woman wanted to include lots of people, but her fiancé wanted a smaller, more intimate wedding. Given this difference, what criteria should be used to decide? After some discussion, they discovered that the woman wanted a festive event, but the man wanted a feeling of intimacy and privacy. Could they come up with a wedding that was both festive and intimate? They agreed that the wedding itself would be small, in a parent's home, but a large reception with lots of guests, food, and music would follow later that day in a hall rented in town.

Having looked at general principles of interpersonal communication, let us now turn to some useful guidelines for improving your competence in various interpersonal contexts. First, in the remainder of this chapter, we will discuss communication with family and friends as an important setting for informal, intimate communication. Then, in Chapter 6 we will examine professional communication as an example of moderately formal, moderately intimate communication and also we will present some guidelines for interviewing.

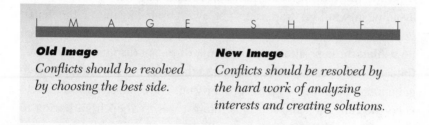

Old Image
Conflicts should be resolved by choosing the best side.

New Image
Conflicts should be resolved by the hard work of analyzing interests and creating solutions.

COMMUNICATING WITH FAMILY AND FRIENDS

Although modern culture is largely a world of work, most people still find their relationships with family and friends their main means of developing connection, identity, support, affection, and meaning in life. Yet, ironically, communicating with family and friends can be fraught with difficulty in our society. When we ask students in our classes to discuss communication problems they have had, most examples pertain to family and friends.

Many of these problems involve some of the factors discussed earlier in the chapter—establishing coordination, avoiding unwanted repetitive patterns, achieving understanding, and managing conflict. These challenges are part of living in a complex society. Don't expect to eliminate relational difficulties, but you can enhance and improve close relationships, and in this section we explore three of the ways—managing contradiction, maintaining dialogue, and expanding awareness

Managing Contradiction

Contradiction is part of modern life. People face it every day—whenever two valued things are inconsistent; whenever one valued goal is disaffirmed by achieving another; whenever one rule is broken to follow another; whenever one desired course of action is vetoed in favor of another.

Contradiction is confusing because people are taught from an early age to be consistent and logical, but the vagaries of modern life make consistency impossible. Life requires balancing, juggling, and weaving;

people are always managing inconsistent elements. For example, if you want to have a good relationship with your parents, you must stay somewhat close to them; but if you want personal autonomy and independence, you must break away. Can you be both independent from your parents and have a close relationship with them? For some the answer is no, but for many it is yes. Those who successfully meet the challenge of independence and closeness have been able to come up with ways to manage this contradiction.

Good communication in relationships, in all walks of life, requires that contradiction be managed. In a friendship, for example, at least three general contradictions are common. First, you want the freedom to depend on your friend, but the freedom to be independent as well. If you have ever wondered how much time to spend with a friend, you have faced this dilemma. If you have ever had a friend call you up one too many times with a problem, you understand. You want to rely on your friend, but you don't want to be a burden. You want your friend to rely on you, but not too much.

The second contradiction frequently found in friendships is affection versus usefulness. Should a friend be valued just as a friend, or can friends be useful for other purposes? Most friends face this question, and most think both are true. Would you ask to borrow a friend's car? Would you ask a friend for a loan? Would you gladly feed a vacationing friend's cat? Again, different friends handle this contradiction in

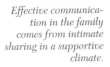

Effective communication in the family comes from intimate sharing in a supportive climate.

different ways, and friends may handle it differently at different points in their lives.

A third contradiction is between judgment and acceptance. Should you accept friends as they are? Of course. Otherwise, you would not be a friend. On the other hand, good friends should be able to be honest about their perceptions, right? If you see a friend doing something wrong, you wouldn't be a very good friend if you didn't share your perception. Maybe. Most people would say both are correct even though they contradict one another.

The rules and patterns of communication established within a relationship function in part to accomplish this difficult balancing of contradictions. How is it done? There are a variety of ways.

Often when confronting a contradiction, we *select* one goal over another. For example, you might decide that it is impossible to be close to your parents, so you develop your independence and let the chips fall.

Other times, you might *separate* the two contradictory elements so that their opposition is denied or downplayed. There are at least two ways in which this might be done. You could, for example, alternate between one element and the other. Sometimes, for instance, you might nurture closeness with your parents and other times maintain distance from them. The second way to separate the contradictory elements is by topic. In some areas like emotional support, you might nurture closeness, while in others like career choices, you might work on distance.

A third general strategy for managing contradiction in relationships is *neutralization*, which takes the sting out of the opposing elements. One way to do this would be to compromise, or do a little of both. You might try to be somewhat close to your parents, but also keep a little distance at the same time. Or you could act ambiguously, so that it would be unclear which of the two sides is being developed. Here, you might act in such a way that your behavior could be interpreted as closeness or as distance, whichever you prefer at the moment.

Yet another way in which contradiction can be managed is through *reframing*—redefining the contradiction so that it is no longer a contradiction. For example, in relating to your parents, you might redefine autonomy as another form of closeness. You might tell yourself,

"My folks always wanted me to be my own person, so by doing so, I am actually nurturing a kind of closeness with them."

Indeed, contradiction is ever present in relationships, and the above examples are just a few of the ways people handle it.

Maintaining Dialogue

Have you ever been in a "discussion" with someone who did lots of talking but not much listening? Too often in our society, conversation is considered a competition in which the loser is called "listener." The interaction is seen as a **monologue**, a turn at talk, a chance to make your point without much sensitivity to the other person.

The idea that interpersonal communication is one-way breeds two dysfunctional behaviors: insensitivity to feedback cues and poor listening habits. If you believe that you "have the floor" when you are speaking, you will tend to discount the other communicator's responses. You may ignore important cues that would help you adapt to the communication situation. If you believe that listeners simply take messages in, you will be unresponsive, nonanalytical, and inattentive in listening.

In contrast to this typical view of communication, **dialogue** involves open talk, give-and-take sharing, and genuine listening. An acquaintance of one of the authors grew up in such a one-way home. The communication in this household was dominated by a father who did all the talking; the mother and four children listened and obeyed. Although there were some warm and happy moments, there was also a lot of misery and fear. After the children were nearly grown, an emotional split developed between the father and the rest of the family that was only partly repaired years later, when the father was retired and aging. All the members of this family, including the father, suffered a good deal of emotional wear and tear as a result of the powerful monologic spirit that pervaded their family life.

People in dialogue engage others as important human beings, not as objects.[4] People in dialogue seek to understand, not to manipulate. The well-known theologian Martin Buber called this orientation an I-Thou relationship. It contrasts with an I-It relationship, in which people treat others as objects to be moved in order to meet selfish needs.[5]

Communication as dialogue involves a few important attitudes:

1. *Genuineness.* Open communicators tend to be direct and honest about how they feel. They communicate with minimal pretense and do not put on a false front.
2. *Accurate empathic understanding.* Empathy is the quality of seeing something from another's point of view, of feeling about a situation as the other person does. The best understanding between people involves empathy. It involves entering into the feelings and meanings of the other person.
3. *Basic respect.* The best intimate communication involves genuine warmth and respect between the communicators—even when disagreements are expressed. When people regard each other positively, they affirm each other's right to individuality.
4. *Presentness.* In good intimate communication, each person gives undivided attention to the other. Presentness is the quality of being "all there." When this quality is well developed, each person is capable of being in touch with the totality of the other person.
5. *A spirit of mutuality.* This characteristic is manifested by treating other people as human beings rather than objects. Status and role considerations are suspended, and the communicators relate person-to-person.
6. *A supportive climate.* In good dialogue, the participants encourage each other to express themselves completely. Communicators listen well without hasty or harsh criticism, without interrupting, and without refuting.

As we have seen, then, viewing interpersonal communication as a situation in which one person talks (actively) while the other person listens (passively) is counterproductive. A transactional orientation, in contrast, emphasizes the idea of active listening.

Active listening involves two important qualities. First, it means listening for as much meaning as possible. Active listeners realize that a message entails more than verbal statements. If you listen actively, you attend not only to the words of a message but also to the other person's voice. You monitor nonverbal cues carefully and provide feedback through questions and restatements to test whether you have understood correctly. In ideal interpersonal communication, both people actively speak and listen at the same time.

Active listening is a mutual process.

Second, in active listening you must postpone judgment of the other person's message long enough to understand what is meant. Active listening is therefore nonjudgmental. It focuses on understanding the message; evaluation must wait. There is a simple rule to follow in interpersonal contacts, especially when you anticipate disagreement, conflict, or defensiveness. First, try to understand the point of view, the meanings, and the feelings of the other person empathically. Then, when you believe you know what the other person means, evaluate it in terms of your criteria. Listen, understand, and evaluate. This is not always easy, but such an approach will help you avoid difficulties that arise through miscommunication.

If you think you are being judged prematurely, you will feel pressure to withhold important feelings and become defensive. Active listening communicates openness to self-disclosure. It removes the threat of immediate judgment and encourages the communicator to explain the message clearly and completely.

For example, a husband discloses his anger about something his wife said or did, and she listens attentively and restates the message, giving him a chance to correct any misunderstanding. In her behavior the husband perceives the message: "I am listening, and I want to understand how you feel and why. It's OK to disclose your anger, and in return I have the right to let you know how your disclosure has affected me."

With a good deal of experience and some failure, many adults come to "discover" the factors that create openness in dialogue. The authors' own lives illustrate this well. During our twenties, our focus was on productive activities, but as we emerged into our thirties, we began to realize how important intimate sharing truly is. In a sense, our values shifted from getting things done to sharing ourselves with others. At the same time, we discovered how fragile intimate relationships can be. We have learned to nurture dialogue, but only after some painful self-examination.

Expanding Awareness

One advantage of using the transactional perspective is that it helps people become more sensitive to communication as a whole. In interpersonal communication, this means respecting the importance of oneself, the other person, and the context. The following behaviors ignore one or more of the three elements of good communication and thereby can damage family relationships.

Placating. Placating overemphasizes agreeing with others. Placaters are so concerned about others liking them—so concerned about not hurting others—that they simply cannot take a stand of their own. Placating messages are not very honest, because they ignore the self in the transaction. Placating messages place the other person in a superior position.

Family and friends placate one another for many reasons. Often families promote rigid role relationships in which certain members are not allowed to express feelings and opinions. For example, some people still believe that children should be seen and not heard. Sometimes fear lies behind placating messages. Battered spouses report being afraid to express ideas or feelings that oppose the viewpoints of their partners. A common reason for placating is insecurity. This is especially true in new love relationships in which one or both partners are so afraid of losing the other that important feelings and opinions are held back. Sometimes these insecurities linger into marriage; occasionally they last a lifetime.

Placaters deny each other the opportunity to understand their deepest feelings. They inhibit each other's self-discovery because they do not provide the feedback needed to know how they are affecting others.

Blaming. It is natural for everyone to blame others occasionally. But chronic blaming is a real communication problem. Blaming is not the same as disagreement. When people disagree, they can still listen and recognize each other's right to take a stand. Genuine respect abides even in disagreement. A chronic blamer, on the other hand, seems to need to dismiss others as being less important. Chronic blaming is an attempt to control others because it takes the position "I'm OK, but you're not OK."[6]Chronic blamers seem to need to exercise complete power over others. It is not surprising that placating and blaming often go together in a relationship and promote each other. If, for example, a child is continuously told that he or she has little value or personal worth, the child may accept that view and learn to placate others. Chronic blaming presents a barrier to openness by creating a hostile, threatening atmosphere. It takes a lot of nerve to disclose oneself to a blamer; the ego threat is simply too great for most people, so they withhold their feelings.

Being Superreasonable. The superreasonable communicator focuses entirely on the data from the context, ignoring his or her own inside feelings or those of the other person. To a superreasonable mother, for example, feelings have no place in decision making. She might say, "I'm tired, harried, and upset, and I need a moment's peace; but it's Jimmy's birthday, and I'd better bake his cake."

Part of the tendency for some people to be superreasonable stems from our culture's teaching that people are basically rational and that the best decisions are based strictly on logic. Our culture also reinforces the feeling that males should not express emotion, which encourages many fathers to act like business executives even with their families. Obviously, such an attitude inhibits openness because it fails to allow for the most important kinds of self-disclosure.

Being Irrelevant. Some people are able to ignore their own feelings, the feelings of others, and the context. For example, a father might say, "Chris, I told you earlier that you wouldn't be able to go outside and play until your room was cleaned." This statement, however, gets this response: "Dad, I'm hungry. Can I have lunch?" A wise parent will recognize this strategy and quickly put the child back on track.

Of course nobody is perfect, and we all catch ourselves in damaging modes of communication from time to time. The important thing is to aim for increased clarity and congruence in intimate communication.

SUMMARY

Interpersonal communication is the hub of human experience. People's relationships determine in many ways who they are. In this chapter we explored the ways in which relationships are constantly constructed through communication, and how communication in turn is affected by the rules of the relationship.

The rules of a relationship establish certain patterns of interaction that occur within it. Every message has both a content and a relationship dimension, and the participants must coordinate their actions within these dimensions. Sometimes efforts to coordinate are successful, and sometimes they are not. These efforts to coordinate are important, in part, because they help people meet certain needs for inclusion, control, and affection, and because they also permit people to meet one another's face needs.

Relationships are partly defined by the control patterns that emerge as the participants interact. Understanding almost always emerges as an issue in relationships. People become conscious of understanding when it becomes difficult, when they have a hard time understanding where others are coming from, or when they themselves do not feel understood. Understanding is especially problematic during times of conflict, and handling conflict is itself a challenge of interpersonal communication.

Communicating with family and friends is especially important to most people, and it does not happen easily in every case. Communicating with family and friends almost always means managing contradictions; it requires maintaining dialogue; and it means expanding awareness of many subtle influences in self, other, and context.

The fundamentals of relationships covered in this chapter apply to virtually all settings in which interpersonal communication takes place. In the following chapter we consider one such setting—the workplace.

6 Understanding and Improving Professional Communication

Every fall millions of new college seniors return to school with a mixture of excitement, anticipation, and apprehension. The senior year is considered to be especially stressful because most fourth-year students do not know where they will be or what they will be doing a year hence. Most are concerned about getting a good job and performing well once they land it.

If asked, "Who are you?" most middle-aged adults would respond with a statement about their vocation, identifying themselves as a computer programmer, a painter, a nurse, or whatever. Indeed, almost half an adult's waking hours are spent working and thus communicating within a work context. Although some professional communication involves group, public, or mass communication, it far more frequently entails some kind of interpersonal communication. For this reason, virtually all of the points discussed in the previous chapter also apply in professional settings. In this chapter, we explore additional themes pertinent to professional communication.

This chapter is divided into three sections. In the first, we discuss the topic of entering a career. In the second section, we address interviewing, one of the most common and important kinds of professional communication. And in the final section, we explore supportiveness and assertiveness as basic elements of all professional communication.

ENTERING A CAREER

Getting established in a profession is a topic of immediate concern to many college students. The process of entering a career involves three essential aspects of professional communication: general preparation and goal setting, applying for jobs, and making a final decision.

General Preparation and Goal Setting

As you consider possible careers, you will think about your goals. Your academic major and minor will suggest possible careers, and professions such as teaching, law, and social work require special certification provided by certain college majors. Nonetheless, you need not let your college major limit your choices.

We are very firm about this: You can work your way into a great career if (1) you actively use your *entire education*, including major, minor, general education, and electives; (2) you build general career skills, not just field-specific knowledge; (3) you are bright and enterprising and sell yourself well; (4) you are mobile and willing to consider employment in various geographical areas; and (5) you have job experience. The last point is always important, so plan to get experience through volunteering, internships, work-study, community outreach programs, summer work, part-time work, or other opportunities.

So if you think that your major is the only thing that will ensure a good job, you may be sorely disappointed. Your major is not nearly as important as the whole package you create for yourself. Anthropology majors may be hired by investment firms to study the cultures of the nations with which they do business; archeology majors work for the highway department because of their ability to spot and study ancient sites uncovered in highway construction; and humanities majors are hired by corporations because of their communication and language skills. Communication majors and minors can be especially attractive if they combine their communication skills with work in other fields in the context of overall career planning.

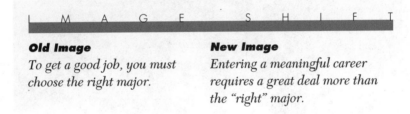

IMAGE SHIFT

Old Image
To get a good job, you must choose the right major.

New Image
Entering a meaningful career requires a great deal more than the "right" major.

We would be remiss in this book if we did not emphasize the importance of oral and written communication competence in getting a good job and building a career in any field of endeavor. Being able to express yourself clearly and articulately; to listen attentively and empathically; and to work with people are fundamental attributes sought by employers of all types.

Goal setting requires consideration of both general and specific career goals. Before you pin yourself down too definitely, explore the general types of careers that might interest you. Most important in this stage is a serious look at your values. What do you want out of life, and what are some of the ways of achieving it? Consider more than personal values such as income and place of residence; think about what you want to accomplish for society during your working years.

Think also of the kind of "work style" that would suit you. You may feel comfortable in an eight-to-five job that leaves you free at the end of the day to pursue personal interests at home, or you may want a more life-absorbing kind of work. You may want a lot of time flexibility, or you may feel more comfortable in an established routine. You might

Setting goals for a career requires careful consideration of one's values and needs.

feel like working in a variety of locations, welcoming travel as an aspect of your work, or you might want a more predictably local position.

All of the above are value issues. In setting general goals, you need to test your aptitudes and interests as well. What are you good at? What kinds of work would maintain your interests? Do you prefer to work with objects or people? Do you like the challenge of problem solving, or do you prefer to apply established procedures?

Does the work environment—including hours, amount of travel, and office space—fit your professional goals and personal values? A higher-paying job may involve longer hours and more stress than you want. Some people are more service-oriented, while others may want more upward mobility, prestige, and material reward.

Finally, geography may be important. You may wish to live in a particular section of the country near family and friends, or you may prefer a rural over an urban setting. Some people are limited to a particular climate because of allergies or other health problems. Other things being equal, however, geographical flexibility is a plus.

Careful consideration of these factors as part of your general plan sets a kind of "magnetic north" for your search for a satisfying career. Every college and university has a career development center to help students explore these issues, and this service is almost always free. We strongly encourage you to work with the career center on your campus. Its staff can administer aptitude and interest tests, introduce you to interactive computer and video programs to explore your career values, provide training in résumé writing and interviewing, and even arrange job interviews on your campus. Most career centers also run a job placement service.

Obviously, career planning is not something that should wait until you are a junior or senior. General goal setting and preparation must begin as you plan your college program, even as early as your freshman year. Deciding exactly what kind of job you want in your first or second year, even in the third or fourth year, may be premature, but goal setting and exploration should definitely begin as early as possible.

One of the things you will learn from your career center is that several career possibilities can meet your main goals. Once these possibilities are presented to you, you can explore them in more detail and begin to establish more specific goals. Specific goal setting does not mean determining precisely what kind of work you will do and what organization you will work for, but it should narrow the list. Give yourself some flexibility in career goals, and don't be surprised if you end up changing careers several times. That is the nature of the society in which we live.

Applying for Jobs

Some people begin their careers as entrepreneurs, designing their own job and working for themselves. Many more, however, begin by applying for a position in an established organization. Thus the question of how to get a job is uppermost in most college students' minds.

Researching the Job. Once a range of career options become available to you, you can begin the application process. Before applying, be sure to do as much research as possible on the organization and position. This step is important because it helps you decide whether the position is right for you; it also serves as a first step in "audience analysis" in case you get an interview. Your career center can help you with this research, and you may want to write directly to the company for additional information. Annual reports, newsletters, and brochures can be helpful. Find out as much as you can about the unit in which you would work, the manager of that unit, and even the person who would interview you.

The Résumé. Your **résumé** is a brief document containing your qualifications for employment, including your education, skills, experience, and achievements. Along with a cover letter of application, the résumé is designed to land you an interview. As a rule it should be brief, with the items most relevant to the particular job appearing first.

All résumés should be headed by your name, address, phone number, and goal statement. For a job that requires certification, such as teaching, accounting, or day care, your résumé might begin with your educational background and certificates earned. For a job requiring specific expertise, such as computer programming, you might begin with your training and experience in that area. As a general rule, include only job related information on the résumé. It is discriminatory and often even illegal for employers to consider nonrelated information such as sex, religion, or race. For this reason, personal data such as height, weight, hobbies, and marital status are generally inappropriate for résumés.

Information in your résumé should be organized in categories such as career objective, education and training, experience, and skills and achievements. These categories can be arranged either chronologically or by topics that best fit the job for which you are applying.

We suggest that you keep a master résumé on your word processor. Add to this every time you achieve something new, each time you get a new job, whenever you accomplish something special, when you receive an honor, when your educational program changes, or whenever any other new development occurs. Beginning early in your college career, get in the habit of adding to this master résumé regularly, so you will not have to remember every detail of your life when it comes time to apply for a specific job. This procedure makes résumé construction easy!

With a word processing program, you can make a different résumé for every application. When you apply for a job, select items from your master list that are relevant to the position. Put together a specific résumé for each job application, and adapt each résumé to the job requirements and company.

One last point: The attractiveness of your résumé matters. Be careful about formatting features, spelling and grammar, and print style. Make the résumé look professional. Figures 6-1, 6-2, and 6-3 illustrate three résumé forms.

Application Letters. Instead of a single "letter of application" you should consider a possible series of letters, including initial cover letter, follow-up, thank-you, acknowledgment, and acceptance or regret. These letters are detailed below.

The first and perhaps most important is the *cover letter* for your résumé. The purpose of the cover letter is to tempt the employer to read your résumé. Short and compelling, it need not summarize all of the information in the résumé but only those items or issues that will attract attention and focus on the most important reason the organization may want to hire you. The cover letter should show an interest in the organization by being tailored for the specific job and demonstrating that you have researched the organization. In a study of *ethos* among personnel managers, Jabusch, Faules, and Alexander found that character and dynamism (motivation) were more important than expertise or training to the people who do the hiring. Finally, you

SAMPLE RÉSUMÉ

(Chronological - Emphasizing Education)

DON HAWKINS

1245 Gosset Avenue   191 Meadow Lane
Arcata, CA 95521   Walnut Creek, CA 96301
(707) 822-3456   (415) 833-7221
(until June, 19XX)   (permanent address)

EDUCATION

B.S. Degree, Oceanography major, Biology emphasis, Humboldt State University, Arcata, CA, May 19XX. Pertinent courses include (semester units):

Biological Oceanography	Chemistry (14)
Physical Oceanography	Physics (8)
Chemical Oceanography	Calculus (12)
Marine Phycology	Marine Field Techniques
Seminar in Oceanography	Statistics
Zooplankton Ecology	General Oceanography
Verebrate Physiology	Invertebrate Zoology

RESEARCH

• A determination of the total primary productivity for the coast off Humboldt Bay, 19XX.
• A bioassay determining the toxicity of crude oil on surf perch, 19XX.
• A zooplankton study for the coast off Humboldt Bay, determining the location of different species of zooplankton, 19XX.

SPECIAL QUALIFICATIONS

Experience working on a large oceanographic research vessel where I used different types of sampling gear as well as common oceanographic instrumentation. Experience in small boat handling. SCUBA certification (NAUI).

WORK EXPERIENCE

Tour Guide. Organized and directed tour groups. Lectured to the public on marine intertidal invertebrates. Marine World, Vallejo, CA, Summer 19XX.

Park Aide. Provided information and directions in Visitor Information Services and led campfire programs. Richardson Grove State Park, Garberville, CA, summer 19XX.

Cannery Worker. Assisted in a variety of processing tasks in a tomato cannery, including quality control. California Canners and Growers, Salinas, CA, summers 19XX and 19XX.

SPECIAL INTERESTS

Intertidal invertebrates, pollution, bioassay techniques, diving, sailing.
References available upon request.

Figures 6.1, 6.2, 6.3 *The sample résumés on pages 180, 181, and 182 are reprinted with permission of the Humboldt State University Career Development Center.*

SAMPLE RÉSUMÉ

(Chronological - Emphasizing Experience)

SUSAN PETERS   1220 Janes Road
                                                                     Arcata, CA 95521
                                                                     (707) 822-3800

Objective: Primary elementary teacher in rural or semi-rural CA

EDUCATION

Multple Subjects Teaching Credential (Clear), June 19XX. Supplementary Authorizations: ESL and English

Workshops: Conflict Management Feb 'XX, Self-Esteem Mar 'XX

Bachelor of Arts, Liberal Studies Major, June 19XX. Humboldt State University, Arcata, CA.

SPECIAL QUALIFICATIONS

Speak Spanish fluently; play guitar and piano. Ability to coach volleyball and soccer.

TEACHING EXPERIENCE

Student Teacher—2nd Grade. Jefferson Elementary School, Eureka, CA. Taught all areas of study in learning centers as well as individualized instruction in reading and math. Worked with ESL and Resources Specialist in providing services for students with special needs. Taught special units in Spanish, creative dramatics, nutrition, and music. September 'XX - June 'XX.

Alternate Student Teaching—5th Grade. Coordinated Science Fair Activities.

Teacher's Aide, McKinleyville Elementary School district, McKinleyville, CA. Coordinated educational and behavioral programs for five 4th grade emotionally disturbed boys. Organized and supervised swimming lessons for Special Education students. September 'XX - June 'XX.

Children's Drama Teacher—Camp Counselor, Camp Somerset, Oakland, CA. Bunk counselor for ages 8 to 16. Taught creative dramatics to ages 6 to 16. Directed 80 to 100 children in productions of Rogers and Hammerstein's **Cinderella**, **The Wizard of Oz**, and **Oklahoma**. Summers 19XX, 19XX, and 19XX.

Camp Counselor, Camp St. Michael, Leggett, CA. Group counselor for ages 10 to 14. Taught swimming, archery, crafts, and primitive camping skills. Summer 19XX.

OTHER EXPERIENCE

Senior Staff Dormitory Supervisor, Humboldt State University, Arcata, CA. Supervised six living group advisors. Coordinated educational and recreational programs offered to a complex of 400 residents. September 'XX to June 'XX.

Clerical Aide, Humboldt State Library. Part-time 19XX - 19XX.

HONORS AND ACTIVITIES

Who's Who in American Colleges and Universities, 19XX.

Counselor, Humboldt Orientation Program, H.S.U., 19XX.

Member, National Speech and Debate Honorary Fraternity, 19XX.

President, Newman Community, H.S.U., 19XX.

(Teaching resumes are often 2 pages. Other things you should include are professional workshops, special skills such as computer, music, art, drama, related hobbies.)

SAMPLE RÉSUMÉ

(Chronological - Functional)

GRETCHEN CARRILLO
1470 Sunset Avenue
Arcata, CA 95521

(707) 822-2345

JOB OBJECTIVE: Challenging position in Human Resources.

EDUCATION

Bachelor of Arts Degree. Humboldt State University, Arcata, CA, May 19XX. Major: Psychology, Minor: Economics, G.P.A. 3.40

Associate of Arts Degree. College of the Redwoods, Eureka, CA, May 19XX. Graduated with honors.

SKILLS

Administrative and Management Skills

—Supervised staff, budgets, and facilities in business and non-profit organizations.
—Attention to detail (gathered sophisticated information as research assistant).
—Processed orders for meat company, routed truck logistics (increasing efficiency by 20%).

Human Relations and Communication Skills

—Experience writing training curriculum and news articles
—Supervision, counseling, problem solving skills
—Seasoned interview skills as "stringer" for city newspaper
—Develop rapport successfully with diverse client populations

EXPERIENCE

Assistant Manager for Inventories. Meat Wholesale Company, Eureka, CA. Assisted in maintenance of inventories, processing of orders, and directed transportation strategies. June 19XX - present.

Supervisor. Counselors Program, Eureka, CA. Recruited, trained, and supervised staff for program to educate high risk students about self-management skills. September 19XX - June 19XX.

Journalist. Sacramento Bee, Sacramento, CA. Worked as part-time "stringer," conducting interviews, gathering facts, writing news and features. Published 50 articles. June 19XX - May 19XX.

Other Part-Time and Summer Experience. Student intern in Psychology Department; tutor in English, math, and other subjects; waiter; and camp counselor.

INTERESTS AND ACTIVITIES

Vice President of Senior Class, 19XX.
Member of Student Council, Debate, and Swimming Teams.
Exchange student in Australia for a year, 19XX.

should proofread the letter carefully, because poor writing skills can cause your application to be rejected without serious consideration. It is even a good idea to have a professor, staff member of the career center, family member, or friend read the cover letter and résumé to point out errors and make suggestions for improvement.

Should your cover letter and résumé evoke a favorable response or an interview, you will want to write a *thank-you letter* to employers or their representatives who have shown you consideration. If you receive no acknowledgment of your application or a delay in an answer from the employer, you may want to nudge them with a brief *follow-up letter*. When you receive an offer or rejection from the organization, you should respond with a *letter of acknowledgment*, discussed below.

The Interview. Every job applicant wants an interview; this is a crucial step in the employment process. When you get this far, you have been at least partly successful. We devote an entire section to interviewing later in this chapter, so we mention it here only briefly.

Whether your interview is successful or not, be sure to send an acknowledgment letter. If you receive a job offer, state your understanding of the terms of the offer, and your decision or the date by which they may receive a decision from you. (Actually, in many cases this information will be handled by phone, although a brief letter of acknowledgment should always go out anyway.) If you are rejected for the job, resist the temptation to write an angry reply. Acknowledge the rejection in an objective and professional manner, since you might want to apply to the same organization at a later date. Besides, such a response is the professional and respectful thing to do.

If you are successful, you will get an offer and be in the happy circumstance of making a decision.

Making the Decision

Because prospective employees are so preoccupied with getting an offer, they often forget that the final decision is in their hands. Making the decision is a crucial stage in the employment process and can affect your life in significant ways. The job-application process runs two ways. It allows employers to evaluate applicants, but it also allows applicants to evaluate employers.

Here is where your goal setting can serve you well. If you know what you want, you can match potential employers to your goals and values. When you make your final decision, you will write a *letter of acceptance or regret*. In your letter of acceptance, state your understanding of the terms of employment. You may also want to clarify such arrangements as starting date, moving, etc. You should always write a brief but polite letter of rejection to any employer you decide against. If you were interviewed, in addition to a letter, always call the employer to deliver your acceptance or rejection personally.

INTERVIEWING

Several times each week students enter our offices to talk about their academic progress, the possibility of pursuing a degree in communication, or other matters relating to their lives. In short, they arrive with something on their minds, and our communication focuses on those issues. Everyone frequently participates in interviews of various kinds, whether visiting the doctor, shopping for a stereo, or chatting with a counselor. It is our purpose here to discuss how interviews can be made more efficient by improving one's insights into the interviewing process and by improving one's personal preparation for an interview.

An **interview** is dyadic communication that focuses on a specific content area and for which at least one communicator has a preconceived purpose. Because of the purposive nature of interviewing, we will stress the development of efficiency that helps communicators achieve their purposes in an interview. As in any human interaction, certain variables seem to influence the interview more than others.

Control and Flexibility

What happens in an interview depends largely on how its participants share control. In every dyad, both participants help to determine or control the direction and content of the communication. If the participants share the same purpose, they should share the control of the interview in order to achieve that purpose efficiently. Nonetheless, control is rarely shared equally in an interview, nor should it always be.

For instance, in an initial medical interview the shared purpose of the doctor and patient might be to attain the most accurate possible diagnosis of an ailment. Being more familiar with the various possible ailments, the doctor might exercise more control over the interview at first, but if the discussion moves away from the symptoms that the patient is experiencing, the patient will want to assume more control by focusing on the overlooked symptoms.

If the participants do not share the purpose of an interview, there might be a struggle for control; the participants might disagree about which purpose should be pursued. Consider, for example, an interrogation interview, in which the interrogator seeks the greatest amount of accurate information, whereas the person being questioned wants to reveal very little. The entire interview could be a contest for control.

Another key element in efficient interviews is flexibility. Achieving a purpose in an interview is much like finding one's way through new territory with a poor map (or no map at all): there are many false starts, blind alleys, and unproductive directions. Participants must be flexible enough to adapt to what happens in an interview. The interviewer must be ready to follow through when unanticipated types of information, questions, or even objections are raise by the other person. Conversely, the interviewee should be prepared to adjust when the interviewer raises unanticipated questions or areas of information.

Like control, flexibility can be either cooperative or competitive, depending on the degree to which participants share a common purpose. If the purpose is shared, as in the case of doctor and patient, participants should be willing to move flexibly into new areas. But if purposes differ, as in the case of a political press interview, the participants must be flexible enough to handle unanticipated and perhaps leading questions.

Types of Interviews

Interviews are often classified according to content, such as a sales interview, a grievance interview, or a medical interview. In keeping with our focus on efficiency, however, we will classify interviews according to their purpose. Thus we will examine informational, decisional, and developmental interviews.

Informational Interviews: Collection and Dissemination. The purpose of an **informational interview** is to share, as accurately as possible, information about a particular area. Thus a survey interviewer attempts to gather the most accurate information possible about interviewees' opinions on a particular issue. Or a doctor uses an informational interview to share with a patient the diagnosis of a disease. In the first interview the purpose is to collect accurate information; in the second, the purpose is to disseminate information in a way that is most advantageous to both parties.

Three common types of interviews are used to collect information: the survey, the diagnostic interview, and the investigative interview. The first two types are similar in that they involve the participants' cooperation in working toward a common purpose. The investigative interview may or may not involve cooperation; usually it does not.

Every day newspapers or TV news broadcasts reveal the results of *surveys* concerning particular issues or the popularity of political candidates. The data for such polls are usually gathered from either face-to-face or telephone interviews. Less well known is the fact that most political and marketing organizations survey public opinion in order to adapt their appeals to specific groups of people. Not only do the interviewers want to obtain accurate information in the shortest possible time, but they also want interviewees' opinions to be represented accurately in the survey; thus a premium is placed on efficiency in the interview procedure.

Diagnostic interviews most frequently occur in the medical setting, but frequently teachers, religious leaders, and even friends need to find out what is going on in order to help in a given situation. In a diagnostic interview, as in a survey, it is in the interests of both parties to share the most accurate information in the shortest possible time.

Investigative interviews differ from surveys and diagnostic interviews in that the purposes of the participants are frequently at odds. We have noted already, for example, that the participants of an interrogation have different purposes. Similarly, in a journalistic interview the investigator wants to "get to the bottom" of a situation, whereas a politician or public figure wants to create the best public image possible.

Besides collecting information, interviews can *disseminate information*. In the medical context, a doctor must tell a patient about a diagnosed illness in a way that helps the patient handle and respond to the information appropriately. We suspect that many malpractice suits stem not from poor medical care but from unskillful, inefficient interviews between doctors and patients.

In a business context, information is disseminated through **appraisal interviews**, in which an employer evaluates the performance (whether good or bad) of an employee. An appraisal interview could also involve a grievance that an employee registers with a superior in the organization. Since appraisals usually deal with personal characteristics that may be highly ego involving for the interviewee, they need to be particularly well planned and conducted with great care.

Decisional Interviews. In **decisional interviews**, one or more of the participants aims to influence the other person's decision. Although this purpose can occur in virtually every interview context, decisional interviews take place most often in relation to personnel and marketing aspects of business organizations. Most decisional interviews involve employment, recruitment, placement, and sales.

Employment interviews and **recruitment interviews** involve a decision about hiring an individual for an organization. Both types require the participants to agree about the employment. However, an employment interview stresses the employer's decision, whereas a recruitment interview stresses the employee's decision.

Placement interviews occur in an organization during or after a person's employment and are designed to place or replace that individual. A placement interview is like a diagnostic interview in that a maximum of accurate information must be shared, but it goes beyond appraisal.

Sales interviews are among the most common and complex of all decisional interviews. Who has not had a conversation with a salesperson about a stereo, an automobile, some item of clothing, or a home appliance? Although the communicators may share the common purpose of effecting the purchase of some item—say a computer—they are frequently at odds about which particular item will be purchased, so influence is exerted on the decision. Indeed, except for mass advertising, most selling occurs in the dyadic interview context.

Developmental Interviews. A **developmental interview** combines the elements of sharing information and arriving at a decision in an effort to enhance the personal development of one or more participants. We have put this interview into a separate category not only because it combines information sharing and decision making but also because we think its process is somewhat different from the other types of interviews.

The structure in an interview depends on its purpose and on the amount of cooperation offered by the person being interviewed.

A personal development interview deals primarily with the participants themselves as the content of the interview. Furthermore, it facilitates insight about the self and may lead to a decision about what kind of person the participants are or will be.

Counseling interviews are designed to help people understand themselves and arrive at decisions concerning their lives. Counseling can center on educational, marital, theological, medical, or even legal issues. Although counseling interviews frequently deal with problems, they usually cover what society might define as a "normal" range of behaviors.

When issues or behaviors fall beyond the range accepted as normal by society, the interview is commonly known as a therapeutic interview. Counseling and therapeutic interviews are beyond the scope of this book, for they entail years of professional preparation and should not be conducted by nonprofessionals.

Teachers and students frequently become involved with academic behavior problems such as plagiarism, late or missed assignments, and the like. Whenever people are in relationships within an organizational structure, issues concerning the correction of behavior arise; **correctional interviews** are designed to address such matters. Thus, teachers and students, supervisors and subordinates, and parents and children use correctional interviews to examine positive and negative approaches to personal development.

Types of Questions

A primary form of communication in an interview is the use of questions. Generally, questioning is designed to encourage the other communicator to participate. The types of questions asked can profoundly influence the responses received. A reporter who asks, "Mr. President, what is your policy concerning Bosnia?" will probably not learn what the president thinks about Asia or Latin America. On the other hand, if the reporter asks, "What has been the most difficult issue you have faced in the past six months?" the answer might cover a broad range of foreign and domestic matters.

Although questions differ in many respects, we believe that the most significant distinguishing variable is the degree to which questions restrict or predispose the respondent's answer. Thus we will classify questions on a spectrum from unrestricted (open) to restricted (loaded) (see Figure 6.4). Bear in mind, however, that this spectrum has an infinite range of degrees of "restrictedness."

Open Questions. **Open questions** allow the respondent the most choices. How would you answer the comical question "What do you think when you don't think anything else?" The cartoon character Bugs Bunny frequently asks the consummate open question: "Eh, what's up, Doc?" Open questions offer the advantage of giving respondents freedom to determine the content of the response, which usually increases their participation. Counselors, for example, often begin with a new client by asking: "What brings you here today?" On the other hand, open questions yield information that is difficult to record and analyze quantitatively, and they may keep the interview from moving into the areas of interest to the interviewer.

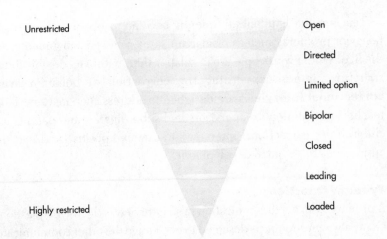

Unrestricted

Highly restricted

Open

Directed

Limited option

Bipolar

Closed

Leading

Loaded

Figure 6.4
Types of questions.

Directed Questions. **Directed questions** partially restrict the content of the response. You might ask a person, "What do you think about the drug crisis in the United States?" Although this question is still quite broad, it excludes more answers than it encourages. You could restrict the answer even further by asking, "What do you think has caused the current drug crisis?" or "What do you think about the idea of legalizing drugs?" Although increasingly directive, these questions still have the advantage of not revealing the questioner's bias; they allow the respondent considerable leeway in answering while at the same time focusing on the content area of interest to the questioner. Directed questions are among the most useful of all interview questions.

Limited-Option Questions. Sometimes an interviewer wants data that can be quantified and analyzed, such as the information reported by public opinion surveys. In this case it is necessary to restrict respondents to a fixed number of possible answers. Similar to a multiple-choice question on an examination, this type of question is called a **limited-option question**. A surveyor might ask, "Which of the following candidates do you favor at this time: Candidate A, Candidate B, Candidate C, or Candidate D?" Although limited-option questions allow respondents little flexibility, they can produce data that are highly amenable to quantification and analysis.

Bipolar Questions. Even more restricted are bipolar questions, an extension of limited-option questions. A **bipolar question** gives the respondent only two options from which to choose. Most bipolar questions seek a yes or no answer. Bipolar questions elicit highly specific answers, but they severely restrict the respondent—making it almost impossible to respond further.

Closed Questions. An even more restricted question is the **closed question**, which asks for a single, specific datum that frequently is demographic or biographical. Examples include "Where do you live?" "What is your date of birth?" "Who was that person I saw you with last night?" Closed questions sometimes are needed to obtain specific data that can be analyzed in terms of a preconceived classification, but—like limited-option and bipolar questions—closed questions severely restrict respondents' answers.

Leading Questions. A **leading question** is a type of closed question that leaves the respondent virtually no choice at all. In a sense, the questioner gives the respondent the desired answer. "Nice day, isn't it?" we may ask. What can the person say? "No, I hate sun"? An employment interviewer might ask, "Of course, you wouldn't want a job that required irregular hours, would you?" Leading questions indicate the position of the questioner. They have the disadvantage of not allowing respondents any choice, and in a sense they deny the respondents' right to think for themselves.

Loaded Questions. A **loaded question** predisposes the respondent to give a particular answer by loading the language in favor of or against a particular response. Examples are "Did you vote for that corrupt Nixon?" and "Do you prefer this acid-tasting coffee or the mild one?" Such questions are not designed to get information but to make a rhetorical point.

Questioning Sequences

The various types of questions do not, of course, occur in isolation. Questions are used to follow up on previous questions until the purpose of the interview is achieved as efficiently as possible. The specific sequence of questions depends somewhat on the advantages relating to types of questions. It also depends on whether the interviewee is cooperative or uncooperative, talkative or reticent. Among the most common question sequences are (1) funnel, (2) inverted-funnel, (3) art-form, (4) tunnel, and (5) quintamensional.

Funnel Sequence. The **funnel sequence** begins with relatively unrestricted questions and then becomes increasingly restrictive. Thus, an interviewee might be asked,

> What do you think of the president's approach to the war on drugs?
> In your opinion, what is the most important aspect of the problem?
> What effect do you think the legalization of drugs would have on the courts and prison system?
> Do you favor the legalization of drugs?
> What specific drugs do you think should be legalized?

Inverted-Funnel Sequence. The **inverted-funnel sequence** proceeds from relatively restricted questions to less restricted ones. The interviewee might be asked,

> What, if any, drugs should be legalized?
> What effects do you think the legalization of drugs would have on the courts and prison system?
> What is the most important aspect of the current problem with drugs in the United States?
> What do you think of the president's approach to the war on drugs?

The funnel and inverted-funnel sequences offer different advantages. In interviewing a person who talks freely or who needs the greatest latitude, the funnel sequence might be useful. If, on the other hand, the interviewee is reticent or the interviewer wants to obtain specific information in the shortest possible time, the specific-to-general, inverted funnel should be used.

Art-Form Sequence. A special case of the inverted funnel is a specific-to-general sequence we will call the **art-form sequence**. Originally designed to elicit discussion of various art forms such as paintings, pictures, sculpture, movies, and so on, the art-form sequence can also be applied to issues. The stages in the art-form sequence are (1) objective, (2) reflective, (3) interpretive, and (4) decisional.

Objective questions focus on specific data or images that the interviewee recalls; for example, "Where have you seen or read about homelessness?" or "What words or phrases do you recall from that play?" Reflective questions ask the interviewee to relate to the objective data; for example, "How do you feel when confronted with homeless people?" or "What scenes in that play surprised you?" Interpretive questions ask what the interviewee thinks is the meaning behind the issue or art form; for example, "What do you think causes most cases of homelessness?" or "What do you think Shakespeare was trying to say in that scene?" Finally, decisional questions ask the interviewee to make a decision about the object of the interview. These would be used only in decisional interviews, whereas informational and personal development interviews could stop at the interpretive level. Thus, the interviewer might continue by asking, "What can we do to deal with the homeless?" or "What does this drama tell us about our own lives?"

Tunnel Sequence. The **tunnel sequence** moves along the same level of restriction in a series of parallel questions. The interviewer might begin by asking what the interviewee thinks about a certain model of automobile, model A. Then the same question would be asked about models B, C, and D. This sequence has the advantage of obtaining data that can be compared easily without loading or biasing the response in a particular direction.

Quintamensional Sequence. The **quintamensional sequence** was developed by opinion researchers to determine the intensity with which opinions are held. The five steps of the quintamensional sequence are

1. *Awareness:* What have you heard about the Balanced Budget Amendment?
2. *Uninfluenced attitudes:* What do you think about it?
3. *Specific attitude:* Do you approve or disapprove of the amendment?
4. *Reason:* Why do you feel that way?

5. *Intensity of attitude:* How strongly do you feel about the Balanced Budget Amendment?

In concluding this discussion of question sequences, we must return to our previous point concerning flexibility. Not every interview will follow the sequence that has been planned. Interviewees sometimes refuse to answer a question, give nonanswers, or answer a question that was not yet asked. Then the interviewer must be prepared to relate the answer to the appropriate question and must be ready to follow up with a question that will move the interview toward the desired purpose. It is not uncommon, for instance, to begin a funnel sequence with an open question that receives no response. The interviewer must then proceed to increasingly directed questions until a response is received; then the questions can again become more general. In a sense the interview moves back and forth along the "funnel."

Preparation: Situation Analysis

Before beginning an interview, it is useful to analyze the components of the situation in order to be ready for any eventuality and to adapt to the specific constraints involved. You should analyze the purpose of the interview, its setting, yourself as an interviewer or interviewee, your co-interviewer, and the time available.

Analyzing the Purpose. Since one distinguishing characteristic of an interview is its purposiveness, it is a good idea to analyze your purpose and, if possible, the purpose of other participants. Everyone, of course, should know the general purpose of the interview (employment, sales, medical, or the like). But what about its specific purpose? Most salespersons know, for instance, that few sales are concluded in the first interview. Although they should always be flexible enough to close a sale if the opportunity emerges, they should also be clear about what goal—short of closing the sale—they would like to accomplish. Similarly, people may not be hired for a job after an initial employment interview (perhaps because there are no openings), but they can create such a favorable impression that they will be hired as soon as an opening occurs. You should consider such secondary goals as seriously as primary goals, and you should know your specific purposes as well as your general purposes for the interview.

Analyzing the Setting. The setting of the interview should also be considered carefully. If you have control, determine what the most advantageous setting might be and strive to create it. If you do not have control over the setting, analyzing it will help you adapt more flexibly to whatever situation you encounter. Most insurance representatives, for example, prefer to discuss finances with a couple in the living room or kitchen of their home, without the interruption of children, telephones, and the like. If the setting is an office, most businesspeople try to make their offices exude success, which tells the client nonverbally that the company is a good one with which to do business.

Analyzing Yourself. Another factor of considerable importance in preinterview analysis, but one frequently overlooked, is yourself. Knowing yourself makes you a more efficient interviewer or interviewee. What are your needs and motives, attitudes and opinions, and insights or blind spots in terms of the subject of the interview? Equally important is your emotional state at the time of the interview. Are you tense or relaxed? Indifferent or too ego involved? Finally, how have you related to the other person in the past—if at all? Is the relationship based on trust, or do you feel suspicious?

Analyzing Your Co-interviewer. It is perhaps too easy but also accurate to say that the better you know your co-interviewer, the more likely you are to have an efficient, if not successful, interview. We suggest that you ask the same questions about the other person that you ask about yourself. If your superior has unexpectedly called you in for an appraisal interview, it is important to analyze that person's point of view, his or her feelings about you, and even his or her current emotional state.

Investment representatives often spend literally hours researching a prospective client before the first interview. If such preinterview research is not possible, a significant portion of the first interview should be devoted to "casual conversation" designed to find out as much as possible about the other participant, within the time constraints of the situation.

Analyzing the Time. Some interviewers are more preoccupied than others with time, and sensitivity to that can make a great difference. If time is severely limited, you should focus on a limited objective—

major issues only—and probably should use more directed questions. For example, while conducting research in the nation's capital some years ago, one of the authors was able to interview one senator at length over lunch, but he had to streamline his questioning for a hurried interview with a second senator in a reception room off the Senate chambers.

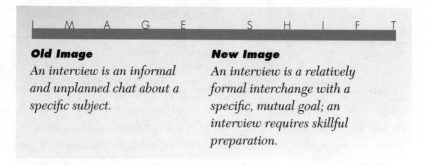

Old Image

An interview is an informal and unplanned chat about a specific subject.

New Image

An interview is a relatively formal interchange with a specific, mutual goal; an interview requires skillful preparation.

The Interview Schedule

After analyzing the interviewing situation, you are ready to prepare an interview plan, or **interview schedule**. The interview schedule should be in outline form and should contain a purpose statement, a brief opening, an outline of your questioning sequence, and a brief closing statement.

The *purpose statement* should state in a single declarative sentence the results you seek to obtain from the interview. For an employment interview the statement might read, "As a result of this interview I wish to be employed by ABC Company as a computer programmer."

The *opening* of the interview simply introduces you to the co-interviewer, states briefly the subject of the interview, and elicits the cooperation of (and perhaps motivates) your co-interviewer to participate constructively.

The outline of the *questioning sequence* constitutes the major part of your interview schedule. We suggest a general-to-specific outline form with open spaces for responses and specific spaces for checking off responses to limited-option questions. The partial Senate interview schedule in Figure 6.5 illustrates the points we have made.

Purpose: To gather accurate information about factors influencing the passage of the IMF treaty in the U.S. Senate.

Office of Senator_____

Person answering these questions_____

Position_____

A. Personal Convictions

  1. How many senators were influenced by personal convictions concerning the IMF treaty?

    All (°)   Many (°)   Some (°)   Few (°)   None (°)

  2. How many senators were influenced by personal convictions other than those raised by the treaty itself (e.g., national autonomy)?

    All (°)   Many (°)   Some (°)   Few (°)   None (°)

  3. How much effect did the personal convictions of the senators have on the passage of the bill in its final form?

    Great (°)   Considerable (°)   Moderate (°)   Little (°)   None (°)
    Comment:

B. Opinion of Constituency

  1. Were any senators influenced by the feelings of their constituencies?

    Yes (°)   No (°)

  2. How was this influence exerted? (Indicate all appropriate answers.)

      a. By Letters   (°)
      b. By lobbyists   (°)
      c. By campaign contributions   (°)
      d. Through the press   (°)
      e. Other   (°)

  3. In your judgment, how much influence did the constituencies have on passage of the bill in its final form?

    Great (°)   Considerable (°)   Moderate (°)   Little (°)   None (°)
    Comment:

C. Strategic Compromising

  1. Would you consider the IMF treaty a compromise measure?

    Yes (°)   No (°)

  2. If so, what were the compromises? (Indicate all appropriate answers.)

  3. In your judgment, how much effect did this compromising have on the passage of the bill in its final form?

    Great (°)   Considerable (°)   Moderate (°)   Little (°)   None (°)
    Comment:

Figure 6.5 *An interview schedule.*

SUPPORTIVENESS AND ASSERTIVENESS

Applying for jobs and participating in interviews are common and important types of communication. Another crucial type of communication in professional settings is group problem solving, which is the topic of the following chapter. Professional settings, of course, require many other forms of communication, far too many to discuss separately in this book. In the remainder of this chapter, we discuss two general approaches to professional communication that will serve you well no matter what specific type of communication you may be engaged in.

Supportiveness

Many variables affect professional communication, but the most important is a supportive climate. In **defensive climates** workers rationalize mistakes and are negativistic, critical of others, and withdrawn. **Supportive climates**, on the other hand, not only facilitate the accomplishment of the task but also promote effective communication. Characteristics that distinguish the supportive climate and thus support

The most important basis for professional communication is a supportive climate.

communication are spontaneity, empathy, equality, description, problem orientation, and provisionalism. Let's look at these characteristics in more detail.

Spontaneity versus Strategy. Few people like co-workers who are secretive and devious. When people feel that others are using strategies against them, they become defensive; communication becomes less supportive, and the organization functions less effectively. On the other hand, if professional communication is spontaneous and open, threats are reduced and work proceeds efficiently.

Assertive workers feel free to speak up when they need information or clarification.

Some degree of competition seems to be a good thing in the workplace. It keeps people alert and causes them to work to their capacity. But intense competition creates a threatening climate in which fewer risks are taken, communication becomes less spontaneous, and efficiency is impaired.

We appreciate co-workers who are secure enough within themselves and with the group to be able to respond to a question or to a work situation without weighing every word. Their behavior creates a supportive climate and encourages others to be equally spontaneous. However, such an atmosphere can be destroyed quickly by thoughtless remarks or pointless criticism.

Although spontaneity is usually desirable and fosters a supportive climate, it can be counterproductive if carried to the extreme of allowing everything to be expressed. Professional communication should be appropriate and well timed. To accomplish this, people should temper spontaneity with judgment.

Empathy versus Neutrality. Earlier we defined empathy as the quality of being able to see and feel another person's point of view. When co-workers treat you with empathy, you tend to respond in kind, and the result is a mutually supportive work atmosphere. The development of empathy does not necessarily mean that you like or even approve of everything your co-workers do. But it does mean that you attempt to understand them, which frequently leads to greater acceptance.

The lack of empathy has been termed *neutrality*. Many people want to see themselves as being cool, austere, or distant. Yet, as society becomes more complex, more and more people complain about being treated "like numbers." Such treatment from professional colleagues can be threatening and can lead to suspicion and mistrust within the work environment.

Equality versus Superiority. Although there must be some structure (usually involving a hierarchy) within most work organizations, overemphasis on status differences can threaten the work environment. Consider the attitude of Japanese businesses, in which every employee is valued not according to rank but in terms of the quality of his or her work. In such a system the president of a corporation may bow with respect to a dock worker, and a superior laborer is valued more highly than a mediocre administrator. Each employee is treated with what Carl Rogers calls "positive regard," for everyone realizes that all members contribute to the goals of the organization. This supportive work climate can lead to both high morale and high productivity.

Description versus Evaluation. Driving along a country road one day, one of the authors saw a squirrel dart across the pavement in front of him. Midway across the road the squirrel saw the automobile, stopped, started back, stopped, started across again, and finally cowered in fear as the car passed over it without harm. People behave similarly when they perceive danger. In a work environment where communication is constantly evaluative and judgmental, people may feel so threatened that they are unable to perform effectively because of fear of reprimand and rejection. Even compliments can carry implied threats: "Your work has improved so much this past month" can convey the threat "and you'd better not let it slide backward." Some people phrase almost everything they say in such judgmental terms.

One way to avoid excessive judgment is to replace it with description in your communication. Instead of judging the other person, describe your reaction to what was said or done. This approach relies on "I" messages. For example:

Evaluation: You are lazy.
"I" message: I get impatient when you spend so much time at the water cooler. I need your estimate in order to complete the bid on that office building.

Evaluation is sometimes necessary, but not to the extent that it is offered immediately. Furthermore, the adverse effects of judgment can be lessened by distinguishing between the person and the act. No one is perfect. It is much less destructive to say, "I don't like it when you take my typewriter without asking," than to charge, "You are a thief."

By treating work colleagues with positive regard even though you may not like their foibles or habits, you will enhance the supportive climate as well as increase the chances of being accepted in spite of your own shortcomings. Until such time as everyone can achieve perfection, this seems to be the best approach to effective professional communication.

Problem Orientation versus Control. Do you enjoy being manipulated or controlled? Not many people do. Sometimes in work contexts people feel that they are being persuaded to adopt a plan that they do not really favor. Sometimes they may even feel that a matter has been decided already and that they are merely going through the motions of making a decision. This, of course, communicates a feeling (real or imagined) that colleagues do not value one's judgment.

Contrast such a work atmosphere to one that is problem oriented. In a problem-oriented climate, no solutions are predetermined. Each employee may favor a particular plan, but everyone is willing to make a change on the basis of new data. Communication focuses on investigating the problem rather than on selling the solution. New data are introduced, and all possible solutions are put forward for equal consideration. Only then is the final solution determined. This problem-oriented approach creates a supportive climate and hence improves job satisfaction and ultimately productivity.

Provisionalism versus Certainty. The final characteristic of communication within a supportive work climate is provisionalism. Jack Gibb has pointed out, "Those who seem to know the answers, to require no additional data, and to regard themselves as teachers rather than co-workers tend to put others on guard."[1] Not only does this attitude tend to cut off the flow of information, but it creates feelings of resentment and suspicion among co-workers.

Children need a sense of certainty in order to feel that their world is secure. It is a sign of maturity, however, to be able to recognize and live with uncertainty and even ambiguity and still feel secure. People need to develop a tentative attitude toward communicative claims. "As far as I know . . . [claim]"; "At this point in time . . . [claim]"; and "It is my best judgment that . . ." are three ways of expressing provisionalism without destroying the claim itself.

Conversely, people should not place too much credence in assertions that are expressed without qualification. Indeed, people should suspect unqualified assertions more than qualified ones, since they frequently represent an effort to hide the speaker's insecurity. Unfortunately, assertions of certainty are often given more credence than provisional statements, simply because they sound stronger.

Assertiveness

Our discussion of supportiveness thus far may seem to imply that we think people should be submissive in their professional relationships. But we take a far different view. Submissive people usually are reluctant to ask for what they want or to express their opinions, especially when disagreement seems likely. They frequently find themselves disappointed with decisions for which they have provided little input. Aggressive people, on the other hand, tend to impose their wishes on others, even at the expense of colleagues' rights. They are frequently outspoken and pay little attention to either verbal or nonverbal messages that run counter to their opinions. We recommend a communication style—assertiveness—that falls midway between submission and aggression. Assertiveness has been described as "the positive expression by word or deed, of one's rights, thoughts, feelings, desires, and abilities . . . the positive presentation and protection of oneself."[2]

Most writers agree that an assertive style of relating to others carries certain rights and responsibilities and is characterized by particular ways of talking.[3] If your style is assertive, you know you have the right to express your own opinion, and you accept the responsibility of allowing other people to express theirs. You have the right to disagree tactfully; you do not have to smile and nod in acquiescence. It is appropriate to agree with a compliment or at least to acknowledge it. It is both permissible and desirable to disclose information about yourself as long as you do not monopolize the conversation or disclose inappropriately intimate information.

You also have the right to feel however you want to feel (or must feel), and the responsibility to "own" your feelings. Furthermore, you have the right to express your feelings in your personal way and the responsibility to allow others to express theirs. "Feeling talk" involves an open sharing of feelings and honest responses to questions about feelings. For example, you might tell co-workers, "This week has been rough on my nerves" or "I feel great this morning!" In saying such things, you allow your co-workers to adjust their communication to your feelings at the time. Furthermore, recognizing your right to your opinions and feelings makes it unnecessary to justify your position over and over. You may say to a contentious colleague, "We've talked about this before, and we obviously disagree. I prefer not to discuss it."

You also have the right to question anything you do not understand and to ask why you have been instructed to do something. On the other hand, you have the responsibility to explain yourself so that you can be understood and can work cooperatively on a given task. Too often workers proceed with a job that they do not understand or to which they object. The result is either poor work or an unhappy worker; a quick request for clarification might alleviate both problems.

Still another right is to ask for what you want. Along with this right, however, comes the responsibility to ask for what you expect and to be willing to work for it. Do not expect your co-workers to be mind readers or Santa Claus.

We have pointed out several times that no one is perfect. Everyone has the right at times to be irrational, illogical, inconsistent, or unpredictable. Everyone is entitled to make some mistakes. On the other hand, people have the responsibility to be generally competent colleagues. Co-workers frequently depend on each other to accomplish the work. Self-confident, assertive people usually are willing to admit their mistakes and to accept the idiosyncrasies of their colleagues. However, a person who makes mistakes too often or whose work is too inconsistent or unpredictable might also expect to be looking for a new job.

One of the most important rights is to make your own decisions in life and to defend yourself against attempts by others to limit or infringe on your rights. Along with this right come the responsibilities to determine your own behavior and to grant the same rights to others. Frequently in work contexts, people of higher position in the organization attempt to define who or what others ought to be. This sometimes manifests itself in attempts to subvert the rights or responsibilities of others. In such cases difficult decisions must be made, and compromises must be achieved. For example, you may decide to go along with things that are more important to the other person while firmly asserting the

In some work environments—like this toy factory in Mexico—there is little meaningful communication from employees to bosses.

rights and prerogatives most important to you. If crucial issues cannot be resolved—if the "real you" is incompatible with the objectives of the organization—you may decide to leave the organization.

Imagine that you are at a meeting of co-workers when the supervisor assigns you a job for which you feel you have less time and qualification than another worker does. If you were a submissive person, you might smile and grudgingly accept the job, but later you would complain to several co-workers that the assignment was unfair. If you were an aggressive person, you might speak up at the meeting: "I think you are being unfair and arbitrary to give me that job. Harry isn't working half as hard as I am, and that's one job he can do." If you were assertive, you might handle the situation in several ways. You might say: "I'm awfully busy right now, and that job isn't in my specialty. Could we discuss it privately before you make the final assignment?"

Old Image
Communicating at work is simply a matter of being nice to your co-workers.

New Image
Competent communication at work involves both supportiveness and assertiveness.

SUMMARY

Communication on the job affects just about everyone. In this chapter, we have discussed two important types of professional communication—career entry and interviewing. We also addressed two approaches to communication that help people in almost all professional settings—supportiveness and assertiveness.

Career entry is a complex process of goal setting, planning, and communicating. It means knowing yourself, presenting yourself, and making decisions. Anyone involved in a serious career search will need to know certain fundamentals—research, résumé writing, letters of application, and interviewing.

Interviewing is an especially difficult yet important kind of communication related to employment situations, but it also includes a set of tools that most professionals use continually on the job. Several aspects of interviewing have been covered in this chapter.

Whether in interviews or other types of professional communication, supportiveness and assertiveness can be important tools. At work, supportiveness is required to provide a climate in which people can cooperate and achieve goals together, and assertiveness is necessary to make one's own wants and needs known.

In the following chapter, we discuss another form of professional communication—problem solving in small groups.

7 Understanding and Improving Group Communication

S hortly before noon they began to arrive—through the back gate, along the short drive, and into the portal leading to the West Wing. The guards recognized each of them at a glance, having long since dispensed with the ritualistic flashing of passes. On this Tuesday in November of 1967, the eight suited men knew instinctively where to go.

They exchanged some pleasantries, wondering how long the storm would last. Conversation faded when President Lyndon Johnson entered. He was a big man, physically tall and psychologically towering. He grinned and said, "Hungry? Let's eat."

A few moments later the nine were eating salad and exchanging information about casualty figures and enemy movements. By 1:30 they had made decisions that would affect the lives of thousands of American soldiers in Vietnam as well as millions of anxious watchers at home.

This was the Tuesday Lunch Group: President Lyndon Johnson, Robert McNamara, Earle Wheeler, Clark Clifford, Walt Rostow, Tom Johnson, George Christian, Richard Helms, and Dean Rusk. Over a period of four years, this group made decisions about increasing the draft, deploying troops, bombing targets, and other matters that changed history.

Like it or not, we human beings are affected deeply by groups. Human beings are not solitary animals. We need human contact, and we require cooperation to achieve our goals. At the same time, we seem unable to endure the overload and chaos of large, undifferentiated masses, and so we gather together into small groups. Even huge organizations like General Motors are divided into smaller units, and work gets done through interaction in groups.

UNDERSTANDING GROUP COMMUNICATION

Group communication here does not mean casual, improvised transactions like those occurring at bus stops, supermarkets, and public parks. We are referring to the relatively well-established groups that affect people's lives in enduring ways. Such groups usually have a history and are definable as distinct, engendering a sense of belongingness and common goals among members. Communication within the group is relatively frequent and ongoing. In addition, the group usually evolves standards of behavior and expectations for its members. A pattern of interaction is followed in the group, and this interaction leads to various psychological rewards (and sometimes punishments) for the members.

Think a moment about all the groups in your life that fit these characteristics. Families are groups, and so are cliques. People encounter groups related to work, school, church, and community. Usually people belong to several groups, each with its own pressures, communication patterns, expectations, and rewards.

For purposes of discussion, we will think in terms of two categories of groups. **Natural social groups** develop out of everyday interpersonal contacts. They are not created but instead evolve naturally. Such groups come into existence because of proximity and common interests among a handful of people. Such groups meet people's needs for association and contact. They are fluid and overlap. Social groups do not necessarily meet formally; in fact they may not "meet" at all.

The second kind of group, the **created group**, does not evolve naturally but is formulated for specific purposes. There are several types of created groups, which can serve educational, therapeutic, and task purposes. Such groups are usually designed to involve certain people and to meet regularly according to planned formats or agendas.

Natural social groups meet our needs for association and contact.

Communication is central to all kinds of groups. The concepts and principles of interpersonal communication discussed in Chapter 5 are important in groups too, for interpersonal communication is the basis of group life.

In this book we are particularly interested in **task groups**, which affect everybody in two important ways. First, almost all people are called upon to participate in task groups, where they are required to expend valuable time and energy interacting with others to solve problems and make decisions. Second, group decisions affect people's lives in crucial ways. The fact that you are taking a communication course—especially if it is required—is a result of discussions by a university committee or series of committees. Thus, everyone has an interest in understanding and improving communication in task-oriented groups.

The Transactional Approach

As discussed before, the transactional approach to group communication stresses three factors: process, context, and function. Despite the temptation to think of a group as a collection of individuals, groups are best viewed as a process—a process of communication, a pattern of interaction among the members.

Second, group communication occurs in context. Basically, two kinds of context are important. The *external context* consists of outside expectations for the group, the social climate in which the group operates, and the resources provided for the group. The *internal context* consists of the task or problem facing a group, the human resources in the group, the physical setting, and the group's history. We cannot really understand any particular happening in the group without a broader understanding of these contextual elements.

Finally, the transactional perspective helps us to focus on function in group communication. Communication in groups achieves both personal and group goals. Personally, members can develop and maintain relationships with others within groups. Virtually all the relationship functions discussed in Chapter 5 can occur not only in couples but also within groups.

On the group level, communication functions in two ways: (1) to accomplish the task through shared information, opinions, and ideas;

and (2) to maintain the group by means of positive interpersonal relations. Of course, the outcome of interaction is not always positive. The task may not be completed, or it may be done ineffectively, and group maintenance may decline. (Later in this chapter we provide some guidelines for improving these two functions in groups.)

Functions can also be viewed from another angle. Consider all the energy a group uses in dealing with a task. Everybody puts effort into the group, hoping that the energy will be transformed into something more than the simple sum of individual efforts. This idea—that the whole is more than the sum of its parts—has been called **synergy**, the output of a group.

On the simplest level, synergy can be divided into two parts: the energy expended directly on the task (**task energy**) and the energy that keeps the group together (**interpersonal energy**). Every group has both kinds. The task will not be accomplished if members do not work on ideas and solutions, but the people in the group also require human attention. Part of the time a group deals with the problem or task at hand, and part of the time it works to motivate its members and make them happier, more relaxed, and ready to attack the assignment. Usually these energies are mixed and fulfill both functions simultaneously.

Interpersonal energy is always necessary but when the group spends too much time on that, it exhausts the members' ability to handle the task. Thus, when interpersonal energy is too high relative to task energy, the group will not be able to achieve more than could be done by a single person. The challenge is to optimize interpersonal energy and to maximize task energy so that synergy can be achieved. Under such ideal conditions, group members reap rewards for accomplishing the task and at the same time experience the joys of interacting with others.

So far this probably all sounds quite abstract. But nearly everybody discovers at one time or another just how real the task-interpersonal relationship is. For example, one of the authors once participated in a committee to revise the university's basic speech requirement. The group began by outlining several possible objectives for such a course; then we were supposed to discuss different teaching strategies for achieving the approved objectives. We met every week for an entire year. Finally—after the first chairperson gave up and another person had led the group for a few more months—we disbanded, never having completed our task.

The reasons this group failed are too complicated to list here. It is enough to say that we spent so much time resolving our interpersonal differences that we simply could not get around to solving the task. There were numerous conflicts and differences of opinion, exacerbated by an unbending attitude on the part of a few members. In other words, the proportion of interpersonal energy expended relative to task energy was simply too great. Later a new committee, having learned from the mistakes of the old committee, devised a very good solution to the problem in only a few weeks.

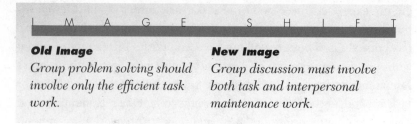

Old Image
Group problem solving should involve only the efficient task work.

New Image
Group discussion must involve both task and interpersonal maintenance work.

Interaction in Groups

Communication in groups can be classified according to interpersonal functions and task functions. Although some messages serve only one function, many serve both.

Messages that function in the interpersonal area involve friendliness and unfriendliness, dramatizing and showing tension, and agreeing and disagreeing. These kinds of messages fulfill or detract from the socioemotional needs of the group and can build or degrade group maintenance. One of the authors knows an administrator who is quite a joker in committee meetings. He repeatedly injects bits of humor into otherwise serious discussions. Committees have come to rely on this dean for relief from group tension. For example, he once likened the university to a "bunch of bare-handed fish grabbers in a world of nets." This kind of dramatizing can allow a group to escape, even if just for a moment, from the tensions that naturally arise within it.

Task-related messages involve giving or asking for suggestions, providing or requesting information, and providing or asking for opinions.

Most commonly messages in groups are designed to give either opinions or information. Unfortunately, people rarely ask for information, opinions, or suggestions.

Networks. Communication within a group is patterned. For various psychological and physical reasons, channels of communication among participants are not equal. Think about your own participation in groups. It is highly unlikely that you interact equally with every other member of the group. Interaction patterns are called **networks**.[1]

Network researchers have noted that some people seem to have more links than others do. In certain groups, lines of communication are distributed more equally than in others. A person with links to most other people in the group is central in position; people with few links are said to display **peripherality**. With **centrality** comes leadership, since central people control the flow of information. When most members of a group are in touch with each other, there is high **shared centrality**.

There seems to be an optimal point of shared centrality. When a number of people are central, chaos may result, since everybody is talking with everybody else. But if only one person is central and the other members are isolated, motivation and satisfaction may wane. Figure 7.1 illustrates high, medium, and low centrality.

At times groups of students in our classes display either too much centrality or too little. One time we asked a group to build a model house from materials like paper, tape, paper clips, glue, and rubber

Figure 7.1
Shared centrality.

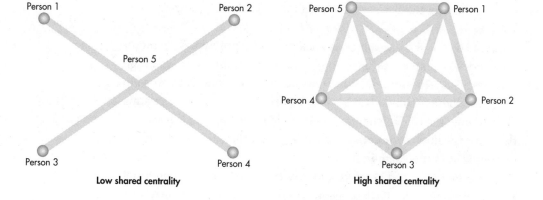

Low shared centrality

High shared centrality

bands. This was a fun exercise. The rest of the class sat around the edge of the room observing a most amazing thing: everybody in the group talked—and they talked all at once. Each member rather independently projected his or her own decision onto the group task without finding out how the group might mesh its efforts. As a result, the group had a lot of fun, but the model house was a catastrophe. The group exhibited high shared centrality, but it had little leadership or coordination. A business would not last very long if it operated that way.

Another student group in the same class was asked to solve an abstract problem. One member of the group asked for ideas. After several moments of silence, another member revealed an idea. This was followed by more silence. The "leader" then asked for more information or ideas. Again, another piece of information was offered reluctantly, followed by more silence. Finally, after about fifteen painful minutes of such "interaction," the leader solved the problem alone. This group accomplished its task, but the process was slow and dull, and the members of the group did not feel very good about the process. In this case the group lacked shared centrality, and one member virtually took control of the task. If you went to work every day to a group like that, you would soon quit or die of boredom.

Coalitions. As communication networks develop in groups, members will probably join together into subgroups, or **coalitions**. The larger the group, the greater the tendency that this will happen. You might relate nicely to four or five other people in a group, but it is unlikely that you will relate equally well to eight, ten, or fifteen members. Coalitions tend to form on the basis of similar communication styles, goals, and beliefs.

In one recent class, a group was asked to solve a problem. Two rather extroverted members of the group immediately formed a coalition against the other four members. Since no one else could get a word in edgewise, these two ended up talking just to each other. By intimidating and ignoring the others, they gained complete control over the group's decision. Coalitions are natural, of course, and they are not always as damaging as in this example.

These examples of networks and coalitions point to the important effects of group size. Groups need to be large enough to provide a broad range of inputs but small enough to remain cohesive and manageable. We deal with group size later in the chapter.

Roles. If we can begin to predict how a person will interact in a group, we are close to defining that person's roles in the group. A **role** is a pattern of behavior assumed by a group member, determined largely by the group's expectations. Expectation and behavior affect each other. After a while the group expects a person to behave in a manner consistent with that person's habits and capabilities. In a sense, roles are patterns of talk; they are expected communication acts for a given person.

Since interaction can advance the task and socioemotional goals of a group, roles tend to cluster around those goals. Roles that fulfill task functions in a group include initiator/contributor, information or opinion seeker, information or opinion giver, elaborator, coordinator, orientor, evaluator/critic, energizer, procedural technician, and recorder. Roles that build and maintain the group include those of encourager, harmonizer, compromiser, gatekeeper/expeditor, standard setter, observer, and followers. People commonly assume more than one of these roles.

Leadership. Leadership is a generally misunderstood concept. Too many people think of leadership as something a person has or does to other people. We prefer to think of **leadership** as a set of functions that persons assume. Any group member can assume any of these functions as necessary. When one person consistently takes one of these functions, he or she is taking a *leadership role.* Some people lead more than others, but leadership is situational; a leader in one situation may not lead well in another situation. Also, several people may assume different leadership functions in the same group.

Another misconception about group leadership is that it involves a single trait or skill, but because there are a number of leadership functions, there are a number of leadership roles. Task leadership consists of functions that move the group toward its objective. Socioemotional leadership consists of functions that build group solidarity and cohesiveness—acts that help members feel better about themselves, resolve conflict, or relieve tension.

Although it is important to think of leadership in terms of functions rather than people, we know that some members assume more responsibilities than others do. In a given group it can be predicted that one member will emerge as a primary **task leader** and another as a primary **socioemotional leader**. Rarely does a single person in a particular group consistently lead in both areas.

Earlier in this century much research was conducted by psychologists and sociologists to discover leadership "traits."[2] This approach did not work very well for a variety of reasons. For one thing, human traits are far from universal, and leadership is highly situational. Second, trait lists do little to improve group leadership because they tend to let people off the hook. A person may conclude, "Since I don't have any of the leadership traits, I will be content simply to sit back and follow." We are very firm on this: All group members have a responsibility to understand leadership functions and to communicate in ways that help the group achieve its socioemotional needs and its task.

This attitude toward leadership has been labeled the **democratic style**. One person—either a formally appointed or an emergent leader— may assume the role of primary leader but allows various group members to assume these roles as they feel necessary, distributing task functions as appropriate among group members.

In contrast to the democratic attitude is the **autocratic style**. In this case the person who is appointed or emerges as task leader jealously guards the task leadership functions and will not share them with other members. Often the autocratic leader is insensitive to socioemotional needs and may suppress attempts of various members to meet these needs.

It sometimes happens that no single person becomes primary task leader. Sometimes even an appointed leader fails to assume primary responsibility for leadership functions, which results in a **laissez-faire style**. This style is not the absence of leadership but the spreading, or diffusion, of leadership functions among members. The difference between democratic and laissez-faire styles is that under the former, one or two people—being group centered and sharing responsibility— take the primary responsibility to see that leadership functions are met; under laissez-faire leadership, however, no specific members take primary responsibility for the group.

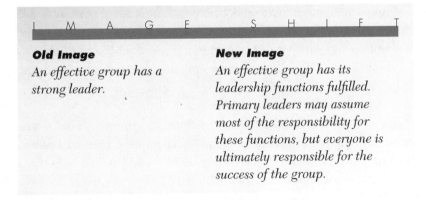

I M A G E   S H I F T

Old Image
An effective group has a strong leader.

New Image
An effective group has its leadership functions fulfilled. Primary leaders may assume most of the responsibility for these functions, but everyone is ultimately responsible for the success of the group.

Group Influence

Perhaps you have been at a party where most of the others were smoking and putting pressure on others to do likewise. Even people who are fully aware of the health problems and addictiveness associated with tobacco may take a cigarette when it is offered. Refusing certain social pressures takes extraordinary self-confidence and independence of thought. The fact is that groups exert powerful influence on people's lives. We rely on groups to help and guide us. Because of our need to identify with other people, groups have strong effects on our values and behaviors.

Conformity to group norms may be largely unconscious.

Groups influence individual behavior for a number of reasons. First, groups give stability, enabling individuals to achieve personal goals. Without "a little help from our friends," we would not be able to accomplish much. In addition, groups provide guidelines for behavior, called norms.

Norms. **Norms**, behavioral expectations for group members, are based on group values, and group membership requires some adherence. Both natural groups and created groups develop norms, and both types of groups have an impact on their members.

This discussion should not give the impression that people are totally subject to the whims of the group. Although groups are powerful, they do not exert total control over individuals. For one thing, an individual belongs to a number of groups, each of which has its values and norms. Keep in mind too that a group is not an amorphous mass. It consists of individual human beings who influence one another. Thus the group itself is subject to change. Although the group as a whole will influence its members, those individuals will also affect the group. The group and the individual change each other through interaction.

Conformity. **Conformity** is acceptance of group norms, but a person can accept them to varying degrees. Here we discuss three levels of conformity—compliance, identification, and internalization.[3]

Sometimes people go along with others simply because they want to be accepted. They conform for the reward of approval. This first level of conformity is called **compliance**. It is public, as opposed to private, conformity; that is, others can observe your conformity, whether you genuinely believe in what you are doing or not.

Compliant people need to have their conformity known; otherwise no social reward would be available. For example, one young man was rather compliant as a child. As an approval seeker, he would usually follow the crowd in order to be accepted. For instance, he tried very hard to support the sixth-grade football team, even though he privately hated the game. Later, as an adult, he continued to fake an interest in sports because males in our culture are expected to "talk sports." At some point, however, he realized that it was not necessary to continue this pretense in order to be accepted.

The second level of conformity is **identification**, which is motivated by a need to affiliate with the group. A person thus goes along with the group in order to maintain a satisfying self-image. Conforming helps the person take roles in the group, and the roles themselves are the source of satisfaction. We might call this "believing in believing." One churchgoer admits, "I don't believe literally in the divinity of Jesus, but the symbolic act of worship reinforces a spirit of love that makes me a better person." Her identification with the church and its beliefs is itself a satisfying act. Like compliance, identification is also primarily a public form of conformity.

The third level involves private and public commitment to the values and norms of the group. **Internalization** occurs when a person integrates the group's norms into his or her private value system. It is not the act of conforming that is rewarding but the actual belief itself. When a young adult first affiliates with a political party, for example, he or she may adopt its stands on the issues in a kind of intellectual and surface fashion. After years of membership, however, internalization takes place, and the party deeply influences the person's true attitudes and values.

There has been a good deal of research into the sources of conformity. We have noted that cohesiveness within the group leads to a "we-feeling," which generates greater group influence. Basically, it is fair to say that two overriding sources of conformity prevail.

The first basic factor affecting group influence is the degree of personal uncertainty the members feel. You tend to conform when you are unsure of your own judgments and when you feel that the group has an answer.

The second factor is the degree of credibility, trust, and solidarity in the group, captured by the term **cohesiveness**. Cohesiveness is the quality of mutual identification among members. The more cohesive the group, the more solidarity exists. The Three Musketeers—"all for one and one for all"—exemplify this spirit. The more the members rely on the group to attain mutual goals, the greater the cohesiveness is likely to be. The more cohesive the group, the more influence it will exert on the lives of its members.

Cohesiveness is a powerful force and can work for or against a group. Normally, cohesiveness is an asset because it facilitates interaction and motivation. But when cohesiveness is carried to extremes, it can be damaging.

Groupthink is an extreme form of conflict avoidance that occurs in highly cohesive groups that prize friendship and togetherness. In such groups, especially if there is a very strong leader, the group will suppress conflict and end up with poor decisions.

There are eight symptoms of groupthink: (1) an illusion of invulnerability; (2) collective efforts to rationalize; (3) unquestioned belief in the group's inherent morality; (4) stereotyped views of out-groups as being evil, stupid, or weak; (5) direct pressure against deviance; (6) strong tendency toward self-censorship (keeping still about doubts); (7) shared illusion of unanimity; and (8) an ultimate emergence of mind guards.

One way to avoid groupthink is to break into subgroups to discuss an issue.

COMMUNICATING EFFECTIVELY IN GROUPS

In this section we look at a number of things group members can do to enhance their productivity and satisfaction. The first step usually entails analyzing the task.

Analyzing the Task Situation

Groups communicate in a rich context, but too often members are oblivious to this fact and fail to thoroughly understand the situation they face. Following are some important points for group members to consider as part of the situational analysis.

Considering External Demands. No group works independently of its environment; every group is constrained by what goes on around it. External demands are especially important in organizations, in which a single group constitutes only one small part of a complex system. Three external demands are especially relevant: expectations, social climate, and fiscal and time resources.

Groups need to be sensitive to the expectations of people outside the group. Often an organization establishes decision-making groups to achieve certain objectives, which not only guide the group but also partly shape its climate of interaction. At universities, for example, complex sets of policies govern the operation of departmental personnel committees, which make recommendations on faculty appointments, tenure, and promotions. Through experience committee members have learned that other committees and administrators expect strong compliance to the rules. Certain departmental committees that have not been sensitive to these expectations have been forced to spend many hours correcting mistakes—or worse, seeing their recommendations rejected by higher authorities. All groups feel such pressures to a greater or lesser degree.

The second aspect of the external environment that a group must take into account is the social climate. Consider the plight of a board of directors that must handle a corporate merger in an atmosphere of anger and fear about layoffs and reorganization. Even if the members of the group are not involved directly, the external social climate creates pressures that affect what happens inside the group.

Almost every decision-making group receives its financial resources from an outside entity. The group has only so much money or staff time with which to do its job. Few groups receive unlimited funding. An even subtler resource-related constraint on groups is the time that members can make available for meetings. The overall organization and other external interests prevent groups from participating endlessly in discussion. Members must think about these constraints on resources when preparing for group work.

Understanding the Problem. A group's task usually involves some problem or set of problems. The group is expected to make a series of decisions that solve the problem. An amazing number of groups spend hours discussing possible solutions before somebody finally says, "Hey, what's the problem?"

Occasionally a group in our class decides to discuss the problem of parking on campus. Not infrequently they begin with a discussion of new parking areas, parking malls, and a variety of complex solutions until someone asks, "How many cars are registered on campus, and how many existing parking places are there?" Faces go blank. Realization dawns that until these and other questions are answered, the group will not even know if there is a problem, let alone its extent or complexity.

Much problem definition takes place in the group itself, but individual members need to give considerable thought to the problem on their own.

How a group defines its problem has much to do with how effectively it accomplishes its task. Accurate problem definition reduces the chance of defensiveness and increases the chance for creative problem solving. Poor definitions may create undue defensiveness and closed-mindedness in the group. The following guidelines are useful.

The problem should be stated in situational rather than behavioral terms. A behavioral definition implies that somebody did something wrong; it therefore creates a tendency to try to solve the problem by correcting the errant party. Yes, people do make mistakes. But if a problem calls for a group solution, it will not be solved by correcting "misguided" individuals. Consider the following examples of behavioral and situational definitions:

Behavioral: Workers on the line have not been fastening their safety belts.

Situational: Too many accidents are happening on the line.

Behavioral: Operators are using telephones for personal calls.

Situational: The telephone system is not adequately handling incoming calls.

The problem with behavior-oriented definitions is that they presume the group already knows which behaviors are at fault. Behavioral definitions severely limit the group's creativity in discovering all origins of a problem and in generating appropriate solutions. Sometimes, of course, analysis leads to the inescapable conclusion that the problem originates in some person's behavior, but such a case calls much more for individual action than for group discussion.

Try not to imply a solution in the definition of the problem. Groups often unwittingly limit their creativity by defining the problem in a restrictive way. Notice the difference in the following alternate definitions:

Restrictive: How can we get line workers to fasten their safety belts?

Open: How can management and employees improve safety on the line?

Restrictive: How can we stop operators from making personal calls?

Open: How can incoming calls be handled more efficiently?

The problem also should be stated in terms of mutual interest. People don't usually care about solving a problem in which they have no interest. It stands to reason that groups motivated to deal with a problem will be more creative and energetic in solving it. Consider the following examples:

Singular interest: How can the company cut its safety costs?

Mutual interest: How can safety costs be cut without creating hazards for employees?

Singular interest: How can we cut down on the number of personal telephone calls?

Mutual interest: How can personal as well as business calls be handled most efficiently?

Only one objective should be included in the statement of a given problem. It is true that complex problems require complex answers. But too many groups attempt to attack a complex problem without first determining its components. At first a complex problem may appear fuzzy, but it almost always consists of several concrete aspects. The group should try to determine the specific problems and define them separately. Avoid problem statements that embody several objectives. Consider the following examples:

Multiple objectives: How can safety equipment be improved, and how can we get the line workers to use it more often and more completely?

Single objective: How can safety equipment be made easier to use?

Multiple objectives: How can we get more funds to increase the number of telephone lines and also get people to make fewer calls?

Single objective: What system can we develop to handle the increasing number of telephone calls?

One of the most important outcomes of problem analysis is the decision concerning whether to use a group or an individual to solve the problem. Table 7.1 outlines some factors that may affect whether a group or an individual is best suited to solve the problem.[4] Remember, it is not always fruitful to involve several people in group problem solving.

Analyzing the Group. An ongoing, active group analysis will help members maintain a clear understanding of their situation. Of course, group analysis should go well beyond looking for signs of trouble. It is one thing to feel that all is not well and quite another to understand

Table 7.1 Criteria for Individual versus Group Problem Solving

USE A GROUP IF . . .	USE AN INDIVIDUAL IF...
1. The problem is *complex*; i.e., several steps are necessary to solve it.	1. The problem is *simple*; i.e., the process is relatively simple.
The solution will be difficult to verify.	The effectiveness of the solution will be obvious.
The problem solving requires a division of labor.	The problem solving can be done easily by a single person.
There are many parts to the problem.	
2. The problem is perceived as impersonal by members of the group.	2. The members of the group are personally involved in the problem.
3. The problem is m*oderately difficult* for the members of the group; i.e., the problem solving requires more information than a single person is likely to have, or many work hours are required.	3. The problem is *easy* for individuals to solve; i.e., the problem solving requires information that one person may have, or little time is required.
4. Individuals will have to assume a great deal of personal responsibility for the problem.	4. The problem involves little personal responsibility.
5. The proposed solution will probably be diverse, or many solutions are required.	5. One or few proposed solutions are expected.
6. Attitudes toward the problem are likely to be diverse.	6. Little disagreement is expected.
7. The group probably will maximize task energy.	7. Much nontask behavior is expected.

why. We hope that the principles discussed in this chapter will enhance your understanding of the dynamics of group communication.

Determining Personal Needs and Tendencies. Self-understanding is an important prerequisite for any communication. This point was driven home in a conversation between two university employees. One was complaining about having to go to an annual departmental meeting.

"How can you complain about that?" the other asked. "We have a meeting in our department every week."

The first one gasped: "Every week! That's incredible. What do you do in all that time?"

His friend explained that they had to make decisions about the job, personnel, and other department policy. "We're very democratic," he explained.

The other employee quipped, "That's what we pay our department chairperson for!"

It may appear that the first employee was irresponsible to withdraw from departmental responsibilities, but people differ in their desire and need to join groups. Not everybody is eager to participate.

Of course, self-analysis involves more than simply knowing whether or not you like groups. You also must know how well you are prepared to discuss particular problem topics, and which roles you tend to take in groups. As a member of the group, you represent certain attitudes and biases. You cannot rid yourself of prejudices, but you can recognize them and take them into account. Realizing that group problem solving is a process of give and take, good participants try to know what is important and why. In analyzing your attitudes and preferences, beware of the tendency to bolster your ideas against attack. People often justify prejudices on the basis of rational-sounding premises, but such mental gymnastics are simply rationalizations.

The following **bolstering tactics** are common in decision making: (1) exaggerating favorable consequences of the preferred alternative, (2) minimizing unfavorable consequences, (3) denying negative feelings about the preferred solution, (4) delaying commitment in order to delay negative consequences, (5) hiding one's true feelings so that the preference cannot be judged by others, and (6) shifting responsibility for one's actions to others.[5] Each of these tactics simply reinforces one's preferences without allowing consideration of new ideas. The tactics thus impair honest communication with others about possible alternatives, and they discourage members from joining in creative problem solving.

Group members, then, must not only understand their biases but must also avoid bolstering tactics that prevent them from being committed to the group task.

Analyzing the Physical Setting. The importance of the physical setting cannot be underestimated. Members should recognize the constraints arising from the physical space and layout. Later in this chapter we discuss how to take advantage of physical factors. For now, let us consider an example of setting analysis.

One group used to hold its meetings in the ugly, cramped living room of an old house fondly called the "squad room," dominated by a large table that took up most of the space. Members would crowd around the table, but there was never enough space for everyone. A few people always had to sit near the walls, away from the table and away from the group. Finally, to improve its communication, the group decided to improve the setting. The table was discarded, and members donated chairs and a couch, which they placed around the perimeter of the room. Carpeting, new window valances, and a coat of paint also improved the physical setting. Of course, these changes did not solve all the problems of group communication, but they helped considerably.

Preparing for the Discussion

All planned communication requires preparation. Almost always there is some lead time in which to prepare for a given discussion, and often, especially in organizations, group decision making is an ongoing process, so preparation is continual. One may begin preparing for group problem solving well in advance, but the preparation process continues throughout the problem-solving period—often for weeks or months. The following considerations are important in preparing for decision making.

Assessing the Situation. Always look for possible causes and effects of the problem. As you think about and discuss the problem and alternative solutions, be aware of possible conditions and factors that may have led to the problem. Note also what has resulted from the problem. Your problem analysis may require special research or information gathering, but it should continue during all phases of the problem-solving process.

Identifying Alternatives. Part and parcel of decision making is the creation of alternate solutions. Astute group members will look for alternatives on their own, recognizing that initial ideas merely offer a starting point and that the final solution will be a group product.

Identifying Objectives. What is the goal of the group's work? What is the group trying to accomplish? What benefits do the members seek?

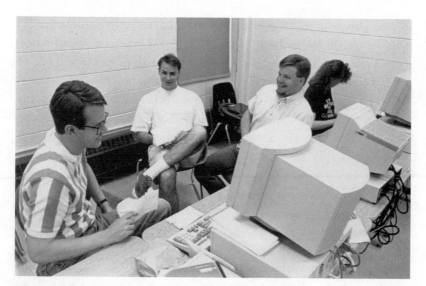

Task groups are often formed to solve a specific poblem.

What is important and not important? What qualities will constitute a good decision for the group?

Assessing Consequences. Group members also need to consider the possible positive and negative consequences of various solutions. Every decision has consequences, and almost every decision has both good and bad effects. The goal is to maximize the positive in relation to the group's objectives and values.

The group should be in constant touch with new information that bears on the problem and on alternate solutions. Often this stage involves an active search for information. Library study and various types of research may be needed. A chief advantage of group problem solving is that it extends informational resources. Each individual may be a specialist in a particular area related to the problem, and each participant should take the role of information seeker.

Decisions are not made in a vacuum. Alternatives are weighed on the basis of available information. Effective group problem solving entails a constant interaction between information and evaluation.

Making a Choice. The group should consider practical problems of enacting the decision. Each participant should come to understand the pragmatic aspects that affect the final decision. Few decisions can be implemented without some effort, and often money. Understanding what will be involved in administering the group's output is an important part of preparing for discussion.

The important point about preparation is that it is an active process involving all members of the group. If members can avoid the notion that they simply have to show up and talk, they are on the right track for success.

Enhancing the Interpersonal Environment

The task work outlined above is crucial for effective group decision making, but it will go nowhere if the group's members do not establish a good working relationship. Here we discuss two aspects of the interpersonal environment—promoting supportiveness and managing conflict.

Promoting Supportiveness. Remember that group communication is simply one of the contexts within which interpersonal communication takes place. All the principles of effective work-related interpersonal communication apply to the group setting as well. Supportiveness involves a genuine respect for the other person and a willingness to listen openly to that person's viewpoints. Supportiveness is the opposite of defensiveness, in which people are emotionally guarded and ego-involved to the point of closing off other perspectives.

Within a supportive climate, people are more creative and more willing to share ideas when they believe others are really listening. People are more cooperative and more willing to join in a team effort when they believe members of the team respect each other as individuals.

There are two approaches to group decision making. For the selling approach, which is usually counterproductive, participants thoroughly prepare their positions beforehand; selling those positions is their primary goal. The other, more productive approach involves defining the problem clearly as a group and sharing ideas creatively and supportively for the mutual benefit of group members. After all, the primary reason for using groups for decision making is to ensure a broader range of human resources. The selling approach breeds defensiveness, whereas problem solving requires supportiveness.

One trap that inhibits supportiveness in groups is the *hidden agenda*, a self-benefiting objective that remains unspoken. The goal is not brought out into the open and addressed explicitly by the group. Rather, it is dealt with nonverbally. For example, on the surface members of a student study group may be sharing information and test-taking strategies for mutual benefit on a coming exam, but the hidden agenda of one of the members may be to get information from the others so he won't have to study.

Managing Conflict. If people are honest with one another and understand each other's points of view, conflict or disagreement is bound to result. Conflict is no fun; it almost always creates tension and discomfort, so people often retreat from conflict situations or avoid them. Despite its irritating qualities, however, conflict contributes to better decisions that lead to growth and change.

Conflict may be disruptive or productive. **Disruptive conflict** is defensive and involves disrespect, dishonesty, inflexibility, and egotism. **Productive conflict**, on the other hand, involves an honest statement of beliefs, openness to new ideas, flexibility, and critical thinking. Most important, productive conflict centers on issues or ideas, not on personalities. Persons in conflict can debate their views vigorously yet still respect and like each other.

Problems arise in groups when members seek consensus and conformity without thinking critically and without being open to important alternatives. When groups attempt to avoid conflict, they come to agreement too quickly. As a result, they may miss important information or suppress good ideas.

Ideas must be challenged, and points of view should be analyzed critically in order to formulate the best, most creative decisions. Groups therefore have a tricky balancing act to perform, optimizing productive conflict and minimizing disruptive conflict. Table 7.2 lists some differences between the two forms of conflict. Clearly, productive conflict offers advantages to group decision making, whereas disruptive conflict raises problems and leads to inefficiency.

In a discussion, people need to be conscious of two principles simultaneously. They should avoid the tendency to suppress disagreement, which leads to groupthink, but they should also guard against escalating dispute.

Table 7.2 Differences Between Productive and Disruptive Conflict

CRITERION	PRODUCTIVE	DISRUPTIVE
Target	Primarily issues, not persons	Primarily persons, not ideas
Language	Tends to be descriptive	Tends to be inflammatory
Nonverbal elements	Tend to be calm	Tend to be excited
Rationale	Tends to be thoughtful and rational	Tends to be emotional
Degree of openness	Tends to be direct and honest	Tends to involve hidden agendas and covert manipulation
Response	Tends to elicit thoughtful consideration of ideas	Tends to elicit defensiveness and ego threat
Feelings	Tend to elicit confidence in self and respect for others	Tend to elicit anger and self-doubt
Motive	Concern for the task	Concern for self
Orientation toward others	Involves interpersonal respect and caring	Does not involve respect and caring

Several practices can be helpful. For example, it is important to separate issues and people. State your objections in terms of ideas, not persons, and do not consider others' objections to your own ideas as an attack on you. Be flexible, tentative, and willing to change. Rely on problem solving rather than selling. Listen actively, as described in Chapter 5.

Often, especially in large groups, issues can be settled by majority rule or simple voting. But in small groups in which goals are shared and commitment is high, consensus is a better form of decision making. Decision by **consensus** occurs when all members of the group agree on the final decision. Everybody has a degree of satisfaction with the outcome. Although some conflict is important in achieving the best possible group decisions, what if the group is stalled and cannot achieve consensus? There are no firm rules for dealing with conflict situations. Much depends on whether group members are sensitive to each other's needs and are creative enough to see fresh alternatives.

By all means, talk about individual and group goals. Seek a clear understanding of what the conflicting sides want to achieve. Communication is not a panacea for resolving conflict, but it helps— especially if it is supportive. Try to agree on group goals first. Ask what the group as a whole wishes to achieve. Then try to devise a proposal that addresses agreed-upon goals. When group members have strong personal goals, be creative in finding ways to fulfill as many individual goals as possible.

When there is a strong tendency to avoid conflict, and groupthink is a danger, the group should take steps to test its ideas. Each member should play the role of critical evaluator, freely expressing objections and uncertainties. Groups need to establish a climate that encourages disagreement and discourages self-censorship.

People in leadership roles should avoid guiding the group's thinking from the outset of discussion. Have you ever attended a group decision-making session at which the chairperson announced the desired decision at the start of the meeting? Bad practice. Wise group facilitators learn how to help the group define the problem without implying a solution. We believe it is important for appointed chairpersons, coordinators, supervisors, facilitators, and other task leaders to remain somewhat in the background, especially at the beginning of the discussion.

A group should seek independent evaluation of its ideas, if possible. This suggestion is especially desirable for very important decisions. Independent evaluation can be incorporated in a number of ways. The group can divide into two or more subgroups, each devising its own evaluation and solution. Members can seek outside advice from trusted associates, later sharing this external input with the group, or outside experts can even be brought into the group to evaluate its ideas.

Sometimes it is a good idea to assign one member to play the role of devil's advocate. This is an excellent way to encourage criticism without threatening anyone's ego. And after the final decision is made, a wrap-up meeting can always be held to give members one more look at the proposal and have one more chance to express doubts.

When these practices are followed, the group will be able to promote optimal, productive conflict, increasing the likelihood of the best possible decisions.

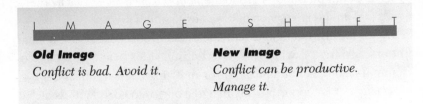

I M A G E　S H I F T

Old Image
Conflict is bad. Avoid it.

New Image
Conflict can be productive.
Manage it.

ASSUMING LEADERSHIP FUNCTIONS

Nearly everybody at one time or another will be called upon to facilitate a group. For some of us, this may become a way of life. Traditionally, the word *leader* has been used to label the person "in charge," but, as we noted earlier, anyone in a group can and should promote task and social functions. Thus the word leader is not quite right, even though it often happens that a single person is designated "chair," "convener," "president," or such. We prefer to think of this person as a facilitator. In most groups the facilitator takes a strong task leadership role that involves three main responsibilities: planning the agenda, conducting the meeting, and organizing the resources.

Planning the Agenda

An agenda lists the order of business for a meeting. It consists of a rather specific schedule of topics or problems for the group to handle. Committees typically deal with several items at a given meeting, and a particular problem area may extend across a number of meetings. Agendas help to sort out the items, indicating which are new and which are old. Agendas help to order the discussion in the most functional manner. Following are some questions to ask in planning an agenda:[6]

1. What is the best sequence for the material?
2. How much time should be devoted to each topic or problem area?
3. How much interaction is expected on each item?
4. How important is each item?
5. How complex is each topic, and how much information sharing will be necessary?
6. What is the objective of discussion on each topic (for example, problem solving, information sharing, motivation)?

Keep in mind that an agenda is a plan for group communication, not an immutable law. A good agenda serves as a highly flexible guide, and adaptive groups will make a variety of adjustments, depending on their spontaneous needs.

Conducting the Meeting

The facilitator has three important functions in most meetings: guiding, stimulating, and controlling.

The group facilitator stimulates and guides participation.

Guidance. Facilitators guide the group by helping it cover necessary ground and meet objectives. One of the most important resources for guiding is a thorough knowledge of group processes, particularly decision making. There are no rules for guiding a discussion; mostly, it involves interpersonal sensitivity and task awareness. The facilitator should have an idea of the direction the group ought to take in creating a decision, and that depends on the problem and the group.

Stimulation. In addition, the facilitator may need to stimulate group discussion by creating interest and motivation among members. Most important, the facilitator may need to demonstrate the importance of the problem being discussed in terms of common interest. There is nothing worse than being involved in a meeting at which members do not feel motivated or interested. If the group is carefully chosen to include interested parties, stimulation may not be particularly difficult.

One way a facilitator can provide stimulation is by sharing pertinent information with the group. Such information may help motivate interest in the problem. (You should have seen the hands go up at the sales meeting when the director began by quoting data about projected market declines.) A guest speaker or film can also help stimulate the group. In our classes we find that students are more willing to discuss ideas after they have participated in some structured activities.

Most of the time, though, facilitators maintain interaction by asking questions. Good questions stimulate thinking and draw attention to the need for clarification, further information, and discussion. Consider the following types of stimulating questions.

1. *Requesting a definition.* "What do you mean by 'quality control'?"
2. *Seeking an experience.* "What has it been like working under reduced light in the shop?"
3. *Probing opinions.* "How do you think we can increase lighting without increasing costs?"
4. *Sharing information.* "How much wattage would be needed to get the required footcandles of light in the shop area?"

Control. Controlling may be the facilitator's most difficult job. The facilitator must make optimal use of time, allowing productive conflict yet steering the group away from disruptive conflict, a difficult task. People need to be heard, but unnecessary repetition only wastes time and creates tension. The group must spend ample time sharing information, but eventually it must make concrete decisions. The discussion must be orderly enough so that people can channel their energy toward achieving the group goal, but it must be free enough to encourage creativity.

Obviously, there are no clear-cut principles for controlling discussion, although the following hints might be useful. First, suggest an overall strategy to the group. Call attention to it when members begin to stray from the agreed-upon pattern. Announce time limits. Divide the labor, making use of subgroups if necessary. Make frequent use of summaries, and provide transitions for the group. Take the role of clarifier, synthesizing information and ideas for the group.

Managing Resources

Group facilitators manage money, time, space, and human resources.

Money. There is usually some monetary cost to group decision making. The group may need an operating budget for supplies and services. Travel money may be required, or new equipment may be needed.

Time. Time resources may be more difficult to deal with. An oversimple but instructive way to determine time costs is to compute the number of person hours being devoted to the group project. For example, a one-hour meeting of ten executives who each earn a hundred dollars an hour would cost an organization one thousand dollars. That might be enough to hire a consultant for a day or two. Of course, time is not really money in the strict sense of the word, and so it is better to consider time as a separate resource.

Suppose you were a supervisor of a group of production workers whom you wished to involve in a discussion of some production problem. In order to call a meeting, you would have to shut down the line. How long would the meeting last? How could you optimize the group's effectiveness in the given time period? Obviously, both the planning and conducting functions of the facilitator are important aspects of time management.

Space. Space is often a neglected resource. How a group uses space makes a big difference in how its members perform. Facilitators should consider several guidelines in planning space resources.

First, the attractiveness of a room affects how well people work. The often overlooked aesthetic dimension plays an important role in influencing discussion. The appearance of a space seems to affect not only how people feel toward others but also how they feel toward themselves. Ugly spaces tend to make people tired, irritable, and bored.

Also, the amount of interaction is affected partly by how the group is set up. For example, three types of seating arrangements are common in classrooms. The traditional setup is arranged in straight rows—described in one book as "something like tombstones in a military cemetery."[7] Students are seated in a horseshoe arrangement, and less frequently they sit around tables in a modular arrangement. The traditional arrangement seems to inhibit interaction, although some people remain very active. This straight-row arrangement seems efficient for public speaking or lecturing, when information sharing is the primary goal. The horseshoe arrangement encourages interaction in large groups, but it will not necessarily draw everybody into the discussion. People who tend to avoid interaction will still remain quiet. However, this arrangement is useful for a lecture-discussion format. The modular arrangement facilitates small group discussion. Although sitting around a table will not motivate everyone to talk, it will help somewhat.

People sitting in certain places talk more than others do. It has been demonstrated that people sitting in front and in a line down the middle of a traditional arrangement interact more than do those along the sides and at the back. In a horseshoe arrangement, people at the back facing the instructor interact more frequently than those along the sides. People at the head of a table usually do more talking than those along the sides.

Does one's place in a group affect interaction, or do highly verbal people tend to choose certain places? Probably both are true. People who tend to be apprehensive about communication will choose inconspicuous spots and prefer communication-inhibiting arrangements such as the straight-row setup.

Members expect different things from people sitting in different places. Classically, people expect the "leader" of a group to sit at the head of the table. People at the head of the table are usually given more status, and they tend to talk more than other members of the group. There may be some practical reasons for this expectation. The person at the head of the table can see most of the others clearly and can therefore coordinate discussion readily.

People prefer different seating arrangements for different tasks. In casual conversation, people tend to prefer sitting opposite each other at the end of a table or next to each other across the corner of a table. Sitting at opposite ends or midway across the table is preferred for competition. When people are working on separate jobs, they prefer more space, sitting at extreme opposite corners of the table.

People will seat themselves differently according to their degree of motivation. It seems that the more motivated a group, the closer the members wish to sit and the more eye contact they wish to have. Competition also brings about the desire for more eye contact, but parties will tend to space themselves farther apart.

In using space, as any other kind of resource, the facilitator should be adaptive. No one arrangement is best. A facilitator should consider the following questions when planning the physical arrangements for a meeting. How large is the group? What equipment does the group need? What is the primary purpose of the meeting? What kind of interaction is expected? How can participation be maximized, given the physical setting?

Human Resources. The final type of resource is the most important of all. Human resources include whatever ideas people bring with them in their heads. Groups are used for decision making primarily because they extend the human resources available for solving a problem. Two important questions arise regarding the use of human resources: Who should participate? And how many people should be involved?

The question of whom to include in a group effort is crucial. The following points should be considered in making this decision: Who has the appropriate information to help solve the problem? Who are the interested parties in the controversy? What groups need to be represented in the discussion? Who has positive communication skills to contribute to the discussion?

One of the authors once had to design an organizational self-study. This task involved creating a steering committee and twelve subcommittees to examine virtually every function of the organization. The task was interesting and rewarding, particularly because of the need to optimize human resources. The author remembers vividly the day the organization sat down to decide who should participate on the steering committee. We considered all the guiding questions above and generated a list of about twenty people who represented various aspects of the organization. After considerably more thought and some consultation, we whittled the list down to fifteen members, but we still faced a dilemma. The optimal group for good decision making contains about five to seven people. We anticipated difficulties in trying to get fifteen people to make decisions quickly and smoothly. We considered what such a large group would mean in terms of time resources. Then we had to decide whether to keep the larger committee, pare it to a smaller size, or find some compromise. With the help of the president, we were able to create a smaller, more manageable committee that also optimized the human resources available.

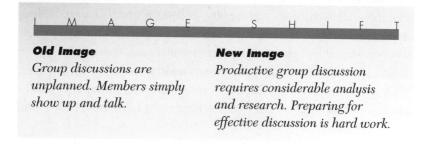

Old Image
Group discussions are
unplanned. Members simply
show up and talk.

New Image
Productive group discussion
requires considerable analysis
and research. Preparing for
effective discussion is hard work.

SUMMARY

Group communication is a process to be viewed within external and internal contexts. It serves personal needs; it maintains the group; and it helps the group accomplish its task. Group energy, or synergy, can be fruitfully analyzed within these categories. Thus group interaction is interpersonal, in that it meets socioemotional needs of the members, and it is task related in that it helps the group solve problems and make decisions.

Group interaction tends to be patterned. A network is a system of communication links among members who are not necessarily linked equally to all other members. A person with many links to others is central; one with few links is peripheral. Shared centrality is the overall completeness of linkages among members. Ideally, groups should have a moderate level of shared centrality. Coalitions are formed as people link to become subgroups in the network.

Roles are behavioral expectations for specific members. A role consists of a predictable pattern of behavior for a particular person in a group. A variety of task, maintenance, and personal roles emerge in group interaction. Leadership is that set of functions that furthers the group's task or its socioemotional maintenance.

Group influence is a powerful force in our lives. Individual uncertainty and group solidarity contribute to conformity. Compliance is strictly public conformity. Identification is primarily public conformity, although it involves more private conformity than compliance does. Internalization is complete public and private commitment to the norms and values of the group.

Conflict in groups can be either productive or disruptive. Productive conflict should be sought and managed, despite the tendency to avoid it. Extreme conflict avoidance leads to groupthink, with the following symptoms: illusion of invulnerability, collective efforts to rationalize, unquestioned belief in the group's inherent morality, stereotyped views of out-groups, direct pressure against deviance, self-censorship, shared illusion of unanimity, and emergence of mind guards.

Group communication consists of an interpersonal component and a task component. Guidelines exist for improving both aspects of group communication.

The interpersonal environment can be improved first by maintaining supportiveness. A good interpersonal environment also consists of optimal, productive conflict in which disagreement is neither avoided nor escalated to a disruptive level. The outcome of optimal conflict is productive synergy.

The task environment consists of several interrelated dimensions, all of which must be dealt with by group members. First, members should analyze the situation, including external demands, the problem, the group, personal needs, and the physical setting. In addition, members should prepare for discussion by canvassing alternatives, assessing objectives, weighing alternatives, seeking new information, reexamining alternatives, and considering problems of implementation.

In dealing with the task environment, the facilitator has three main responsibilities: planning the agenda, conducting the meeting, and managing resources.

8 Public Communication: Analysis

The year is 1886. In a luxurious and spacious banquet hall, the New England Society of New York is holding its annual banquet. A quick glance around the audience reveals some three hundred of the wealthiest and most influential people in the northeastern United States. Financier J. P. Morgan, the Reverend T. Dewitt Talmadge, and General William T. Sherman are easily recognized. Following dinner, several people make brief remarks, including a tribute by the Reverend Talmadge to the Civil War veterans of the North, and some statements by General Sherman that disparage the South. After these two speeches, the normally subdued and conservative audience leaps up and lustily sings "Marching through Georgia." The next speaker to be introduced is a young, mild-mannered stranger named Henry W. Grady. A native of Athens, Georgia, and editor of the Atlanta *Constitution,* Grady is to address the society on the topic "The New South." Facing an extremely difficult speaking situation, he jokes, compliments, cajoles, and ultimately wins over his audience to a more favorable impression of the post–Civil War South. The next day *The New York Times* reports the results: "No oration of any recent occasion has aroused such enthusiasm in this city."

Although such dramatic examples of public speaking are rare in our age of mediated sound bites, public speaking remains a serious form of communication, one in which most professional people engage. For some, such as trial lawyers, ministers, and teachers, public speaking is a necessary skill used regularly. For others, such communication may occur less frequently, but when it does, it is usually important.

We discuss public speaking in two parts in this book, which we call analysis and synthesis. These terms will become clear as we work our way through these chapters.

PERSPECTIVES AND CONCEPTS OF PUBLIC COMMUNICATION

The scholarly study of communication began with the study of public communication. The ancient Greeks, who called this study rhetoric, were concerned about the average citizen's ability to communicate ideas in the legislative assembly and courts of law. (Imagine living with the possibility of being sued and having to serve as your own lawyer.) Today, communicating with large numbers of people in a face-to-face setting remains one of the major communication contexts. Whether lawyers in court, teachers in classrooms, or business executives addressing employees, virtually all of us sooner or later face the necessity of communicating in public. As one college president put it, "Each year as my administrative responsibilities increase, I spend less time at my professional specialty and more time communicating, especially in public."

Perspectives on Public Communication

Most early theorists of public communication operated from a transmissional perspective, which emphasizes the transmission of a message from speaker to audience. This approach is not necessarily "wrong." Indeed, the writings of the ancient and medieval rhetoricians contained substantial intuitive wisdom about public communication. This perspective does lead, however, to an inordinate emphasis on the speaker and the message and insufficient focus on the audience and other aspects of the total situation. Furthermore, it reinforces a natural, though somewhat counterproductive, tendency of every potential public speaker to be self-centered rather than transaction oriented. This self-centered approach may lead the speaker to ignore the needs of listeners and can heighten anxiety about the speaking event.

In the public speaking context, a behavioristic perspective focuses on the response of the audience. Although focusing on the needs of listeners is an important aspect of public communication, carried to extremes it can lead to ignoring other important aspects of the situation and even to uncaring and unethical public communication. The behavioristic perspective may (though not necessarily) lead the speaker into the pitfall of believing that "anything goes" in order to get the desired response from the audience. It also implies a denial of the needs, gifts, and limitations of the speaker.

Most public speaking texts today are written from an interactional perspective, which places equal emphasis on audience, message, speaker, and feedback during the public event. Many writers describe a "circular" process in which a speaker delivers a message, the audience responds through feedback, the speaker adjusts to that feedback, and so forth over the duration of the speaking event. Because a public speaking event has a clear beginning that is almost always initiated by the "speaker," the interactional perspective has been both natural and useful in the study and practice of public speaking.

For several years we have taught public speaking from an interactional perspective that balances speaker, listener, and message. This view also accounts for feedback and continuing audience analysis and the speaker's adaptation to the audience. However, it is clearly still a linear view of what seems to us to be a more dynamic process.

We have observed that some listeners get more out of a lecture or speech than others do. Not only do they process the message as it is being presented, they actually supply aspects of the message in order to share meaning with the speaker. In discussion after a speech, some listeners can offer their own examples of an idea in the speech or may even phrase a central idea of the message more cogently than the speaker did. Certainly, such listeners are "reaching out" (as though to shake hands on a transaction) to share with the speaker the responsibility for the communicative effectiveness of the speech. In dyadic or group communication the roles of speaker and listener change, and the transactional nature of communication in those settings is therefore more obvious. In this chapter we will argue that—although it is less obvious, because the roles of speaker and listener remain somewhat constant—public communication is basically a transactional process. By using this transactional perspective, speakers can enhance their public communication competencies.

Public Speaking Concepts

Before discussing the specific aspects to be analyzed in any public speaking context, let us consider two general concepts that permeate every stage of a public speaker's development. The first has to do with the speaker's image of the public speaking process itself, and the second relates to how a person learns public speaking.

Conversational Mode. Most beginners see public speaking as a performance. Indeed, when asked what first comes to their minds when they hear the term "public speaking," many students say they picture a stage with footlights, a podium, and even their name in lights outside the auditorium. But imagine the following scene instead.

Public speaking is an expanded conversation.

You have just had a fantastic experience that you need to share. You begin talking animatedly about it with a friend in the lounge of your residence hall. Two or three more acquaintances stop to listen, and soon four or five more friends are standing around. Now imagine, theoretically, ten, twenty, even thirty inquisitive people stop by to listen. Now, at what point did that "conversation" become a "speech"?

We maintain that both communication events are basically the same; that is, public speaking should follow an essentially spontaneous or conversational mode.[1] Of course, in speaking publicly you must talk louder to be heard, perhaps must stand up to be seen and perhaps organize your comments more formally. (We will discuss such special aspects of public speaking in this chapter and the next.) However, if you can view public speaking more as a conversation than as a performance, you will avoid some of the pitfalls of the transmissional perspective and will more rapidly develop transactional effectiveness.

I M A G E   S H I F T

Old Image
Public speaking is a performance by a person on a stage in front of a large audience.

New Image
Public speaking is part of a communication event that can be viewed as an elevated conversation.

Learning Public Speaking. Another concept that influences your development as a public speaker is your attitude toward learning public speaking skills. According to one attitude, "Public speakers are born. I'm not a 'natural,' so I can't learn." This, of course, could not be further from the truth. Most verbal behavior is learned. As with any competency, some people learn public speaking more easily than others, but virtually every student who works at it can achieve basic competence. Many truly outstanding speakers in history were not "naturals." Both Abraham Lincoln and Winston Churchill, for example, had to overcome early disadvantages through study and practice in order to achieve the eloquence for which they are remembered.

Other attitudes can be equally debilitating. Some students who have previous speaking experience or perhaps have been on a debate team feel they have nothing more to learn about public speaking. Others feel that they have been talking all their lives and that anyone can talk. But most public speaking classes have not been approached from a transactional perspective, and debate is anything but conversational. Indeed, these kinds of previous experiences may have created habits that speakers must unlearn before they can improve their public communication skills.

We have found that public speaking is a particularly deceptive subject. The principles contained in this chapter and the next frequently seem obvious to students. On the contrary, however, our observation has been that, left on their own to do "what comes naturally," beginning public speakers frequently do exactly the opposite of these principles. Consequently, they are less effective than they might be if they had studied and mastered the recommended methods of preparing for public communication events.

ANALYZING THE RHETORICAL SITUATION

Every speaker faces essentially the same general situation or problem: "What do I say to this particular audience at this particular time and place, with this particular purpose? Indeed, what should be my purpose?" In his discussion of "The Rhetorical Situation," Lloyd Bitzer has suggested that the speaking situation itself places severe constraints on what a person should say. One does not give a campaign speech at a funeral. Recall the constraints placed on Henry W. Grady in addressing the New England Society—constraints arising from the setting, audience, preceding remarks, and his own background.

An analysis of the rhetorical situation should include yourself, the audience, the social situation, and the topic. Although it is convenient to approach these subjects in roughly the order given, they necessarily overlap; you are likely to experience some false starts and backtracking as you proceed with the analysis. Furthermore, the analytic processes described here represent the speaker's thinking, or what he or she might write in an outline, not necessarily what the speaker would say in the speech. That is to say, the following discussion describes a speaker's thought processes before the speaking event, not the speech itself.

Analyzing Yourself

As speaker you are one of the most important aspects of the public speaking event. Speakers commonly tend to be preoccupied with themselves, sometimes indiscriminately so. In short, when most people are scheduled to "give a speech," they feel varying degrees of anxiety. However, most professional observers agree that the first step toward solving a personal problem (and initially a speech presents a very personal problem) is an accurate assessment of one's capabilities, limitations, and desires.

Although we do not wish to reinforce the tendency to be self-centered and, hence, anxious, we suggest a systematic, objective analysis of oneself as the first step in approaching public speaking from a transactional view. This self-analysis includes examining one's anxiety, knowledge, desire to communicate, attitudes, and limitations.

Anxiety. Some years ago we taught public speaking to a class of about twenty steelworkers. These men worked either among the caldrons of molten metal in a steel mill or on the construction of high-rise buildings—very dangerous work. Yet when these tough, brave men began to speak before their peers, they reported feeling severe anxiety and even fear. Such anxiety is perhaps the most common of all phenomena related to public speaking and is the one problem that beginning speakers worry about most.

When we speak of anxiety, we are not referring to "communication apprehension," which is an intense fear of all communication situations.

We define anxiety as a feeling of tension during public speaking. If you feel extremely apprehensive about public speaking, you should confer with your instructor.

The thought of speaking before an audience is a cause for anxiety in all of us.

The basic origin of ordinary speech anxiety is the speaker's self-preoccupation, which stems essentially from a transmissional perspective of public speaking. More specifically, anxiety comes from the speaker's perception that the event is important, poses a threat to the speaker, and has an uncertain outcome. Every speaker experiences this kind of anxiety to some degree, depending on his or her perception of the significance of the speaking situation. The authors of this book always experience strong anxiety when addressing a group of administrators or peers in the university senate or at a professional convention. Indeed, there are still times when our knees literally knock together.

Another cause of anxiety is perception of the public speaking situation as a threat to one's being. Whereas such activities as skydiving, mountain climbing, and working atop a skyscraper would pose a physical threat, public speech poses a psychological threat to the speaker's self-esteem. Whether the threat be real or imagined, the effect is the same: tension.

A third cause of anxiety is the uncertainty of the outcome. The speaking event could be both important and threatening, but if the outcome were certain, the speaker would feel less anxiety. But a speaker never quite knows how an audience will react. In some cases the speaker may not feel adequately prepared. Beginning speakers especially feel that they do not know how to prepare.

How can speakers go about controlling anxiety, once they know what causes it? We speak of controlling anxiety because almost no one can eliminate it altogether and because we are convinced that, properly controlled, anxiety is a good thing. It lends the intensity and dynamism needed for effective delivery. However, a speaker can control anxiety through three means: preparation, practice, and focusing on the transaction.

Let us return to our group of steelworkers. Why were these men afraid of public speaking but not of their extremely dangerous work? The answer, we think, involves two variables: preparation and practice. At work the men knew what they were doing and had done it many times before. In short, they were prepared and practiced. As public speakers, however, they were unprepared and inexperienced. If you want to control anxiety as a public speaker, you must "do your homework" through careful analysis, extensive research, and clear organization. Then you will develop the confidence that comes from knowing you are well prepared.

Practice will also help you reduce and control anxiety. The speeches that you give for the class with the help of your instructor and classmates will be immensely useful. Practicing your speeches before delivery is a necessary process, which we will discuss more fully in Chapter 9. If your preparation is substantial and follows recommended principles, and if you have practiced your speech several times, you will reduce the threat to your self-esteem by substantially reducing the uncertainty of the outcome.

The final way of reducing anxiety is to focus on the communication transaction rather than on yourself. We know this is difficult to do, but ask yourself, "Where is the audience with respect to my topic? Are they 'with' me? Do they understand?" By focusing your attention away from yourself and onto the transaction between your ideas and the listeners, you can control anxiety and make it work for you.

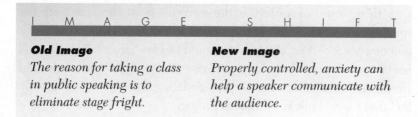

IMAGE SHIFT

Old Image

The reason for taking a class
in public speaking is to
eliminate stage fright.

New Image

Properly controlled, anxiety can
help a speaker communicate with
the audience.

Knowledge. One aspect of your "self" that is most relevant to your role as a public communicator is your background, or knowledge. Many students think that they have little or no personal resources from which to draw for public speaking, yet, after answering a few questions, they find that they have more to offer than they realized.

To begin with, what are your interests? How do you spend your spare time (assuming you have some)? People display an amazing diversity of interests. Some rock hounds, for example, are semiprofessional geologists. Many people have studied the history of their city, county, or state. Still others are art or music buffs. Some people are "doers" and can tell a great deal about physical activities, crafts, or activist causes. Virtually everyone has interests, and most people could develop even more. What interests you?

Another topic to consider is documentary television shows you have seen or books you have read recently. Television coverage of *Voyager's* Neptune photos or programs on the Civil War may have stimulated your interest in astronomy or history. Documentaries on oceanography or the human brain may have excited you about those areas. Books by writers of every kind have inspired people about topics ranging from ancient civilizations to strange inventions to sports figures.

Besides considering what you have seen or read lately, think about what you have been studying. Which courses have particularly interested you? In which ones have you done especially well? Many adults today take courses part-time in order to pursue some interest that has lain dormant for years. Perhaps the first question people ask you as a student is, "What is your major?" They really are asking, "What is your chosen field of study?" The more time you devote to your major study and later spend in your vocation, the more you will be able to draw on your experience for material as a public speaker.

Another important aspect of your background relates to where you have lived and where you have traveled. Much of what you know about places and people you learned by "being there." What have your observations taught you about how people from different walks of life react to such things as work, marriage, childrearing, leisure time, and values?

Our final and perhaps most serious question is, "What life situations have you experienced?" Certainly, the older you become, the more experiences—pleasurable and traumatic—you will have. But that doesn't mean you haven't already dealt with important life dramas. Three recent television documentaries about cancer, pornography, and crime all pertained to young people. And two of the most effective and influential speeches one of the authors has heard were delivered by students who had been adopted as children; they used their experiences either as the subject of the speech or as data to support a claim within a speech.

Life constantly teaches, and we all know more than we suspect. Take the time needed to reflect on your interests, reading, television viewing, studies, vocation, and life experiences, and you will be surprised at the amount of knowledge you have to draw on.

Desire to Communicate. Have you ever been frustrated by being misunderstood? Have you ever tried to explain something to a young child or to someone from a different culture who did not understand what you were talking about? The experience can be most annoying, for it thwarts your fundamental desire to communicate. Consider how many areas of your life create a desire to share a particular meaning with other people. The need can sometimes be urgent. For example, at one time the teachers in our state were on strike, and one of the authors felt strongly about it, not only because he is a teacher too, but also because his children were of school age. The need to express himself resulted in an outburst: "People just don't understand the teachers' situation. There are so many myths about education in our state; some of our citizens need to be set straight!" The spontaneous desire to communicate resulted in a speaking engagement, for the program director of a local service club had overheard the outburst and knew the professor had something he wanted to say.

Beliefs, Attitudes, and Values. Because of their significance in any communication context, you must assess your attitudes, beliefs, and values before you speak in public. In general, are you an opinionated person, or are you fairly accepting of other people's ideas, beliefs, and lifestyles? What attitudes and values are particularly meaningful to you? Will they be shared by your audience? How closely do they relate to your topic? In some cases your most valued attitudes may become the subject of the speech; at other times attitudes that seem irrelevant to your topic may raise communication problems between you and your audience. In any case it is important that you be in tune with your attitudes and feelings so that you can deal with them constructively during public communication.

Limitations. Most beginning public speakers are all too aware of their limitations. Some people shy away from opportunities or even obligations to speak to groups because they exaggerate their own limitations. On the other hand, a few people fail to recognize that they have limitations or that there is any topic on which they are not qualified to talk. Most have both gifts and limitations, strengths and weaknesses, and must assess them as objectively as possible before assuming the responsibility of speaking in public.

Are there any biases or blind spots that will affect your preparation or the speech itself? Do you have any psychological or physical weaknesses for which you must compensate? By objectively assessing your limitations, you can usually decide that they are not so great that you should avoid speaking in public. On the other hand, a mature awareness of limitations will enable you to correct them or compensate for them in a way that improves your public communication.

In summary, a public communication transaction is a two-way street; as both speaker and listener you are an important part of the transaction. By becoming sensitive to your anxiety, your knowledge, your desire to communicate, your beliefs and attitudes, and your limitations, you will become a more productive participant in any public speaking transaction.

Analyzing the Audience

Although a speaker must consider the audience in somewhat general terms throughout every stage of analysis, it is necessary to make a detailed analysis of the specific audience in preparing for each public speaking event. Indeed, if public speaking is a two-way transaction, it follows that the better you know your audience, the more effectively you will be able to find areas of common meaning. Understanding your listeners usually becomes more complex as their numbers increase. Generalizations become more difficult to make. If your audience is extremely heterogeneous (dissimilar in age, background, interests, or other important traits), it is better to know that beforehand; and if it is relatively homogeneous (similar in important characteristics), you can use that information to adapt your material to their particular needs. In analyzing the audience, you should consider demographic characteristics as well as any variables that are specific to your topic.

Demographic Analysis. Regular readers of public opinion polls are aware that people's meanings (attitudes and understanding) tend to cluster around certain observable personal characteristics or social groupings. In similar fashion, audience characteristics can be grouped into the categories of age and sex, vocation, religion, education, geographic location, and lifestyle.

Age constitutes one of the more obvious physical characteristics that can be used to analyze your audience before a public speaking event. Much has been written and said about generation gaps in communication. Although this phenomenon is probably exaggerated, it is clear that people in different phases of life tend to have somewhat different interests, values, and experiences. Social scientists have long recognized adolescence and old age as periods of significant concern and adjustment for many people. More recently, it has also been recognized that middle age requires many people to make significant adjustments in career, marital relations, and other aspects of life. Typically, young people are concerned with selecting a mate or career and with seeking recreational opportunities and social change. Middle-aged married people are frequently concerned with career advancement, managing a home and family, educating their children, and future security. Elderly people seem more concerned with maintaining their financial independence and good health; they want to continue to be useful, contributing members of society. Even though these generalizations do not always hold true, it is useful to analyze the relationship between the age grouping of your listeners and your anticipated topic.

Gender, of course, has long been recognized as an important communication variable. Fortunately, the women's movement has begun to break down sexual stereotypes, but centuries of tradition and role expectations are difficult to change. Although the interests of women and men may be growing more similar, there still remain numerous interests and values that are more common to one sex or the other. Thus, regardless of which side of the issue is taken, women tend to be more interested than men in such topics as child care, abortion, and contraception. Similarly, men tend to be more interested than women in gun laws, home construction and repair, and football. However, speakers should avoid reinforcing such stereotypes. Your goal should be only to understand the interests, values, and language expectations of the audience, which includes an evaluation of the similarities and differences between women and men in your particular audience.

Most adults spend at least half their waking hours in the world of work. A craft or profession thus constitutes a major preoccupation as well as an *occupation*. People in similar jobs seem to value and be interested in similar things. For example, many of the author's friends are in the academic community and are interested in such issues as literacy, funding for education, and freedom of expression. Friends in the business community, however, seem more concerned with the growth of the economy, taxes, government regulations, and unemployment.

Various *religious* groups emphasize different beliefs and values. Catholics tend to oppose abortion and, to a lesser degree, birth control. Moslems stress a prior life and shun the use of alcohol. Quakers value human rights and oppose violence. Although such focusing of beliefs and values around a religious tradition is useful in analyzing an audience, caution is in order. It has been the authors' observation that the differences between "liberals" and "fundamentalists" within a particular religion may be as great as or greater than the differences between religions. In general, liberals tend to emphasize the similarities between religions, whereas fundamentalists stress the differences. You should consider this tendency toward polarization within religions during your analysis, especially with audiences that appear to be homogeneous or polarized in terms of religious variables.

People's attitudes, as reflected in public opinion polls, vary on many issues according to the level of *education*. Furthermore, education seems to make a difference in the way people approach problems and issues. More highly educated people tend to look at issues in varying degrees, or shades of gray, whereas people with less education view issues on a right-or-wrong, black-or-white basis.

Several years ago one of the authors was asked to teach a public speaking class to a group of employees of Deseret Test Center. Not knowing much about the group, he assumed it would be a typical cross-section of adults who had elected to improve themselves but were not deeply committed to difficult reading or research. He planned the course accordingly and selected a somewhat jazzy text to keep them interested and motivated. Imagine his surprise when he discovered that the entire class was made up of college graduates, many with advanced degrees in science, engineering, and mathematics. Furthermore, they had been required to take the course in order to become more competent at making public presentations for government grants. Needless to say, the speaker changed his plans for the course, as well as the text. The educational level of the audience had to be taken into account.

Geography must also be taken into account when analyzing your audience. During America's bicentennial celebration in 1976, the authors had the opportunity to participate in several town meetings at which citizens discussed issues that concerned them and wrote specific proposals to deal with those issues. Although we were struck by some of the similarities among concerns, it became apparent that people from different geographic areas also had some different concerns. People in the eastern United States were suffering from freezing temperatures and flooding; those on the Pacific coast were dealing with drought. More important, people in different regions of the country often took different positions on such issues as farm supports and gun control. In addition, it may make a difference whether an audience is drawn from an urban, suburban, or rural area. For example, in some states people from urban areas favor more wilderness to which they can retreat on vacations, while people who live in rural areas near the wilderness favor more economic development of their locale.

Lifestyles in the United States are becoming more heterogeneous (or, at least, different lifestyles are more readily accepted). This has been reflected somewhat in housing. Single-unit homes now have

A university audience is fairly homogeneous.

fewer formal living rooms and dining rooms but more family rooms and a somewhat more open atmosphere. Furthermore, single-unit dwellings and apartment buildings are giving way to condominiums, apartment villages for families, and other forms of multiple-unit housing.

Changes in lifestyle are also reflected in marital status and family arrangements. With the divorce rate around fifty percent, many sociologists point out that the nuclear family (husband, wife, and children) has become a minority type of household. Fewer couples feel the social pressure to get married or to have children. Married people who have children may relate differently to your topic than do married people without children, divorced people with or without children, or people who have chosen a single lifestyle. In the area of California between San Francisco and the Oregon border there are thousands of counterculture people, once referred to as hippies. On the other hand, the original population of that area could be considered quite traditional, or straight. A public speaker would need to know what blend of these lifestyles an audience contained in order to have the best chance for a successful transaction.

Topic-Specific Audience Analysis. Analyzing your audience according to observable demographic characteristics is useful but somewhat general. At best it is only a preliminary step toward an in-depth analysis of your audience and specific topic. You must apply your interpersonal sensitivity in considering a specific audience. The typical college communication class, for instance, is rather homogeneous in age and includes about fifty percent women and fifty percent men; all members are high school graduates at least, and are intelligent, oriented toward business or a profession, and usually rather uniform in terms of religion, ethnic groupings, and lifestyles. With such an audience you could talk about almost any topic, and you might assume that you need analyze your audience no further. This is not the case, however, as one young woman found out in speech class. She had prepared well in order to present a clearly organized, solidly supported speech about why people should stop smoking. After complimenting the speaker on her skillful delivery, the professor asked how many members of the audience smoked. No one responded; the class was made up entirely of nonsmokers. The speaker had spoken beautifully, but she had been talking to herself. If she had analyzed her audience more carefully, she might have spoken about why people should never begin smoking or why smoking should be banned in public places. She could have used much of the same data, but the change in focus would have been significant.

In analyzing the audience, you must ask yourself what those people know about your topic. What values and attitudes are they likely to have toward your subject? Are they doing anything about it? A young man in class once wanted his audience to believe that the government should support farmers at ninety percent of parity. Topic-specific analysis revealed, however, that most of his listeners were from cities and were indifferent to the plight of farmers; furthermore, few audience members even knew the meaning of parity.

You may wonder how you can find out specific information about an audience. If it is a group to which you belong or to which you have easy access, you should ask a representative sample of your audience what they think about your topic. Suppose you plan to speak about capital punishment. Analysis of that subject would produce such questions as:

1. What are the capital crimes in the United States? In your state?
2. Do you think capital punishment is administered equitably among the sexes and ethnic groups?

3. Do you think capital punishment deters crime?
4. Do you think the execution of falsely convicted persons is widespread?
5. Are you in favor of capital punishment? Why or why not?

Asking a sample of your audience to answer such questions would give you a fairly clear idea of what your listeners think about the selected topic and would indicate how you should focus the material in your speech.

If you do not have direct access to audience members ahead of time, you can use indirect methods of analysis. For example, you can get both demographic and topic-specific information about your audience from the person who invites you to speak. Interview the person in charge of the program, focusing on questions pertaining primarily to the characteristics of the audience. Remember also that many organizations and clubs publish newsletters that can help you analyze the membership. One speaker we know, when speaking in a strange city, waits to have his hair cut until he arrives in town; then he pumps the barber for information about current events and public opinion. If you are sensitive to the need for topic-specific analysis, you will find ways to learn about your audience.

Continuing Audience Analysis. It is also important to continue analyzing audience variables during and after your speech. Although some public speaking involves a single event, many speakers address the same audience more than once. Teachers meet with the same class for as long as a year, and religious leaders may address the same congregation at least once a week for several years. Continuing analysis allows you to adjust your message not only while you are speaking but also in subsequent messages.

Analyzing the Social Situation

The social situation includes the psychological and physical context for a public speaking event. It is this context that imposes the constraints that Lloyd Bitzer noted in "The Rhetorical Situation."[2] Such constraints strongly influence the choices a speaker must make about what to say and how to say it. Furthermore, the context imposes constraints on the listeners, which must be considered as well. In this section we will see how the psychological climate and the physical setting influence the public speaking situation.

Psychological Climate. On November 22, 1963, one of the authors was scheduled to meet with a public speaking class in order to hear and evaluate some student speakers. About an hour before the class began, John F. Kennedy was shot by a then-unknown assassin in Dallas, Texas. The news spread rapidly, and by class time it was confirmed that the president was dead. Remarkably, most students were present as the class convened. They discussed the news for a few minutes, but it soon became clear that everyone was preoccupied with the dramatic event and that some were in a state of shock. The psychological climate in that class was so unsettled that purposeful communication was virtually impossible. We adjourned.

Some factors in the psychological climate that may constrain speaker and audience include beliefs, attitudes, documents, facts, traditions, images, and interests.[3] We have already discussed beliefs and attitudes, and later we will analyze facts, documents, and interests as they relate to speech materials and content. Here we will briefly discuss how images, traditions, and current events affect the public speaking situation.

Kenneth Boulding has noted that all people carry pictures or images in their heads that profoundly influence their behavior. Individuals as well as communities have stories about themselves that, in a sense, they act out. For example, a baseball player who dons a New York Yankee uniform may begin to picture himself as a winner, and his performance on the field may improve. Similarly, a psychologist friend recently admitted that she was unable to quit smoking until she had shifted her self-image from that of a smoker who was trying to quit to that of a "nonsmoker."

It is your job as a public speaker to analyze the total situation to determine what images your audience holds. You should at least be aware of these images—either to associate them with your desired response or to circumvent them if they might hamper communication. Indeed, it is frequently the purpose of the speech to change an audience's images.

Everyone is constrained by traditions. Although the influence of tradition is perhaps most obvious among older people, the need for tradition, or at least routine, also is strong among the young. Even though many teenagers seem to rebel against tradition, they might be extremely upset if all traditional constraints were removed. Most traditions have been embedded in our culture for so long that people scarcely know when they began. Religious celebrations, patriotic memorials, the disposition of the dead, marriage ceremonies, and the like are deeply rooted in traditions that date back hundreds of years. On the other hand, some traditions may have become significant to a group in a relatively short period. The Shakespearean Festival in Cedar City, Utah, is an example. Only a few years old, the festival has become not only a tradition but the central event in community life during the summer months.

Our example about the assassination of President Kennedy demonstrates how profoundly current events can influence the psychological climate of the speaking situation. Doubtless you can think of similarly pertinent examples. Your analysis of the psychological climate should include current events as well as images, traditions, and the other sources of constraint on the rhetorical situation.

Physical Setting. When you think of a public speech, you probably imagine a typical auditorium with a good public address system, a stage, attractive surroundings, and so on. Although most speeches by prominent people occur in such a setting, many speeches are delivered in school cafeterias or in banquet halls or from the front porch of a house or the back of a truck. Because settings can vary so greatly, you must analyze the location, arrangement, equipment, and decor.

The *location* is crucial to the success of your speech. In some cases you can control its selection. If so, you should choose a setting that is (1) appropriate for the image you want to create and (2) the correct size for the audience, with physical characteristics that meet your needs for acoustics, lighting, and so forth. If you cannot control the choice of location, you should arrive early enough to determine its adequacy and how you can make adjustments to reduce the constraints it imposes. It is far better to have the audience sitting close together, even if you must rope off the back sections of a large auditorium. It is also better to provide too few seats than to have them scattered over a large area (seating can

be added if the audience exceeds expectations). Your goal is to secure a location that most enhances the communication transaction you seek.

The *arrangement* of the physical setting can also enhance or detract from your transaction with the audience. One of the authors once addressed a fraternal lodge in a large room in which the members sat against the walls in a circle. A more effective arrangement had as many as two hundred people sitting at tables arranged tightly in concentric squares.

Listeners respond not only to the speaker but also to each other. It is important, if possible, to arrange the physical setting to provide for maximum interaction between the speaker and every member of the audience and for interaction among the listeners themselves. Although an auditorium provides little flexibility in this regard, many other settings can be adjusted to suit your needs.

The success of most speeches depends in part on some type of *equipment*. When the audience exceeds forty or fifty people, for example, most speakers need some type of voice amplification. Unfortunately, public address systems are notoriously unpredictable. Before speaking, assure yourself that the system is working, and learn how to control it from the microphone. You should practice, at least briefly, to make sure you are familiar with the characteristics of a particular public address system.

If your speech involves audiovisual materials, you will need at least an easel and probably a variety of recording and projecting equipment. Be sure such equipment is available, and check its wiring and connections under the exact conditions that will apply. Some speakers carry their own extension cords as well as spare projector bulbs and batteries to use in the event of an equipment failure.

Decor has to do with the way that the physical setting is decorated. For example, we have all seen television broadcasts of political nominating conventions. The convention hall is invariably decorated with flags, bunting, balloons, and pictures of the candidates. A festive, pep rally mood is created to enhance the communication transaction.

Speeches are greatly influenced by the nonverbal symbols used in the decor. Wall hangings as well as centerpieces on tables can enhance the transaction. At town meetings, quotations from famous Americans often adorn the walls in addition to the usual red, white, and blue banners. The audience can read the quotations before the formal activities begin, thus enhancing the desired patriotic atmosphere.

What type of mood do you wish to create for your speech? Should the atmosphere be festive, worshipful, mournful, arty, studious?

Analyzing the Topic

An obviously important aspect of the public speaking situation is the subject matter itself. Most beginning public speakers are particularly concerned with such questions as "What will I talk about?" "What slant will I give the subject?" and "What am I trying to accomplish?"

Choosing a Subject. It is normal to want to give a speech that will involve and excite your audience. However, this desire may lead you to look outside yourself and your situation for a ready-made topic. That mistake was made by a student who introduced himself as having lived in Germany for two years, among other interesting experiences. The class expected him to select topics related to this background, but his first speech was about seat belts and his second speech was about speed skiing. By midterm he was doing poorly. When asked about this, he admitted that the speech about seat belts had come from *Reader's*

Digest and that he thought the audience would like the discussion of speed skiing.

In selecting a topic, you should first consider what you know and care about and what will be significant to your listeners. Choosing the subject is one of the few areas where we recommend that you be somewhat self-centered. Ready-made speeches about "natural" topics are not found "out there" someplace. They are uncovered by analyzing your own experiences, interests, and beliefs. What interesting places have you lived in or traveled through? What is your chosen career? How do you spend your spare time? What have you studied or read recently?

Another important concern in selecting a topic is its appropriateness in terms of audience expectations. Most audiences come together because of a common interest or purpose. Thus a literary society is likely to have different expectations of a speaker than a mountain climbers' club. Although you should begin by analyzing your own expertise and convictions, audience expectations may constrain your choice.

Other concerns when choosing a topic relate to the occasion, context, and resources available. Such occasions as a court trial, funeral, or political rally virtually dictate the topic. Other occasions may be less constraining but still may suggest a topic. Furthermore, the context— such as recent events or some local news story—may inspire a particular subject. You should also consider whether adequate resources are available to prepare your speech. Research is almost always necessary, and it is frustrating to discover too late that some crucial data are beyond your research capabilities.

Focusing the Subject. One of the most difficult and often neglected steps in preparation is limiting, or focusing, the subject. Depending on time and circumstances, every speaker has to ask, "How much can I cover?" or "How will I ever be able to talk for that long?" Indeed, it is common for beginning speakers to wonder how they can fill the time allotted. This concern reflects the transmissional, self-centered point of view. Thus, the key to focusing the subject lies in your concern for the interaction between (1) the needs of your listeners and (2) the time available.

You must first analyze the material related to your topic so that you can establish priorities. What portions of the material must be communicated within the constraints of a given time period? What do your listeners most need to know about your subject, given five minutes, ten minutes, or an hour? A young outdoorsman was once asked to speak to a group of students about the wilderness areas of his state. Think of the countless aspects of outdoor life that might be interesting: the beauty, the sites to visit, the activities available, plant and animal life, laws and regulations, and so on. With only ten minutes to speak, however, he decided to focus on what was potentially the audience's greatest need—survival in the wilderness. Yet the topic was still not focused. From among the four major aspects of survival (attitude, shelter, water, and food) this speaker decided to eliminate food and water because in most cases people are rescued before these needs become critical. The final speech focused on mental attitude and shelter as matters of immediate and preeminent concern.

Besides creating priorities, focusing on the needs of listeners helps you avoid missing the point altogether. For instance, most golf instructors begin by discussing the basic swing. Instead, we would focus first on the etiquette of golf. Why? Because most golfers cannot tolerate someone who disrupts their game by thoughtless behavior. Thus, instead of focusing on what you or the audience might like, focus on what your audience most needs to know in the time available.

Gathering Materials. After selecting a topic, you can begin the research needed to produce the specific data on which your message will be based. One of the founders of the modern field of speech, William Brigance, has referred to this process as "earning the right to speak."[4] If you have taken the opportunity to influence people in a public speaking situation, you have also assumed the ethical responsibility for the accuracy and currency of your data. We suggest you concentrate your research in four areas: self-analysis, library research, interviews, and government and private agencies.

Self-analysis can produce a significant amount of subjective data. Over a lifetime you have made many observations. Your experiences plus those of people you have known provide excellent examples, analogies, and illustrations for ideas in speeches. They also demonstrate your involvement in the subject and thus tend to increase your credibility with listeners. Furthermore, your experiences may have been shared by your listeners, which strengthens the transactional bond with your audience.

College students know a considerable amount about library research, and so it is not our purpose to review that process. Yet we would like to reinforce those aspects of library research that are useful in speech preparation. For most topics, indexes of various publications can speed your initial investigation. Although some libraries still have a card catalog, most have moved to a computer data retrieval system. It is beyond the scope of this text to detail how such systems work for each library, so we suggest that if you are not already familiar with your library's system you request an orientation from your librarian.

In addition, *The Reader's Guide to Periodical Literature, The New York Times Index,* and other indexes in specific subjects are particularly useful for general research. Most of these are now available in electronic form. Particular data can be found in various statistical abstracts, almanacs, and collections of quotations. As you begin reading books or articles about your topic, watch for footnotes citing further reading on particular subtopics. Besides printed matter, most libraries have multimedia materials that may bear on your topic. Remember also to consult with the reference librarian, who can help you locate additional material.

Most people who have pursued a particular profession are familiar not only with the issues involved but also with the best sources of information about topics related to their work. A brief, well-planned interview with a competent person whose job bears on your topic can produce rich dividends and save time by helping you avoid false starts or inferior sources. Keep in mind, though, that time is precious to most people, particularly when they are at work. You should be exceptionally well prepared for such interviews through prior analysis and research on your own. Look again at the discussion of interviewing in Chapter 6 to refresh your memory about interview preparation.

Recent years have brought a significant increase in government and private agencies designed to care for social ills, and in activist organizations attempting to alter the social structure. It would be difficult to select a speech topic about which some agency has not already done considerable research. Such organizations and agencies are usually anxious to share their ideas and information. In some cases—especially when private, activist organizations are involved—the data and arguments may be one-sided and in a few instances inaccurate. If possible, you should contact both public and private agencies that represent various sides of the issues. If you intended to speak about abortion, for example, it would be wise to acquire information from both pro-life and pro-choice groups.

This raises a most significant point concerning your responsibility as a public speaker. Research into a topic should be designed not to prove a point but rather to validate ideas. This is done most effectively by remaining as open-minded as possible during the research phase. Remember that so far you have only chosen and limited the topic; you have not necessarily decided on the purpose of your speech or its final focus. One student wanted to advocate an idea that his professor considered indefensible on the basis of familiar data. Nonetheless, the professor simply urged him to conduct extensive research before making a final decision. A week later the student was prepared to advocate the opposite side of the same issue.

Formulating a General Purpose. Some rhetorical scholars have classified public speeches according to three general purposes: information, persuasion, and entertainment. We prefer to distinguish among speaking events according to the kinds of communication transactions that occur among speaker and listeners. In other words, what kind of meaning or response is shared? In general, speakers and listeners can share understanding, beliefs and attitudes, emotion, and overt behavior. Although this classification is strongly analogous to the traditional concern with purposes of speeches, we think this system focuses on the transactional response rather than on the transmitter's (speaker's) intentions. The two classification systems follow, in Table 8.1; notice how the categories relate to each other.

The transactional nature of these goals can be illustrated by an experience one of the authors had with the Pony Express trail. In 1991 he and his wife were asked to find, survey, and record the Pony Express and Overland Stage stations in Utah. After over five hundred hours of volunteer effort they knew a lot about the stations and were asked to conduct driving tours of the trail. It was a true exchange of information;

Table 8.1

SPEAKER'S PURPOSE	TRANSACTIONAL PURPOSE
To inform	Shared understanding
To entertain	Shared enjoyment
To persuade	
to convince	Shared, strengthened, or attenuated attitude
to stimulate	Shared feeling

to activate	Shared overt behavior
	  Adoption
	  Continuation
	  Discontinuation
	  Deterrence

although they did most of the talking, a number of the tour participants were more knowledgeable than they on specific details about individual stations. Each tour gave them new clues and claims to track down.

It should be pointed out that these "general purposes" are not discrete but represent a spectrum of potential responses. For instance, most teachers may want all their students to understand a lesson perfectly, but they settle for a variety of partial insights. Similarly, you might want all your audience to quit smoking. Realistically, however, you might expect—from even a great speech—that a few people will quit, some will reduce their consumption (for various time periods), and some will continue their smoking unchanged.

Theorists also argue over the distinction between informative and persuasive speaking. Some say that all speaking is persuasive; that is, it is impossible to gain new understanding or even enjoyment from a speech without having your attitudes toward its ideas changed somewhat. Although we tend to agree with this view at the most theoretical level, our attitude has been expressed best by Gary Cronkhite:

> I would prefer to speak of the "informative" and "persuasive" elements or dimensions of a communication. To the extent that a communication introduces items of information new to the audience, one might label that communication "informative." To the extent that the communication produces change in the evaluative or approach-avoidance behavior of an audience, one might label it "persuasive." . . . This approach allows for communications which are highly informative and highly persuasive, not very informative but

Writers like Alex Haley, author of Roots, *usually have no problem knowing what an audience expects of them.*

highly persuasive, not very persuasive but highly informative, and for the overwhelming number of communications which are neither very informative nor very persuasive.[5]

A further characteristic of persuasive speaking in public or private is that it involves decision making. In public meetings this can range from informal consensus building to more formal decisions on policy and budget. Some meetings of as many as two hundred people arrive at decisions by consensus. On the other hand, when formal decisions are being addressed, the chair may invoke Robert's Rules of Order to ensure that the decisions are made within a context of formal rules that will stand the test of time and, possibly, litigation.

Although most communication situations can be considered either informative or persuasive, more specialized types of transactions occur frequently enough for us to discuss them individually. These include speaking occasions where the general purpose is to entertain, assert individuality, build community, articulate a perspective, pay tribute, perform a courtesy, justify yourself, or refute an opponent.

Speeches to entertain are designed to share enjoyment with listeners on a particular topic. Of course, humor or other entertaining content is frequently found in informative and persuasive transactions; here we define entertaining speeches as those whose primary purpose is entertainment or enjoyment. Although speeches to entertain may be called for in a variety of situations, they most frequently occur in after-dinner situations or celebrations.

A specialized type of speech to inform articulates a perspective, as explained by Foss and Foss: "When this is your goal, you share information about a subject and present your point of view on it in order to enhance understanding of the subject by all participants in the interaction." They go on to point out that when articulating a perspective the speaker should, ". . . bring to bear on the subject all of the resources available to you in serious, reflective consideration."[6] This implies that the speaker not only has investigated the subject thoroughly but also should share information with the listeners in a cooperative, conciliatory way rather than confronting them and getting if off his chest.

Another specialized type of communication to inform is meant to assert individuality. Although people are continually attempting to clarify (and sometimes obscure) who they are and "where they are coming from," individuality is more formally asserted when people introduce themselves to a class, an organization they have recently joined, or even some people they would like to know better. Foss and Foss state, ". . . the interactional goal of asserting individuality, then, is one in which you share yourself and encourage others to do the same to establish an atmosphere of trust, respect, and familiarity that encourages continued interaction."[7]

A general purpose not easily categorized as informative or persuasive is to build community. So many issues that worry people today—crime in the streets, poverty, feelings of alienation—are related to the strength or deterioration of communities. Speaking that builds community emphasizes shared understandings, beliefs, traditions, myths, and especially values. Building community focuses on the things that people have in common rather than on the issues that divide them.

Another type of communication goal is to pay tribute. This specialized transaction occurs at commemorations, dedications, commendations, and memorial services. Although tributes are not designed to change people's beliefs, values, or behavior, they could be considered persuasive in that they frequently induce resistance to change by reinforcing beliefs, attitudes, and especially values.

In addition to tributes, numerous occasions require short speeches of introduction, nomination, welcome, farewell, or presentation. These occasions of *courtesy* are usually persuasive in that they either create or reinforce a favorable attitude toward an individual, reinforce values that are shared within an organization, or suggest behavior in the form of more active support for the individual or organization. Such speeches are usually both positive and noncontroversial.

At the other extreme are combative transactions. These situations involve apologizing for or justifying one's own conduct and refuting an opponent's arguments on a controversial issue. Richard Nixon demonstrated consummate skill in self-justification in both his Checkers speech and his farewell speeches following his resignation. Robert Packwood, in answering charges of sexual harassment that had been leveled against him, combined both apology and justification. From presidential debates to town meetings, speakers find themselves answering or refuting claims made by opposing speakers.

We should note further that the general purposes of speeches interact in complex ways. For instance, information and entertainment can be used for persuasive ends. Indeed, some speeches can have each of these outcomes for different listeners. Your primary interest should be to identify the broader goal of your speech.

You may still ask, "Why is the distinction among general purposes important to me as a public speaker?" The answer is simple enough: If the general focus of your speech does not meet the audience's expectations, the communication transaction may suffer. For instance, there are few more sensitive topics than religion. On one occasion the Pittsburgh Theological Seminary asked the Church of Jesus Christ of Latter-day Saints (Mormon) to provide a speaker to tell them about the basic beliefs and organization of the Mormon church. Hugh B. Brown was selected to speak. Since Mormons tend to be known as effective proselytizers, Brown would probably have considered it a coup to convert the entire audience to his religious viewpoint. Realizing the unlikelihood of that, however—especially given an audience of Protestant theologians—Brown chose to give a clear, straightforward, objective description of the Mormon church. Not only did he meet the audience's expectations for an informative speech, he probably created a generally favorable attitude toward his church in the process.

Culmination of Situation Analysis

Your analysis of the rhetorical or public speaking situation is nearly complete. It culminates in the statement of (1) a clear transactional purpose and (2) a central idea. These constitute the goal and cornerstone of your message.

Statement of Transactional Purpose. The transactional purpose of any public speaking event is the response you desire from the listeners during and after your speech. It is the goal or destination of the speech. You should phrase the specific purpose (to yourself) by saying, "I want each member of this audience to . . ." Following are some examples of specific purposes:

1. I want each member of this audience to understand
   a. how a trumpet makes notes.
   b. how to identify yellow journalism.
2. I want each member of this audience to believe that
   a. women should receive equal pay for equal work.
   b. capital punishment does not deter crime.
3. I want each member of this audience to value
   a. endangered species.
   b. the free enterprise system.
4. I want each member of this audience to be able to
   a. quit smoking.
   b. survive in the wilderness.

Of course, such statements of purpose represent your thought processes and will probably be stated on your outline but not directly to your listeners.

Statement of Central Idea. Every formal presentation (written as well as oral) should have a basic concept or overriding theme that summarizes the meaning you hope to share with the listeners through your message.

If the specific purpose is the goal of your speech, the central idea is the means to that goal. The central idea is stated in the outline as (1) a complete sentence; (2) a declarative sentence; and (3) as simple a sentence as possible. Following are some examples of central ideas:

A trumpet makes notes by varying the size and shape of the air column.
Yellow journalism is identified by its sensationalism.
The basic human rights are shared by all people.
If you are isolated in the wilderness, keep calm.

The specific transactional purpose and the central idea of your speech are the culmination of your analytic process. They will serve as the foundation of the synthesis process, which is the subject of Chapter 9.

BRIDGING COMMUNICATIVE GAPS

Perhaps you have heard a speaker remark: "But I told them! Why can't they get it?" The fact is, telling is not communicating. Rather, the actual job of communicating is accomplished through specific supporting materials. Basic communicative gaps exist between you and your listeners; you do not share the same images. You say one thing; your listeners hear another. You are excited; they are bored. You value something highly; they couldn't care less. The following communicative gaps, which correspond roughly to the general purposes discussed earlier, can be bridged by supporting materials:

Listeners' need for clarity.
Listeners' need for comprehension.
Listeners' need for memory.
Listeners' need for interest and attention.
Listeners' need for a particular attitude.
Listeners' need to "ground" abstract concepts in personal experience.
Listeners' need for an overt behavior.

To help bridge these communicative gaps, you must use several types of specific, concrete materials. Different materials succeed with different listeners at different times; variety is essential. Furthermore, although some materials are typically more effective than others for some transactions, most materials help bridge more than one gap at a time. Useful materials include (1) examples, (2) statistics, (3) comparisons, (4) quotations, (5) stories, (6) repetition, and (7) explanation.

Whether general, specific, or hypothetical, examples constitute specific instances of the concept you wish to illustrate. Thus, a driving instructor gives several instances of specific traffic accidents related to alcohol in order to clarify and reinforce the dangers of driving after drinking. In selecting examples, you will sometimes have to use general or hypothetical instances, but the more detailed and specific your examples, the more effectively you will achieve your purpose. You should also make every effort to select examples that are as close as possible to the known interests and experiences of your listeners.

Statistics are numerical statements that illustrate specific instances. Although we do not mean to ignore the more sophisticated use of statistics in predicting probabilities, public communicators are more interested in the relationship of statistics to specific instances. Statistics are powerful for summarizing large quantities of data. Ross Perot used statistics in the presidential campaign of 1992 so effectively that other politicians have adopted his techniques.

Even in the most sophisticated use of statistics, the procedures and conclusions are based on a sample of individuals, or specific cases belonging to a particular population (of mice, college students, medical patients, and so on). Public communication uses informal statistical forms such as ranges, averages, gross amounts, sequences, and the like. They clarify that, for example, of the many people who died on the highways of your state last year, each was an individual tragedy. This point of view suggests some principles for the use of statistics.

First, statistics can be used effectively in conjunction with specific examples. The examples provide the depth (the vicarious experience or image), while the statistics provide the breadth (the scope of the data). Second, statistics should be related to the experiences of listeners. For instance, you might say, "About seventy-three thousand people died from the atomic blast at Hiroshima; that would be like exterminating Harrisburg, Pennsylvania, in a flash." Third, statistics should be simplified or rounded off without distorting the meaning of the original figures. In fact, 72,735 people died at Hiroshima, but the rounded-off figure does not distort the point and actually makes it easier to comprehend and remember.

One form of support often used to increase understanding or clarity is comparison or contrast, which interprets the unknown in terms of the known. Whether analogies, similes, or metaphors, comparisons constitute the most direct way of grounding unknown or abstract principles in the experiences of listeners. For example, a friend of one of the authors was asked—by a person who was raised near the beaches of southern California—why he was so tired from hunting pheasants. His reply achieved almost instant clarity, comprehension, and memory: "Walking in tall grass is like walking in soft sand." For years paleontologists' ideas about dinosaurs were misguided by an early comparison with reptiles. More recent comparisons of dinosaurs with birds have led to more productive study.

Have you ever thought, "I wish I had said that"? Frequently someone states an idea or describes an event so succinctly, clearly, and beautifully that it could scarcely be improved upon. You can make your own speeches much more communicative simply by copying down such *quotations*, filing them, and using them when appropriate. For instance, few speakers could better describe the formation of lava falls in the Grand Canyon than John Wesley Powell did: "Just imagine a river of molten rock, running down about 2500 feet into a river of melted snow. What a seething and boiling of the waters; what clouds of stream rolled into the heavens!"[8] Although collections of quotations are available, we recommend that you simply take the time to note and file particularly useful ones from your daily reading and normal research.

Although other forms of support—especially examples and comparisons—can be told in *narrative* form, we arbitrarily limit the *stories* category to *myths, anecdotes, fables,* and *parables*.

We subscribe to the notion that learning can and should be fun. Experienced speakers know that a humorous story or timely joke can reawaken an audience's interest. *Humor* plays a mixed role in communication. No significant relationship has yet been established between humor and attitude change. However, one researcher found that students who heard a biology lecture that was punctuated with relevant jokes scored significantly better on a standardized test than did students who heard the same lecture without the jokes. Most people have a sense of humor. Why not let yours work for you in communicating?

Many people know the *fables* of Aesop and other storytellers; such stories are powerful in communicating significant, abstract, and frequently difficult concepts, even to small children. The tales of "Cry Wolf" and "The Tortoise and the Hare" carry profound meanings in clear and interesting ways. Fables have great potential for making ideas clear, interesting, and memorable for listeners of all ages.

In the teachings attributed to Jesus by biblical writers, *parables*, along with comparisons, stand as some of the most communicative devices. The parables about the prodigal son, the sower of the seed, the judge and the widow, the brides and the lamps illuminate points of wisdom applicable to all times and people. When asked, "Who is my neighbor?" Jesus did not indulge in a tedious explanation or abstract generalization. His story of the Good Samaritan said it all. We are not advocating that you preach to listeners, especially in denominational terms. But speeches often deal with human relationships, attitudes, and values, and parables are an effective way to illustrate them. Furthermore, parables constitute a somewhat indirect, nonthreatening way of introducing pertinent issues.

Foss and Foss define myth as ". . . traditional stories—either real or fictitious—that explain phenomena or customs and their origins."[9] Myths are stories that communities share to celebrate past events and reinforce community values. By either retelling or simply alluding to the myth, speakers can identify with the audience, particularly if they share a relatively homogeneous cultural heritage.

One primary difference between written and oral communication is that the latter requires almost instant intelligibility. You cannot usually go back and relisten to a speech the way you can reread a paragraph in a book. Hence, *repetition* and *restatement* have long been the stock in trade of many speakers. Recently under heavy attack in classrooms, drill exercises have been criticized as being ineffective and dull. But advertisers have shown us that a certain amount of reiteration is unavoidable and, indeed, desirable. We recommend that you summarize in both your opening and closing remarks. Your transitions will tie your main and subordinate ideas together, and even your forms of support can provide intentional and interesting redundancy.

Furthermore, the use of parallel sentence structures can add interest and even inspiration to otherwise ordinary data. Both Franklin Roosevelt and Winston Churchill used this device with great effectiveness. For example, in a speech on May 13, 1940, Churchill said:

> We have before us an ordeal of the most grievous kind. We have before us many, many long months of struggle and of suffering. You ask: What is our policy? I will say: It is to wage war, by sea, land, and air, with all our might and with all the strength that God can give us to wage war against a monstrous tyranny, never surpassed in the dark, lamentable catalogue of human crime. That is our policy. You ask: What is our aim? I can answer in one word: It is victory, victory at all costs, victory in spite of all terror, victory, however long and hard the road may be; for without victory, there is no survival.[10]

Explanation may be the most overused developmental device of speakers, especially teachers. We recommend explanation only as a last resort, and then it should be used in conjunction with other forms of support. By itself, explanation remains too abstract and uninteresting. Although explanations are useful for qualifying, discriminating, and amplifying concepts, processes, or principles, they should be combined with illustrations for the most effective transaction with listeners.

There is really no end to the ways in which ideas can be elaborated. In their discussion of "elaborating ideas" Foss and Foss discuss a great variety of developmental devices including audience participation, definitions, dreams and visions, exaggeration, figures of speech, poetry, proverb, question, ritual, song and understatement.[11] The point is to be creative and find what you must to meet your own needs and those of your audience and situation.

SUMMARY

To understand the rhetorical situation, you must (1) analyze yourself in terms of anxieties, knowledge, desire to communicate, attitudes, and limitations; (2) analyze the audience in terms of demographic and topic-specific variables; (3) analyze the social situation in terms of the psychological climate and the physical setting; and (4) analyze the topic by choosing and focusing it, gathering materials, and formulating a general purpose. In this way you arrive at a clear, simple central idea and the transactional response that you desire from your listeners.

Communicative gaps arise from listeners' needs for clarity, comprehension, memory, interest, attitude, overt behavior, and grounding of ideas in personal experience. These gaps are bridged through supporting materials, including (1) examples; (2) statistics; (3) comparisons, including analogies, similes, and metaphors; (4) quotations; (5) stories in the form of anecdotes, fables, and parables; (6) repetition; and (7) explanation. Because the actual job of communicating is accomplished by these forms of support, a large proportion of the message should be devoted to them.

9 Public Communication: Synthesis

December of 1941 was a dark period in U.S. history. The powerful Pacific fleet had been transferred from San Diego to Hawaii in order to buttress the oil embargo against Japan. Early on Sunday morning, December 7, the Japanese retaliated with a surprise attack on the ninety-seven ships anchored in Pearl Harbor. In about two hours all eight of the battleships along "battleship row" were either sunk or damaged, and another eighteen ships were out of commission; 2,341 American servicemen were dead, and 1,143 lay wounded. The world was stunned. The next day President Franklin Delano Roosevelt addressed a joint session of Congress to request a declaration of war. He knew that the country was ill prepared for such a conflict, not having fully recovered from the Great Depression. American allies were fighting for their lives against Hitler. Some had even questioned the moral fiber and will of the American people. What could Roosevelt say to rally public opinion behind a war that would surely engulf the globe? The speech he gave was a masterpiece not only of situation analysis and vivid content but also of organization and delivery.

In Chapter 8 we saw that preparing for a speech involves examining the rhetorical situation as well as analyzing, gathering, and assigning priorities to specific supporting materials. Next the speaker is confronted with the problem of synthesizing everything into a unified, coherent pattern—putting Humpty Dumpty together again. In this chapter we will discuss some general concepts of organizing a speech, including how to develop the central idea with transactional focus, how to organize the introduction and conclusion by functions, and how to use common techniques of organization. Then we will focus on delivering the speech as the ultimate synthesizing process.

DEVELOPING THE CENTRAL IDEA

Many people know that most effective messages have an introduction, a body, and a conclusion. But few people understand the functions of these major parts of a communicative message, and even fewer know how to plan them. Many inexperienced speakers begin by writing the introduction and then write the message almost verbatim from the opening sentence on. Actually, however, it is more rational to begin with the body of the speech. After that, you will better know what you should conclude and introduce. And the first step toward organizing the body is determining and developing the central idea.

Original, significant, and substantive ideas in the body of the message derive from and directly support the central idea. They form the foundation for your transaction with the audience. Two general approaches to developing the central idea are the deductive and inductive methods. (Chapter 3 discussed inductive and deductive reasoning in detail.)

Deductive and Inductive Approaches

With the **deductive approach** you can move directly from your central idea to your main supporting ideas by asking yourself, "What ideas must my listeners believe or understand in order for my central idea to be fully developed, amplified, and classified, and in order for my specific purpose to be achieved?" Let us assume that a speaker has the specific purpose of helping the audience "to identify yellow journalism when they see it." Describing the main distinguishing characteristic of yellow journalism, the speaker states the central idea: "Yellow journalism is identified by its sensationalism." Now, in what ways does the sensationalism manifest itself? The answer to this question produces the following main supporting ideas:

   I. The format is tabloid.
  II. The headlines are "scary" or sensational.
 III. The writing style is short and abrupt.
  IV. Stories are selected for their ability to attract attention on the newsstand, not for their news value.
   V. There is extensive sensational photography.

Note that these points share the following characteristics:

They all support the central idea in that they demonstrate "sensationalism."
The sentences are complete in order to state the point clearly.
The sentences are declarative.

The sentences are relatively succinct.

The sentences are few. (We recommend two to five.)

The sentences are relatively parallel or equal in importance.

Having identified and ordered your main ideas, you can use the same process to determine any necessary subordinate ideas. For instance, the fifth point in the outline ("There is extensive sensational photography") could further be qualified:

  a. The front page is usually covered with pictures.

  b. The pictures are usually in poor taste.

After you have arranged the main and subordinate ideas, you decide which forms of support will be most effective for your particular audience and time; you then list the supporting materials under the appropriate ideas.

You also can use the **inductive approach** to develop your central idea. Frequently the analysis process described in Chapter 8 results not in a clear, analyzable central idea but in a specific purpose and a mass of data, notions, and ideas. In this case you can work inductively from the specific to the general by looking for categories of data that illustrate or prove the same point. You can then group the minor points into broader generalizations until you have a few main ideas that can be generalized into a central idea.

Suppose, for example, that your travel club has asked you to speak about your recent visit to Japan so the members can prepare for a tour they are planning. Your purpose is "to have each member of this audience aware of what to see and do in Japan." Your analysis of the topic has produced a long list of interesting things to see and do: Kofukugi, the gold and silver pavilions, Sumo wrestling, Himeji Castle, Kabuki drama, the Toyota automobile factory, and so forth.

As you examine the data you see categories emerging, such as (1) castles, (2) Buddhist temples, (3) Shinto shrines, (4) dramatic productions, and (5) manufacturing processes. Further thought reveals that the castles, shrines, and temples can be combined under "historical landmarks." Such classifying and combining should help you arrive at a

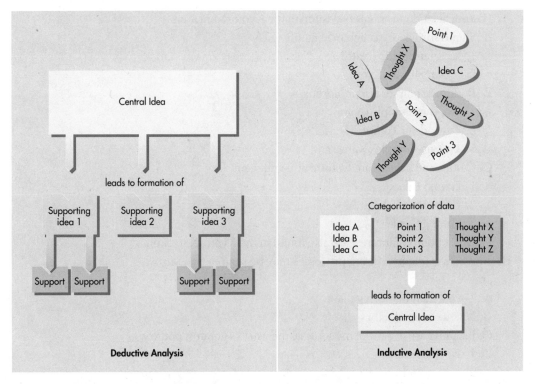

Deductive Analysis

Inductive Analysis

Figure 9.1
Deductive versus inductive analysis.

single central idea such as "Careful planning will enhance the enjoyment of your trip to Japan." As a further step you could phrase the categories as sentences in order to focus your audience's thinking on the most important concept related to each category. The approaches of deductive and inductive analysis are summarized in Figure 9.1.

This speech about Japan also offers a good example of how the anticipated transaction with your audience can help focus your organization. Although the list of topics is rational, covering them all would be useful only if your audience wanted simply to know more about Japan. But we said the purpose of the speech was to prepare the audience for a visit to Japan. If your message is organized by topic, the audience will be confused when they get to Japan, for they will be moving from area to area geographically. So the demands of this particular communicative transaction dictate a spatial arrangement. You thus might arrive at the following general outline for the body of your speech:

I. Historical landmarks may be visited in the Kyoto-Nara area.
  A. Shinto shrines are religiously significant.
    1. Katsuga Shrine (Nara)
    2. Heian Shrine (Kyoto)
  B. Buddhist temples are numerous.
    1. Horyugi Temple (Nara)
    2. Toshodaigi Temple (Nara)
    3. Todaigi Temple (Nara)
  C. Castles and palaces are historically significant.
    1. Gonijo Palace
    2. Emperor's Palace
    3. Himeji Castle
  D. Other points of interest are also found in the Kyoto-Nara area.
II. Interesting manufacturing processes may be seen in the Nagoya area.
  A. Toyota manufacturing plant
  B. Nikon camera factory
  C. Japanese artists producing some of the world's greatest pottery
    1. Noritaki china
    2. Seto pottery
III. Interesting cultural activities are available in Tokyo.
  A. Kabuki drama
  B. Sumo wrestling

Having considered several options for patterning the material, you have, with this outline, prioritized and arranged the material to focus on the communicative demands of this particular speech.

Whether to use the inductive or deductive method of analysis depends somewhat on your familiarity with the subject. The more familiar the subject, the more likely that the deductive method will be useful; the less familiar the subject, the more likely that the inductive method will prove fruitful.

In addition, you can choose from several methods of development, depending on the type of central idea. As we examine these various methods, keep in mind that the development of ideas may precede or follow your compilation of data, depending on whether you use the inductive or deductive approach.

Developing Information and Sharing Ideas

Information falls into several categories, for which different approaches to development work best. The following categories are neither mutually exclusive nor exhaustive, but they serve as useful screens through which to view information as you organize ideas and data: (1) processes, (2) abstract concepts, (3) functions, (4) common misconceptions, (5) theoretical principles, (6) categories, (7) chronology, (8) spatial relations, (9) continuum, (10) web, (11) narrative, (12) comparison and contrast, (13) metaphor.

Processes. Listeners frequently want the speaker to tell them how something is done or how it is made. How is a mountain formed? How is a coffee table made? How does a city dispose of sewage? With such questions listeners usually are searching for the workings of a process or procedure. In developing a speech about a process, the following questions should be answered:

1. What is the raw material or input to the process?
2. What is the product or result of the process?
3. What is the general character of the process? For instance, is it basically a building, or growth, process or is it a disintegrating, or reductionist, procedure?
4. What are the major stages of the process?

The answers to these and other questions that are more specific to the particular procedure will provide a general notion of the ideas you must develop in the message.

Abstract Concepts. Abstract concepts are often the most difficult of all meanings to share. Indeed, the higher the order of abstraction at which you conceptualize and verbalize, the greater the possibility that your audience will provide different interpretations in the transaction. For example, what do people "mean" when they talk about love, ethical behavior, communication, procrastination, inflation, or the gross domestic product?

First, it is helpful to determine the general area to which the abstract construct relates, such as economic, political, cultural, physical, and so on. Second, look for less abstract components or related concepts. Love is a difficult concept to describe, let alone define, but most people would agree that it somehow relates to the more tangible concepts of trust, respect, affection, care, and need. The process is one of grounding your main concept in the listeners' experiences.

Functions. Another way that informative data can be developed is by functions. For example, an automobile mechanics teacher could explain the workings of an internal combustion engine by analyzing the functions performed by the fuel injection system, the ignition system, and other systems.

Common Misconceptions. Almost every informative subject is permeated with error and myth. Frequently, public communication involves not the dissemination of information that is new to the listeners but rather the clarification of misinformation. Generally speaking, the less efficient and less open the communication about a subject, the more misunderstandings will occur. For instance, a speech called "Modern Myths in Education" dealt with the widely held misconceptions that teaching is an easy job and that the public cannot afford better education. Similarly, an executive from a comic book company gave a talk on the common misconception that comics are a children's medium, when in fact most comic books today are aimed at teenagers and adults.

Perspectives. Still another way of developing information is by looking at the perspectives or theoretical principles inherent in the subject. Descriptions of the human personality would differ according to which theoretical stance a speaker takes toward the subject. After considering the needs of your listeners, you may even wish to focus your message on the different theoretical approaches to your subject. Throughout this book we have demonstrated over and over that the transmissional and transactional perspectives lead to different communication principles and behaviors. Similarly, because of their different theoretical concerns, artists, engineers, historians, and psychologists can explain various social phenomena in unique, enlightening ways.

Categories. Even though the other modes of developing information also represent methods of categorizing data, some subjects are not amenable to these approaches. Just as the types of foods can be divided into such categories as fruits, vegetables, and dairy products, so can most subjects be broken down into meaningful categories—or even into more than one set of categories. For instance, foods can also be grouped by nutritional content: proteins, carbohydrates, fats, vitamins, and minerals. Part of your transactional task is to determine which categorical scheme is most germane to your listeners' needs as well as to your central idea. (Note that categorization was the approach used in developing the outline about yellow journalism earlier in this chapter.)

Chronology. A chronological development proceeds according to a time sequence. Historical and biographical data frequently (but not always) are developed chronologically. Again, the development depends on the particular transaction you desire with your listeners as expressed in your purpose and central idea. If you want your listeners to understand the development of the automobile, you might choose the chronological method. However, if you wanted them to understand the causes of the Civil War, you might use a topical or categorical approach, even though the topic is historical. Similarly, if you wanted the audience to understand Abraham Lincoln's development as an orator, you would organize chronologically, whereas if you wanted them to understand his qualities of leadership, you would probably pick the topical approach.

Spatial Relations. Some material can best be organized according to spatial relations or geography. That is, the material is developed from top to bottom, right to left, North to South, and so on, depending on your transactional purpose. Earlier we showed how the speech about Japan could be developed spatially for a group of tourists planning to visit Japan.

Continuum. Most issues and ideas can be placed on a continuum or gradation—simple to complex, liberal to conservative, fast to slow, etc. Although this pattern of organization could be used for almost any topic, it should be carefully selected, and used only when it is the most useful pattern for sharing the information with a particular audience.

Web. Although all organizational patterns should be closely related to the central idea of the message, the **web pattern** is particularly well suited to topics that do not follow one of the foregoing patterns.[1] The web places the central idea at the center. The main ideas radiate out and relate directly to the central idea but have little relationship to one another. Thus, the speaker introduces the central idea at the beginning of the message. Each main idea is tied directly into the central idea before the next main idea is introduced.

Narrative. The **narrative approach** involves story telling. It is the telling of one or more stories, the details of which support the central idea. In its simplest form, the narrative approach consists of a single, extended, detailed story with a moral to it. A student of one of the authors recently gave a speech to help the audience understand the potential impact of AIDS in their personal lives. She could have used virtually any of the techniques listed above in developing this central idea, but none would have been as effective as what she did: telling the story of her uncle who is dying of AIDS.

Comparison and Contrast. In a **comparison** you point out the similarities between two things, such as that between carbohydrates as food and gasoline as fuel for an engine. In a **contrast** you point out differences, such as that between a common virus and a retrovirus. These techniques can be quite helpful for an audience; they come to understand something less familiar in terms of something more familiar. Like most of the other techniques discussed in this section, by using comparison and/or contrast, you relate your ideas to experiences with which the audience can identify.

Metaphor. A **metaphor** is somewhat more complex than a simple comparison. Metaphors are implied or implicit comparisons. They tend to be figurative rather than literal, and they are often embedded in the language chosen to describe the topic. For example, in explaining a difficult period in your life, you might say, "After floating down a peaceful stretch of river, I found myself on the precipice of a roaring waterfall." Often metaphors and narratives are combined, as a story can itself become a metaphor for some other event.

The foregoing methods of developing informative data are not mutually exclusive. Indeed, most topics can be analyzed from more than one of these perspectives. Choosing from among these possibilities is part of the continuing process of focusing the topic on the transaction you desire with your specific audience.

Using Stock Questions

One of the most useful approaches to developing a central idea is to answer a series of **stock questions**. Such questions are called *stock* because they are so frequently encountered. They are stock, too, because their answers are necessary if you are trying o prove certain types of cases. These questions are related to three sorts of issues—issues of fact, value, and policy.[2]

Issues of Fact. An **issue of fact** is a disagreement about a state of affairs. It is a question regarding existing conditions, for which individuals would give opposing answers. Rarely can questions of fact be settled by looking up the answer in a book, because people have different opinions about the state of affairs at issue. For instance, you might ask, "Does the banning of assault rifles deter crime?" Some people say yes, and some say no. When you are speaking on an issue of fact to an audience that does not already agree with you, you will need to bolster your case with evidence, perhaps scientific studies, examples, and expert opinions.

Two stock questions are necessary in making a factual claim:

1. Is the claim backed by good evidence?
2. Is my interpretation of the evidence valid?

Suppose, for example, that you wanted to argue that banning assault weapons would not deter crime. You would need to present evidence

A workers' strike illustrates an issue of values. There are usually several valid points of view about the justification for the strike action and the fairness of the workers' demands.

to this effect, perhaps the experience of other countries, and you would need to show that you are interpreting this evidence in an appropriate way.

Issues of Value. **Issues of value** typically involve choices between two or more alternatives or judgments between two or more things. They are questions that must be answered from one's personal value system, and since values differ, people will disagree about the answer to such questions. Often questions of value center around the standards by which a certain course of action should be judged. Some of the most important questions debated in society are value issues such as these: Is homosexuality legitimate? When is welfare appropriate? Are taxes too high?

You can see from these examples that issues of value may have factual issues embedded in them. For example, the gay and lesbian rights debate has an important factual issue at its center: Is homosexuality innate, a matter of conditioning, or a choice? Thus the stock questions for issues of fact may enter into your development of a case for a value claim. For example, if you argue in favor of gay and lesbian rights, you may want to include an argument to the effect that homosexuality is biologically based and therefore not a moral issue.

Stock questions for a value issue are the following:

1. What are the criteria for making the judgment?
2. Are the criteria linked to the evaluation by sufficient evidence?

The best way to show how these questions might be used in a speech is to work an example. Suppose you wanted to make the case that taxes are too high. The first question requires you to say what is bad about high taxes. This part of the speech would consist of your criteria for judging whether taxes are actually too high. You might claim, for example, that taxes are too high if they (a) remove too much cash from the investment pool, (b) restrict personal liberty, and (c) lead to inappropriate government spending. Next, you would need to show that the current level of taxation meets these three negative criteria, and you would present evidence to that effect.

Issues of Policy. **Issues of policy** involve proposals for change. Questions of fact ask, "What is the state of affairs?" Questions of value ask, "Is the state of affairs good or bad?" And questions of policy ask, "What should be done?" If you are debating whether taxes are too high, the natural next question is, "What should be done about taxes?" or, more specifically, "Should taxes be lowered?"

A policy claim asserts a plan of action. It might be as vague as "Taxes should be lowered," or as specific as, "We should adopt a flat income tax at 15 percent." Whether general or specific, five questions are frequently answered in the development of a policy case:

1. Is there a need for a change?
2. Is the proposed change workable?
3. Will the proposal meet the need?

4. Is this the best proposal for meeting the need?
5. Will the advantages of the proposal outweigh its disadvantages?

If you were arguing for the adoption of a flat tax at 15 percent, you might proceed by showing that (1) there is a need to lower taxes, (2) a flat tax can and will work, (3) the flat-tax proposal will in fact lower taxes, (4) the flat tax would be better than other methods of lowering taxes, and (5) the advantages of the flat-tax method outweigh its disadvantages.

Since you probably will not have the time necessary to develop all of these questions in detail, you will have to make choices based on the needs of your audience.

Problems and Solutions

Problem-oriented speeches may include any of the techniques discussed in this section, but there is an approach to problem-oriented speeches that we would like to discuss separately. This is a special application of the problem-solving process discussed in Chapters 3 and 7. Here are the stages:

1. Define the problem.
2. Analyze the problem—its origins, history, scope, effects, and causes.
3. Suggest possible solutions.
4. Suggest the standards or criteria by which solutions should be evaluated.
5. Identify the "best" solution.
6. Explore what is needed to bring this solution into being.

You will not be able to discuss all the possible answers to all these questions every time you speak about a problem, but in researching the speech you should seek as many of the answers as possible. You then may decide to focus the speech to include only causes or effects or possible solutions, but that will be a conscious decision based on the constraints of the particular situation, especially the immediate needs of your listeners.

Simplified adaptations of the problem-solving sequence focus on subordinate propositions of fact and include problem/solution, problem/ no solution, and best-solution sequences.

The *problem/solution* sequence is perhaps the most common approach designed to change people's beliefs or behavior. With it the speaker develops the problem in terms of effects, causes, or magnitude until the audience is convinced the problem is serious. Then, the desired solution is developed as the "remedy" of the problem. The problem/solution sequence is most effective with either simple topics or noncommitted audiences.

For audiences who are ignorant or apathetic toward the topic, it may be necessary to focus only on the problem itself and to leave the proposal of a solution to a later date—hence the *problem/no solution* approach. Examples would be the recent consciousness-raising in regard to the problems of population explosion, sexual harassment, and environmental degradation.

When discussing problems, it is sometimes useful to examine them from the perspective of their causes and effects. This approach, called the *causal sequence*, can proceed from causes to effects, effects to causes, or from effects to effects. Establishing the connection between causes and effects is tricky and should be done with caution. Problems with causal reasoning are discussed in Chapter 10.

For audiences who are fully aware of the problem but disagree about what to do about it, the *elimination approach* may be used (sometimes called the "method of residues"). Each solution is discussed and alternatives are eliminated until the desired solution stands alone as the "best" one.

Using Supporting Materials

There is virtually no end to the types of material that a speaker can use creatively to elaborate ideas in a speech. The practical question is how to determine what to include. The answer to this question is always a matter of artistic judgment, but we believe that three principles should guide the selection of supporting material.

The Variety Principle. Although specialized audiences may require particular types of supporting material, most general audiences find variety appealing (thus the **variety principle**). Also, when you have different types of people in your audience, a variety of support increases your chance of appealing to a larger portion of the audience. In our classes, the best speeches include not only facts and explanation, but quotations, expert testimony, stories, examples, analogies, definitions, and sometimes even more.

The Depth-Breadth Principle. One of the most common errors made by inexperienced speakers is the tendency to demonstrate that a problem or situation is widespread without showing that it is significant or important. Another common problem is to show that the problem is significant to some individuals without demonstrating that it is a widespread problem. The **depth-breadth principle** says that you should provide evidence for both the individual significance and the extensiveness of a problem or situation. Breadth evidence shows that it is extensive, and depth evidence shows that it is important.

Take the common speech topic of endangered species as an example. Here you must show both that the number of species endangered is large and that this is a worldwide problem. At the same time, you should provide examples and cases of what loss of an endangered species can mean to other animals and plants in an ecosystem. If you were talking about drug addiction, you might present statistics showing how widespread the problem is and then present the example of a friend whose life has been shattered by addiction.

The Adaptation Principle. Finally, as was certainly made clear in the previous chapter, supporting material should adapt to the audience (the **adaptation principle**). You should use material that the audience understands and can relate to. If you are talking about endangered species, give some examples from the region in which most of the audience members live. If you are talking to a college speech class about addiction, use examples of college students.

ORGANIZATION

Some people argue that they can organize their messages in their heads. That approach may be fine and frequently is necessary, especially when someone must speak impromptu, without time for specific preparation. But when time is available for organization, we recommend

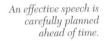

An effective speech is carefully planned ahead of time.

preparing a complete sentence outline. Why? Because outlining is a useful process that helps you test and systematize your ideas. If, indeed, your ideas are already clear enough so that you can organize them in your head, it will take only a few minutes to write them down. On the other hand, if it takes more than a few minutes, you obviously need to spend time to organize your thoughts. Before beginning the actual process of outlining, however, you should plan your introduction and your conclusion.

The point is that your communication with your audience will be greatly facilitated if at appropriate times during the speech the listeners grasp the organizational pattern and central idea of the message. Foss and Foss call this *disclosing form*.[3] For most informative speaking this should occur explicitly, whereas for persuasive speaking when and how to disclose depend upon the mind-set of the audience.

Form can be disclosed directly or indirectly. For the direct approach the speaker states the central idea and main points up front in the introduction. For the indirect approach the central idea and main points are revealed as the message progresses. In either case the audience needs to grasp the form of the message by the end, or communication will be ineffective.

We will discuss the functions of the introduction. Then we will discuss techniques for disclosing the form of the message, which may occur at any point in the message but most frequently are in the introduction and conclusion.

The Introduction

The overriding function of the introduction is to induce the audience to listen to the rest of the speech. That sounds simple enough, but how do you do it? An introduction should fulfill four specific functions: (1) gaining attention, (2) motivating listeners, (3) identifying with listeners, and (4) orienting listeners.

Gaining Attention. Most speakers and listeners, when asked, recognize the importance of gaining or giving attention when they speak or listen. Yet when actually transacting, many people either ignore this knowledge or use some gimmick that can be counterproductive. One student, for example, began a speech by throwing a dinner plate over the heads of his classmates, to shatter it against the back wall. Then he began to speak about flying saucers. This attention-getting device was too dramatic, and it was not really relevant. It is better to use a striking quotation or a pertinent story as a form of support to get attention and introduce your central idea.

Motivating Listeners. This function of the introduction can be seen as establishing the "need to know." Gaining momentary attention is not enough; you must also develop a sustained interest in your topic. Since you have limited the topic to fit the needs of your listeners, you must describe to them—either directly or indirectly—the rationale by which you did that.

You could point to a genuine need, such as their desire to learn about survival tactics in the event they get lost in the wilderness. Or you could create the need to know by arousing curiosity: "Have you ever wondered what it would be like to . . . ?"

Identifying with Listeners. In the introduction you should identify with your listeners by establishing a common bond of acceptance between you and them. You must be concerned about establishing this bond each time you speak to a new group or present a new subject to a familiar group. A speech teacher once introduced the technique of charting (a process that we will discuss later) by telling the class how much he himself had hated outlining as a student. He thus established instant identification with the outline haters in the class.

Orienting Listeners. The process of orienting listeners to your topic varies, depending on whether you want to provide clarity, comprehension, and memory or whether you seek to change beliefs, values, and attitudes. In the first case it is usually best to be direct. That is, you should state your central idea and offer an initial summary of your main supporting ideas. When beliefs, values, and attitudes are involved, however, you may want to orient the audience in a more general and subtle way. You should avoid creating antagonism or closed-mindedness among your listeners.

It is important to realize that we have been discussing the functions of the introduction, not its steps, and these functions can be accomplished simultaneously or separately. Sometimes they are already accomplished even before you speak, and on these occasions, you may need only a brief introduction. The introductions of Winston Churchill's speeches were exceedingly brief. On the other hand, if these functions have not been accomplished, it is foolish to proceed with the body of your speech until you get the audience to listen. Henry W. Grady in his speech "The New South" (described at the beginning of Chapter 8) devoted approximately half of his entire message to the introduction because of the dramatic need for identification which that situation produced.

The Conclusion

The basic functions of the conclusion are to tie the entire message into a coherent, unified whole and then to end the speech. More specifically, the conclusion must (1) encapsulate, (2) remotivate, and (3) terminate.

Encapsulation. The encapsulation function is designed to pull the ideas of the message together one last time. Listeners who either have missed a point when it was discussed or could not get the entire picture during the speech often regain their perspective at this point in the conclusion. Encapsulation usually involves a summary of the main points and a restatement of the central idea. For example, a golf instructor might say, "By developing a grip that allows the hands to move as one, a stance that is firm and comfortable, a backswing that is slow and controlled, a downswing that accelerates the club-head speed, and a high follow-through, you can achieve a consistent swing that will lower your golf score."

Remotivation. Attention comes and goes. Interest waxes and wanes. Accordingly, the conclusion of a speech should contain material that will recapture the audience's attention and build the speech to a motivational climax. This is usually accomplished with some form of support that reiterates your central idea in an interesting way. In short, save your best story or most apt quotation for last, so that it can remotivate listeners and underscore your central idea.

Termination. We have all heard speakers who simply could not stop; they seemed to conclude the speech a half-dozen times. Others quit abruptly, leaving the audience to wonder when to applaud. To avoid just trailing off at the end of a speech, plan your final remarks very carefully. We recommend that you write out the last sentence or two. Actually, if your conclusion has encapsulated and remotivated, your final statement may have already been made or can be simply a brief sentence. Sometimes it is effective to allude back to a story you used in the introduction or to rephrase a quotation from your opening remarks. Frequently, you can review, remotivate, and terminate with a single summarizing statement or form of support.

Accomplishing the Functions

The functions of the introduction and conclusion can be accomplished in a number of ways. Any of the materials suggested in Chapter 8 for bridging gaps or in the present chapter for sharing ideas can be useful. You may begin your speech with a specific detailed example in the form of a *narrative.* Indeed, your entire speech may be a story with a moral to it. *Quotations* are also effective for opening a speech. In addressing McCarthyism, one speaker accomplished all four of the functions of the introduction with a quotation from Shakespeare:

Who steals my purse steals trash; 'tis something, nothing.;
'Twas mine, 'tis his, and has been slave to thousands;
But he who filches from me my good name
Robs me of that which not enriches him
And makes me poor indeed.

Attention and motivation are sometimes achieved with *questions*, which can create the "need to know": "Have you ever wondered what causes earthquakes?" or "Was there a conspiracy to assassinate President Kennedy?" Questions can be an effective technique in the introduction, but they should not substitute for audience analysis that could have been done earlier.

Orientation is frequently achieved, especially in speeches to inform, with initial summaries and overviews.

Similar techniques can be used to disclose form and fulfill the functions of the conclusion. Reorientation is sometimes accomplished by a final *summary* of the main ideas and a restatement of the central idea, especially in speeches to gain understanding. The activation function is frequently a simple *pledge* or straightforward *call to action* such as Patrick Henry's "Give me liberty or give me death!"

More elaborate conclusions can include a *narrative* or *quotation* to remotivate as well as accomplish the other functions of the conclusion. An especially effective technique is to allude back to a narrative or quotation from earlier in the speech, which serves to tie the entire message into a neat package.

Notice how Winston Churchill fulfills the functions of encapsulation, remotivation, and termination by combining several of these techniques in this eloquent conclusion to his speech about the fall of France:

What General Weygand called the "Battle of France" is over. I expect that the Battle of Britain is about to begin. Upon this battle depends the survival of Christian civilization. Upon it depends our own British life and the long continuity of our institutions and our Empire. The whole fury and might of the enemy must very soon be turned on us. Hitler knows that he will have to break us in this island or lose the war. If we can stand up to him, all Europe may be free and the life of the world may move forward into broad, sunlit uplands; but if we fail, then the whole world, including the United States, and all that we have known and cared for, will sink into the abyss of a new dark age made more sinister and perhaps more prolonged by the lights of a perverted science. Let us therefore brace ourselves to our duty and so bear ourselves that if the British Commonwealth and Empire lasts for a thousand years men will still say, "This was their finest hour."

Outlining

Outlining is a technique for structuring ideas and specific data for a more effective public communication transaction. Outlining is governed by certain rules and procedures. We do not believe in rules for rules' sake, but violating the rules of outlining serves as a warning sign of basic problems, indicating a serious error in conceptualization or structure. Let us examine some of the principles of outlining.

1. Ideas should be stated in complete, succinct, declarative sentences under which the forms of support may be listed. Many students of public speaking think a complete-sentence outline entails unnecessary busywork. But one definition of a sentence is that it expresses a complete thought; thus a complete thought cannot be expressed thoroughly in less than a sentence. If an idea is listed in the outline simply as a word or phrase, can you be sure your thinking is precise enough? If you list "format" as your first point in the outline about yellow journalism, will you know what that means? Does it mean that the format is tabloid? That the format can be ignored? That the format is round? Countless ideas, many of which are contradictory, can obviously be indicated by the notation "format." Which idea or meaning do you intend? Clarify your thinking by stating the idea in a sentence. If you are tempted to ask a question, simply answering the question will give you the idea you are after. If you have long compound or complex sentences, examine them to see if in fact they represent two or more ideas that should be stated separately in the outline. For types of support, listing is sufficient; for example, "quote Lincoln" or "story of Joe Zoe." Then in the speech you will read the quotation from a note card or tell the story of Joe Zoe in your own words.

2. Ideas at the same level of subordination should be few. Have you ever played the game of looking into a store window and then seeing how many items you can remember? If so, you are aware that it is easier to remember the items when there are not too many; if there are several items, grouping them into some meaningful pattern improves recall. Consider Figure 9.2. Which pattern is easier to grasp quickly? Which pattern lets you count the items more quickly? Because the mind seeks shortcuts and patterns, look for categories or steps or other ways of grouping several ideas. This will make them easier to understand and remember.

3. "Never an A without a B." This familiar mandate states that any level of subordination in the outline should contain more than one idea.

Figure 9.2
Pattern properties of outlining.

The argument is that you cannot divide an idea into a single part. If you do not have two or more parts, then the point should not be divided at all. For example, the subitem may simply restate the main idea, in which case you are warned that your thinking is not yet clear enough. Or perhaps you have omitted a point—one that could be crucial. Consider the cooking teacher whose outline for a lecture about baking a cake reads like this:

I. Ingredients must be purchased.
II. Utensils must be assembled.
III. A mixing procedure must be followed precisely.
IV. Baking procedure is important.
    A. Temperature

In this case most cakes will emerge from the oven either burned or underdone because point B—"Time"—is missing from the outline. A missing idea in an outline about inflation or diplomatic relations with China may be less obvious. The rule of never having an A without a B helps you catch some but not all mistakes in both analysis and synthesis.

This rule does not usually apply to forms of support. It is possible (but not likely) that a single story or analogy will communicate an idea to an entire audience. In that case you need list only one, for you are not dividing anything; you are supporting it. One form of support may be enough, but do not count on it. More often two or more supports are needed.

4. Physical characteristics of the outline should be consistent. Consistency in numerals, letters, indentations, and capitalization all serve to guide you and your listeners through the pattern of thinking that you wish to share. The outline in Figure 9.3 shows how one speaker incorporated the principles of organization and the techniques for synthesizing into an outline for a five- to ten-minute speech about yellow journalism.

Charting

Some people find the whole business of outlining difficult as well as time-consuming. If you feel this way, you may prefer to use charting as an alternative technique for structuring your message. Originally intended as a method for studying the written messages of others, charting can also be used to prepare your own messages. Charting is based on the same analytic processes as outlining, and it serves the same purposes. That is, it represents the relationships between ideas and their supporting points and data.

To begin charting, construct a matrix with several columns (twelve will do) and five rows. The columns represent an introduction and a conclusion plus five potential main ideas, with space for supporting points and data. In the middle columns write down all the supporting materials and specific ideas you can think of, trying to keep similar ideas and supports in the same or adjacent columns. List ideas near the top of the matrix, and write supporting points near the bottom. Now label each column. After you label the columns, you may have to shift some supporting data into more relevant columns or create or eliminate some columns. Now see whether any of the columns can be clustered into larger categories. If so, label these categories. Continue this process until categories can no longer be combined. Now, across the top of the paper, label the entire chart. In the first and last columns insert the material you will use for your introduction and conclusion. A chart will have as many columns as there are discrete ideas in the speech and as many rows as the maximum number of supports for a particular idea.

Figure 9.3
Model outline.

Title:	Yellow: More Than a Color
General purpose:	To share understanding
Transactional response:	To have my audience understand how to identify yellow journalism
Central idea:	Yellow journalism is identified by its sensationalism.

Introduction

I. Most of you probably read a newspaper every day.
   A. You may get a student newspaper on the way to class; in addition you may get your hometown paper in the mail.
   B. You expect to get honest and adequate coverage of the news so that you'll be well informed.
   C. You probably don't even think about whether you're reading a paper classified as "yellow journalism." I'll examine its outstanding characteristics so that you'll know it when you see it.
   D. Yellow journalism is identified by its sensationalism.
   E. I'm going to look specifically at the characteristics of format, headline forms, writing style, news value, and photography.

Body

I. The *format* is tabloid.
   A. Give a definition of *tabloid*.
   B. Not all tabloids are sensational, but this is the form yellow journalism takes.
   C. Show examples of tabloids (visual aids).

II. The *headlines* are "scary" or sensational.
   A. Give the example of "50-Megaton Blast Hinted."
   B. Give the sensational example of "Wife Stripped, Slain in Triangle."

III. The *writing style* is short and abrupt.
   A. Give an example of Walter Winchell's verbal style.
   B. Give an example of "It was a happy meeting . . ."

IV. Stories are selected for their ability to attract attention on the newsstand, not for their *news value*.
   A. Show an example of a visual aid.
   B. Give an illustration of "The Death of Charles Eliot."

V. There is extensive sensational *photography*.
   A. The front page usually is covered with pictures.
      1. Show visual aid.
   B. Pictures are usually in poor taste.
      1. Give an example of Mrs. Snyder pictured in electric chair right after the current was turned on.
      2. Give an example of "Girlie Pose Advertising for Seventh Husband."

Conclusion

I. The phrase "yellow press" or "yellow journalism" was coined in 1889 when a comic strip character, outfitted in a yellow dress, appeared in the pages of a New York paper that exhibited the features we have just looked at, i.e., the tabloid format, scary or sensational headlines, flashy writing style, news with little true value, and unseemly photographs.

II. I hope the next time you pick up a paper you'll know whether you're being exposed to yellow journalism.

Figure 9.4 is a chart for the speech about yellow journalism. Note that only eight of twelve possible columns were used because the first four main ideas were not divided.

DELIVERY

Having completed your analysis of the situation and content, and having developed a clear, rational outline or chart of your message, you may think that you have completed your preparation for a public speech. But the public communication transaction is not consummated until the actual event occurs. When you face your audience, the variables that you have planned begin to fall into place to form a gestalt that is not only unique to that time and place but that has pattern properties that are greater than the sum of the parts. For this final synthesis to occur during the speaking event and to be as effective as possible, it also must be prepared. Among the factors you must take into account are (1) modes of delivery, (2) functions of delivery, (3) characteristics of delivery, and (4) techniques for preparing delivery.

Figure 9.4
Example of charting.

Introduction				Body				Conclusion
Specific Purpose: To have my audience understand how to identify yellow journalism. **Central Idea:** Yellow journalism is identified by its sensationalism.								
	The format is tabloid.	The headlines are "scary" or sensational.	The writing style is short and abrupt.	Stories are selected for their ability to attract attention on the newsstand, not for their news value.	There is extensive sensational photography.			
					front page covered	poor taste		
1. Mention school newspaper.	1. Define *tabloid*.	1. Give example of "50-Megaton Blast."	1. Give Walter Winchell analogy.	1. Show visual aid.	1. Show visual aid.	1. Show picture of Mrs. Snyder.	1. Summarize.
2. "You expect . . ."	2. Not all tabloids are yellow journalism.	2. Give example of "Wife Stripped."	2. Give example of "It was a happy meeting . . ."	2. Give example of Charles Eliot.		2. Give example of "Girlie Pose."	2. Restate "sensational theme."
3. "You are aware . . ."	3. Show visual aid.						3. Make final statement.
4. State central idea.							
5. Overview.							

Modes of Delivery

Such terms as delivery, presentation, and performance are misleading
in that they imply the linear notion that public speakers do things to
audiences and that the listeners passively receive this transmission.
Instead, we define delivery as the active transaction among speakers

*An effective delivery
synthesizes face, voice,
and body language
with the message.*

and listeners during the process of public communication. Although this discussion focuses primarily on the speaker's behavior, these variables are important only insofar as they contribute to the total transaction. Modes of delivery lie on a continuum of preparation from virtually no preparation to a written manuscript that is either memorized or read.

Impromptu. At one extreme on the delivery continuum is the **impromptu** mode of speaking, in which you are asked to say a few words on the spur of the moment. Some people might say that in this situation the speaker is basically unprepared. We would argue, however, that although you are not prepared for that particular time and place of speaking, you can draw on two sources of preparation. First is the general preparation for public speaking that you accumulate over a lifetime in the form of experience, knowledge, and skills for analysis and synthesis that we have discussed in this book. Second, you can apply those skills spontaneously, while you are speaking. Although the impromptu mode does not allow specific preparation and requires considerable poise along with an ability to "think on your feet," it does have the advantage of increasing spontaneity and contact with your listeners. Let us discuss a few tips for making impromptu speaking successful.

The most important thing to do is to stay as calm as you can. You will have to keep a clear mind to think as you speak. In most cases you will be called upon to speak on a subject for which you are well prepared— a tribute to a friend or colleague, a project on which you have spent considerable time, or an unusual experience you have had. If someone is insensitive enough to call on you to speak on a topic you know nothing about, decline politely.

Given a familiar topic, keep your remarks simple and to the point. The most basic component of organization is the central idea, so think quickly of a single thought that captures the essence of your friend, project, or experience. It need not be perfect or comprehensive—only appropriate. If you think of supporting or qualifying ideas as you go along, so much the better, but this is not necessary for a brief off-the-cuff talk.

Next, try to think of a story, usually a personal experience, that illustrates the point. You can begin your talk with the story while you are thinking of other illustrations. If you think of no further experiences or other forms of support, let the talk be a story with a moral to it, brief and to the point. At the end restate your main point and sit down. You will communicate a worthwhile idea to your audience, look as if you know what you are talking about, and not waste your listeners' time.

Written. At the other extreme on the delivery continuum is the *written* speech, which you either memorize or read from a manuscript. This mode has the advantage of allowing you to choose your words precisely when a misunderstanding or an ill-chosen word or phrase could have severe detrimental effects. However, written speeches have the disadvantage of limiting your ability to respond to immediate feedback and thereby to transact spontaneously with your audience. That is, written speeches may be too transmissional. Furthermore, many speakers fall into the trap of simply beginning to write with the first word of the introduction without taking the time to prepare.

Although we believe that situations demanding a written speech are somewhat rare, if the demand does arise, you should follow all the principles of preparation leading up to the completion of an outline or chart. As you begin to write the speech, try to avoid using your usual writing style, or your speech may sound like "an essay standing on its hind legs." Talk to yourself in a conversational style and write that down. Imagine your audience and talk to them. This approach will provide the best possible conceptual foundation for the imaginary transaction that constitutes the writing process.

After the manuscript is drafted you will need to spend some additional time to (1) memorize it so well that you do not struggle for words and can monitor and adapt to feedback or (2) practice reading it several times with spontaneity so that you can look away from the manuscript and establish contact with your listeners.

As you can see, speaking from a written manuscript is the most time-consuming mode of delivery and should be used only in cases where precise wording is essential.

Extemporaneous. Extemporaneous is an arbitrary designation for a variety of similar modes lying between impromptu and written. Essentially, it involves speaking directly from the chart or outline without relying on the specific wording found in a written speech. Wording is developed during oral practice before the speaking event. Extemporaneous delivery is usually best because speech should be conversational. Surely you would not read a prepared statement in a conversation with a friend. The extemporaneous mode has the advantage of maximizing preparation and spontaneity during the actual speech. We believe that the extemporaneous mode provides the most effective method of synthesizing the communication transaction in most public communication situations.

Functions of Delivery

Because delivery is the final synthesis in the public communication transaction, it must fulfill several functions similar to those discussed previously in other communication contexts. We will examine the functions of (1) intelligibility, (2) attention, (3) credibility, and (4) identification.

Intelligibility. Intelligibility is certainly the most basic and perhaps the most important function of delivery. If listeners cannot assimilate or comprehend a speech, they have little opportunity to transact with the speaker in more complex ways. We have all heard speakers who spoke too softly or too indistinctly to be understood. Although a public speaker does not have to develop an artistic level of delivery, or stage diction, we must stress the importance of a basic level of intelligibility.

Attention. Attention is perhaps more difficult to attain and easier to lose in public speaking than in other communicative contexts because of the necessity to adapt simultaneously to so many different listeners. Nervous mannerisms, repeated words and phrases, or dress and grooming that are inappropriate to the audience or occasion can distract attention from the subject and thereby diminish or destroy the communication transaction. Furthermore, physical movement that is not coordinated with (or that is even contradictory to) the message can be equally detrimental. On the other hand, gestures, facial expressions, vocal variety, emphasis, and effective body movements can help focus attention on the desired meaning of your speech.

Of course, effective listeners do not let ineffective delivery distract their attention from the transaction. A communication event proceeds in two directions at once, and neither the speaker nor the listeners can afford to let attention wander. To do so is to jeopardize the entire transaction and its meaning. Because it is easy to forget about minor things in your hands when you are speaking to an audience, we suggest that you get rid of such things as pencils, paper clips, or other small items that you may play with as you speak. Any distractors are dangerous. Have only your note cards, manuscript, or visual aids with you before beginning the speech.

Credibility. In Chapter 4 we defined source credibility as the bond of trust between speaker and listener. The relationship between credibility and delivery is complex and not well understood. It has been assumed by many speakers that a clear and forceful delivery enhances credibility and thus communicative effectiveness. Some research even supports this contention. Indeed, it is only during the process of delivery that the common (though not universal) factors of credibility such as competence, character, and dynamism are perceived by listeners. Unfortunately, we know little about how this perception can be enhanced.

The interaction between credibility and delivery is further complicated by the possibility that "good" delivery might actually be counterproductive in building credibility with certain groups of listeners. Just as Bill Clinton has been labeled "Slick Willie," it has been suggested that presidential candidate Daniel Webster was defeated (in part) because he was perceived as being "too good to be true." Although we do not suggest that you be intentionally sloppy or inappropriate in your delivery, being "smooth" or "greasing" the audience may actually work against you by eroding the trust bond. Of course, listeners also should be discriminating enough not to reject a speaker just because he or she is too eloquent.

Identification. The final function of delivery is identification. In a sense, all other functions are related to identification; intelligibility and attention are prerequisites to it, and credibility is one dimension of it. Even so, some specific aspects of identification are particularly salient to public speaking.

Earlier we defined identification as involving the meanings, feelings, and behaviors that are shared by communicators. Although identification is a primary concern during every stage of preparation, it reaches its culmination during delivery. A speaker enhances or weakens identification through delivery characteristics and adjusting to audience feedback. Perhaps you have seen a speaker who seemed at odds or out of place with the audience. What seemed to be contributing to the alienation? In some cases it may have been the speaker's reputation or the content of the message, but in others it may have stemmed from delivery characteristics. These characteristics include nonverbal cues, pronunciation, and word choice.

Nonverbal cues such as dress or grooming can enhance or weaken identification, depending on the specific individual and audience involved. Pronunciation and word choice also can form (or sever) bonds of identification with the audience. Language that might enhance identification in a less formal conversation could alienate an audience. The public speaking context calls for somewhat less colloquial phrasing and for wording that has general acceptance. Most people can tell an "outsider" by pronunciation alone, and it would be impossible to adjust to every dialect difference you may encounter. Indeed, a public setting may include several dialects simultaneously.

Because of the situational nature of identification, we cannot set down many rules for developing it. But we can urge you to be conscious of the audience's need for identification. Keep in mind that listeners expect somewhat formal (or at least generally acceptable) language, dress, and demeanor from a speaker.

Another aspect of identification during delivery is how the speaker adjusts to immediate feedback from the audience. Positive feedback comes in many forms. Listeners may smile and nod, or even cheer and applaud. During his "I Have a Dream" speech, Martin Luther King received almost continuous overt, positive feedback from his listeners. On the other hand, negative feedback is not uncommon; listeners may shake their heads, doze off, read the newspaper, or even heckle the speaker. Adjusting to positive feedback is both easy and natural—just keep on doing what you are doing. But what about negative feedback? It sometimes is irrelevant and often is isolated to a small minority or even a single member of the audience. In such cases, try to ignore it. But if a large portion of your audience seems antagonistic to you, does not understand a key point, or rejects your major argument, adjustment is necessary.

In general, it is useless to proceed to your next point until you and your audience have transacted effectively on earlier ones. In the event of relevant negative feedback, you must reach below the surface of your preparation for additional forms of support in order to bridge communicative gaps. Furthermore, by having a clear chart or outline of your speech, you can decide (while you continue to speak) what portions to omit if time is running out. In general, it is better to continue discussing a major point until most of the audience gets it rather than to proceed and take the chance that the transaction will fail completely.

By using transactionally oriented analysis, by speaking extemporaneously from a chart or outline, and by monitoring your listeners, you will be able to maximize identification by adapting to immediate feedback.

Transmissional Characteristics of Delivery

Delivery has typically been described in terms of characteristics that are oriented mainly toward the speaker or transmitter and that follow from a transmissional image of public speaking as a performance or presentation. In Chapter 2 we discussed such transmissional characteristics as voice, physical appearance, body movements, and facial expressions, as well as the more transactional notions of emphasis, intensity, variety, clarity, and appropriateness. Figure 9.5 illustrates the relationship among these variables in delivery. As we discuss how transmissional characteristics apply to the public speaking context, we will look first at vocal characteristics and then at the visual characteristics of delivery.

Vocal Cues. Chapter 2 identified the variable characteristics of the voice as pitch, rate, volume, and quality. We pointed out that all these features contribute to emphasis, intensity, variety, clarity, and appropriateness. In public speaking contexts, primary concern is focused

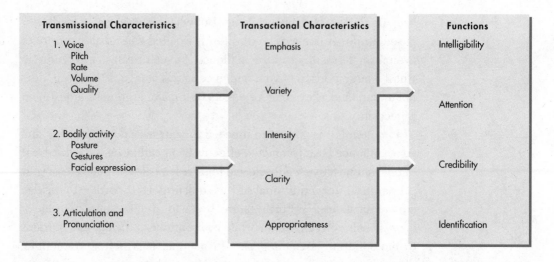

Transmissional Characteristics	Transactional Characteristics	Functions
1. Voice Pitch Rate Volume Quality	Emphasis	Intelligibility
	Variety	Attention
2. Bodily activity Posture Gestures Facial expression	Intensity	Credibility
	Clarity	
3. Articulation and Pronunciation	Appropriateness	Identification

on volume and articulation. Although everyone knows that you must speak up to be heard in a large group, many public speakers talk too softly. We recommend that you practice speaking with what might be called your public voice. If you are trying to get someone's attention at a great distance, you shout. Indeed, some people think the public voice sounds like shouting. Some people actually do shout when a softer tone is called for. You should be sensitive to the problem and should practice adjusting your volume to the size of the audience. It helps to talk to the last row of the audience with your voice (but not with your eyes) and even to ask those in the back if they can hear.

Most large meeting rooms provide a public address system. As we noted in Chapter 8, you should arrive early enough to check all equipment. See that it is working properly, and then briefly practice speaking to ensure that the system is set correctly for your conversational voice.

Articulation. The second important vocal characteristic in a public context is articulation. Although you may be able to get by with careless or sloppy pronunciation in casual conversations, the very size and distance of audiences demand the clearest possible articulation. Again, practice will help. Also recognize that there is a relationship between rate and articulation. If you are not easily understood, slow down a bit. If the problem persists, your communication teacher can suggest some exercises to improve your delivery of troublesome sounds.

Figure 9.5
Characteristics of speech delivery.

There is also a relationship between volume and articulation: the clearer your pronunciation, the less volume you need. You probably have noticed that experienced actors can "whisper" on stage and yet be understood by even a large audience.

Visual Cues. In Chapter 2 we also discussed the significance of visual cues in communication. In public speaking it is usually necessary and certainly desirable to stand up so that your audience can transact with you nonverbally. Furthermore, a slouching posture can attract attention to itself and away from your message; we suspect it even might detract from credibility.

Body movement is also an important factor in public speaking. The timing and frequency of walking, moving your body, or gesturing can either reinforce what you are saying or detract from it. We suggest that you strive for movement that not only feels natural to you but also avoids the extremes of excessive, random activity or stiffness and lack of movement. If you really care about your topic and are adequately prepared, experience will produce the amount of body activity that is appropriate for you.

Facial expression was discussed in some detail in Chapter 2. Here we will just say that, by relaxing and letting your facial expressions

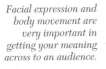

Facial expression and body movement are very important in getting your meaning across to an audience.

reflect the thoughts and feelings you want to share, you can enhance the communicative transaction with public audiences. Of particular importance in public communication is directness, or eye contact, with your audience. Some practitioners suggest that public speakers focus their attention either on the back wall or on a single friendly face in the audience. We contend, however, that this practice cuts off feedback from the audience and limits your flexibility in the transaction. We recommend that you let your eyes roam from listener to listener or, with a large audience, from area to area. This allows you to maintain direct contact with your listeners and also to monitor feedback. (One public speaker is able to identify a single sleeping listener in an audience of four hundred.)

Although the transmissional characteristics described here have traditionally been considered crucial to effective public speaking, the authors' observation of contemporary speakers, along with study of past great speakers, has revealed that many effective speakers succeed without the skillful application of these principles. Abraham Lincoln is considered by most rhetorical scholars to be among the finest public speakers in American history. His delivery was weak, however, as judged in terms of transmissional characteristics. He was tall (six feet, four inches) and somewhat awkward, his movements were ungraceful, and his voice was high and somewhat less than pleasant. More recently, Winston Churchill also succeeded despite several weaknesses in delivery. He had a raspy voice and an articulation disorder. In addition, Churchill was not especially handsome; he was somewhat paunchy, and he slouched. Furthermore, he seldom watched his audience, and he gestured little, preferring to hook his thumbs in the pockets of his vest while he read his speeches from a manuscript. The success of these great orators without the benefit of many of the physical characteristics of delivery poses a contradiction to students of public speaking. It is perhaps too easy to say they succeeded in spite of "poor" delivery. No doubt this explanation is partly accurate, but we prefer to look further.

Transactional Characteristics of Delivery

Chapter 2 covered the transactional characteristics of delivery in terms of emphasis, intensity, variety, clarity, and appropriateness. In public communication contexts these characteristics must be developed more broadly and more obviously than in dyads and small groups. The larger the audience, the greater the expectation of stronger emphasis, wider variety, and heightened intensity. For example, in his message declaring war, Franklin Roosevelt achieved remarkable emphasis on almost every word by combining a slow rate of speaking with the other variable characteristics of his magnificent voice. Almost all public speakers who discuss a serious topic tend to speak with great intensity. If they did not, the effect would be incongruous and sometimes laughable.

We have already pointed out the need for greater clarity. In addition, words and gestures that may be acceptable in small groups or even "polite company" may be considered inappropriate in a public context. Near the end of his term as vice president of the United States, for example, Nelson Rockefeller responded to some hecklers in his audience with an obscene gesture. Although this nonverbal behavior was certainly responsive to audience feedback, many observers considered it inappropriate to Rockefeller's office as well as to the majority of the audience and the public nature of the occasion. Furthermore, it probably did not help Rockefeller achieve his desired response on that occasion, and it may have reduced his communicative effectiveness on later occasions. Since no particular delivery variables are always appropriate, you must carefully consider each speaking situation both before and during delivery. Be mindful of the need for appropriate dress, grooming, gestures, and other aspects of delivery.

Preparing for Delivery

So far we have looked at speech delivery in terms of its components. We have suggested that the transmissional delivery characteristics of vocal volume, articulation, posture, body movement, and facial expression lead to more basic characteristics of emphasis, intensity, variety, clarity, and appropriateness. These, in turn, help fulfill the functions of intelligibility, attention, credibility, and identification. We have reduced delivery to these categories and have analyzed them in order to understand the components somewhat better. However, as the ultimate form of synthesis in public speaking, delivery is a process that cannot be learned or accomplished by analyzing the parts and putting them together. Like gymnastics, skiing, or golf, delivery involves more than the sum of its parts. Delivery must be learned and accomplished as a whole. Among the techniques for developing effective extemporaneous delivery are preparing through practice and focusing during delivery.

Practice. Having completed your analysis and outlining and understanding the objectives and characteristics of delivery, you are ready for your final phase of preparation—oral practice. Since you have not written your speech verbatim, you must develop some tentative wording for the speech. In addition, practice helps you coordinate all the physical characteristics of delivery. But how is this done? There are so many things to think about—voice quality, ideas, gestures, data, feedback, and so forth. When one of the authors was learning to ski several years ago, it seemed that everyone had some advice to offer: lean forward; keep your weight on the downhill ski; bend your knees; and on and on. As one technique was mastered, all the others fell apart. Finally one instructor said, "Think about picking a posy off the heel of your downhill boot." That seemed to put it all together. We suggest that while practicing your speech out loud, you think about the particular thought or meaning you are trying to share with listeners. "Think the thought" as you visualize the coming transaction with your audience. It is important that you practice out loud. Just as the ruts in a dirt road deepen with every car that passes, so each oral practice makes the words and movement come more naturally.

Even though you are not memorizing your speech, and even though the wording differs slightly each time, delivery improves with practice. Just as a story improves with the telling, so will your speech become more interesting and more succinct. By the third or fourth practice session, you may say as much in ten minutes as you said in fifteen or twenty minutes the first time—and you will say it better. Basically, during practice you are developing the transitions by which you proceed from point to point, as well as the explanation or narrative that constitutes your forms of support.

After a few practices, it helps to monitor the visual aspects of delivery. You might practice before a mirror or have a friend observe your delivery and comment on it. If the equipment is available, videotape and observe your delivery. Even experienced speakers practice a speech on a new subject two or three times. Beginners may need six or more practices before the delivery begins to settle down and feel natural.

Focusing. During your speech it is natural to be self-conscious and therefore anxious. We suggest that you focus as much as possible on the relationship between the content of your message and the audience. In a sense you are merely serving as a catalyst to bring about a chemical reaction between your ideas and your audience. How are they responding? Do they understand? Is your message too obvious—or too confusing? By concentrating on the transaction as it occurs, you will be less self-conscious and thus will increase the likelihood of a successful transaction; incidentally, your anxiety will diminish.

SUMMARY

The synthesis process is one of developing your central idea by structuring your supporting ideas and data so that they increase the chances of transacting effectively with your specific audience. You can approach the development of the central idea either inductively or deductively. Specific methods of development include structuring information by procedures, abstract concepts, functions, theoretical principles, categorical breakdowns, chronological sequence, spatial development, narrative, comparison, contrast, or metaphor. Stock questions can be used to develop problems and solutions relative to issues of fact, issues of policy, issues of value. Supporting material can be used according to various principles: variety, depth-breadth, and adaptation.

As to organization, the introduction should fulfill the functions of gaining attention, motivating listeners, identifying with listeners, and orienting listeners; above all, the introduction should make the audience want to listen to the entire speech. The functions of the conclusion are to encapsulate, to remotivate, and to terminate. Outlining and charting are two effective techniques for organizing a speech. Delivery is the ultimate synthesis process in a public speaking transaction. The main modes of delivery are impromptu, written, and extemporaneous. Delivery accomplishes the objectives of enhancing intelligibility, heightening attention, and building credibility—all of which lead to greater identification between the speaker and listeners. Traditional characteristics of delivery include the variable aspects of voice, articulation, posture, body activity, and facial expression. These combine to form more basic properties that are perceived by audiences as emphasis, intensity, variety, clarity, and appropriateness. Oral practice and focusing on the transaction with the audience are techniques for achieving the greatest effectiveness during delivery—the ultimate form of synthesis in transactional public communication.

10 Mass Communication: Reception and Analysis

A t the time this chapter is being written, the United States is marking the twenty-fifth anniversary of the first Apollo moon landing. Even after two decades, this event still seems like a dream. As the world watched, a young American astronaut, Neil Armstrong, stepped from the spaceship *Eagle* onto the dusty surface of the moon. Almost as amazing was the fact that, 289,000 miles away, millions of people were instantaneously watching the event on television. And it had been only a little over a century since the first telegraph made the pony express obsolete.

Ours is a media society. We read best-selling books, news and fashion magazines, tabloids, and daily newspapers. We listen to talk, music, and news on the radio, and we fill movie theaters every weekend. Most of all, we watch television.

Some years ago, one publication estimated that "only sleeping and working claim a greater share of our time than TV watching." By the time of graduation from high school the average American has watched 16,000 hours.[1] Soon most homes will have hundreds of highly specialized channels available, so people will be tempted to spend even more time in front of this glass window on the world.

Because of the pervasive nature of the media, this chapter presents some issues and principles that will help to improve your skills at receiving media messages. In the course of the chapter, we hope to inoculate you against the adverse effects of mediated messages while at the same time helping you to benefit from their many positive aspects. Since this book emphasizes oral communication, our discussion centers on broadcast media.

BASIC ISSUES AND CONCEPTS IN MASS COMMUNICATION

We will first examine some of the issues surrounding broadcast media so that you may better understand the process by which communication occurs in the media.

Perspectives on Mass Communication

Just as communication in general has been approached from many perspectives, mass communication has been described by several models. Some of these are quite transmissional in orientation. If you view media as a simple conduit of information from producer to consumer, you are using the **one-step flow model,** which suggests that information flows in one step from media to audience. A slightly more complex and realistic view is the **two-step flow model,** which includes opinion leaders who spread the influence of media through interpersonal channels. The most complex and realistic transmissional depiction is the **multistep flow model,** which combines mediated and interpersonal lines of influence. Here media and interpersonal channels are believed to work together (Figure 10-1).

To get an idea of how the multistep flow model works, imagine adoption of the minisatellite dish that came out in certain markets in 1994. This new device has been mentioned in limited advertising and news reports, and just a few pioneers are purchasing them. If this innovation is successful, here's what should happen according to the multistep flow model: Some people will hear about the minidish through the media and decide to buy one. They will discuss this decision with

Figure 10.1
Traditional models of mass communication

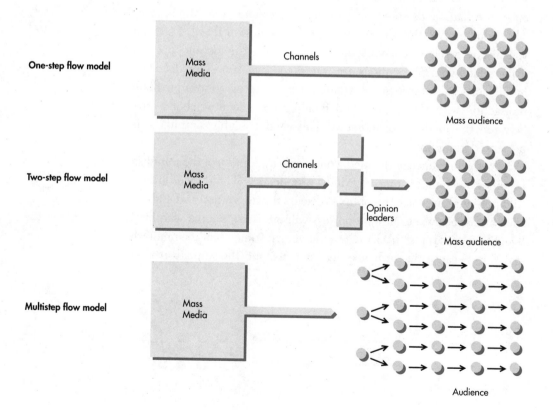

One-step flow model

Two-step flow model

Multistep flow model

their friends, some of whom will not have heard of the minidish before. More and more people will talk about it and decide to buy, and eventually a sizable portion of the video market will come to own a minidish.

Notice that the information and influence about the device do not come strictly from the media, although media do play an important role. Rather, the information and influence spread through a combination of mediated and interpersonal channels.

All these models have a transmissional flavor, varying mainly in the number of interpreters through which the message travels. But if we apply a transactional perspective to mass communication, we can see even more of what is going on. From this point of view, consumers are active participants in transactions with the media. As you watch television or listen to the radio, your attention, motivation, ego involvement, and countless other factors vary considerably among the programs you watch. Furthermore, your selective perception filters out some data, adds some that are not there, and generally screens what you receive. But the transaction does not stop there. Later on you discuss what you have seen or heard with friends and opinion makers, and your perceptions are reinforced, weakened, or distorted by all sorts of interpersonal communication after your immediate transaction with the media. And finally, influence flows both ways between the media and audience. This model, highly simplified, is presented in Figure 10.2.

Now the influence of the media on people's adoption of the minidish becomes much more complex. Media producers will hold focus groups with potential audience members to discuss the innovation and find out what audiences want. News reporters will interview people who have bought one and report back to the audience. At some point the minidish may flop because the audience does not respond the way advertisers

Figure 10.2
Transactional approach to mass communication

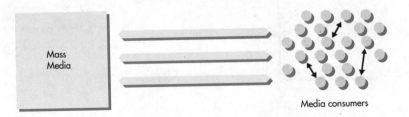

Mass Media

Media consumers

would like it to. Or it may succeed because media producers adapt to the responses of the audience. From the transactional perspective, the results of mass communication are an outcome of a complex and ongoing process of interaction.

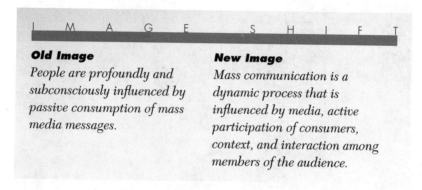

Old Image
People are profoundly and subconsciously influenced by passive consumption of mass media messages.

New Image
Mass communication is a dynamic process that is influenced by media, active participation of consumers, context, and interaction among members of the audience.

Functions of Mass Communication

Few people doubt the impact of the media on our lives, but many question how the media affect us and to what extent. Writers often mention five areas in which media play a significant role: (1) surveillance, (2) correlation, (3) social transmission, (4) entertainment, and (5) advertising.

Surveillance. With the passing of President Nixon, the death of his aide Robert Haldeman, and the publication of Haldeman's diary, Americans have been reminded again of the historic media event called Watergate, a scandal of epic proportions. In covering this 1974 drama, the press fulfilled one of its key functions—to survey the environment for important information for the public—and uncovered a massive conspiracy and cover-up in the administration.

Through investigative reporting, writers for both broadcast and print media serve as watchdogs for a public that has become more and more removed from the centers of power that influence daily life. Regular viewers of the television series *60 Minutes*, we are comforted to know that both television and newspaper reporters in significant numbers are keeping a close eye on the behavior of business, labor, government, and other groups of individuals who might violate laws or exploit people in other ways.

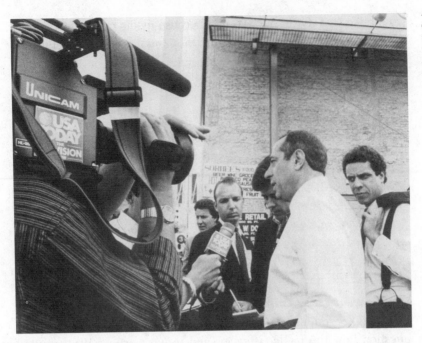

On the other hand, there have been many cases of surveillance dysfunction in which an overzealous reporter, endeavoring to scoop a story, prematurely releases information without adequately verifying the details—and in the process destroys the reputation of an institution or individual. Unfortunately, such faulty stories usually receive prominent emphasis by the media, whereas later corrections and disclaimers are given short shrift. In some cases the damage is irreparable, and the credibility of the media suffers.

Correlation. The media also act as a go-between or gatekeeper that stands between the public and original sources of information. This role is played in two ways: the media selectively screen information, and they then interpret it for the general public. This process of filtering and interpreting is referred to as the **correlation function** of media.

With the virtual explosion of information, people find it difficult to keep abreast of even their professional specialties, let alone their various other interests—to say nothing of topics about which they care little. In a sense the media predigest information for the public.

The media also help people interpret the news. Although this function usually appears in the form of editorials, letters to the editor, and special reports, the process of interpretation also influences what is represented as news. Rarely does an important public figure deliver an address on television without a corps of reporters offering instant analysis both before and after the statement. Although this process is fraught with dangers, few people have the time or expertise to fulfill the interpretive function for themselves. One purpose of this chapter is to make you more qualified to interpret information for yourself so that you can better evaluate the interpretations made by the media.

Education. Every community has a need to transmit its culture from one generation to the next. Preliterate cultures transmitted their heritages for centuries by means of oral communication. With the invention of the printing press in 1450, not only did universal literacy become a societal goal but the printed word became a means for recording social heritage and transmitting it to large numbers of people. Free public education—a relatively recent development of nineteenth-century America—further facilitated this transmission process. However, with the advent of radio and television broadcasting in the first half of the twentieth century, the emphasis once again shifted from written to oral communication and transmission of cultural heritage. Now emerging generations spend twice as much time viewing television as they spend in school, and the media's importance in transmitting culture has become paramount. In fact, Marshall McLuhan referred to our television-oriented world as a "global village."

Although the media serve the useful purpose of transmitting culture, the possibility for dysfunction has increased. How accurately do the media represent past events and cultural values? Is the gradual increase in violence and sex in television a reflection of the past or a self-fulfilling prophecy? We believe that commercial and political influences on the media (which we will discuss in a following section) have somewhat distorted the media's transmission of culture.

The increased emphasis on broadcast media has been blamed, at least in part, for a reduced importance of the written word and interpersonal communication in transmitting culture. One of the authors was surprised to discover during a recent visit to a Sioux reservation that many of the young people had not heard of their tribe's most famous ancestor—Sitting Bull—and yet everyone had a television set and watched it for hours every day.

Entertainment. By far the greatest amount of the time people spend watching television is devoted to entertainment programming. On radio there is greater emphasis on music and news, and the print media balance news, advertising, and commentary, but on the whole, the most widespread function of the media continues to be entertainment. Whether the media will meet the challenge of helping people use their ever increasing leisure time more constructively and creatively remains to be seen.

Advertising. A final function of the media is usually referred to as advertising, a term that unfortunately carries the connotation of merchants influencing, if not manipulating, people to buy their products. We prefer to think of this function more transactionally. Advertising can serve a mutual benefit to both buyer and seller. Dysfunction occurs when merchants use irresponsible advertising practices. For example, some advertisers publicize a special offer at a ridiculously low price but fail to point out that the product is only available in limited quantities. They hope, of course, to attract buyers to the store and then sell them a more expensive product or one on which the profit is greater. Such abuses of advertising are illegal, but regulation is poor, and buyers must still "beware."

Influences on the Media

In the early years of radio the airwaves were relatively free and unregulated. A small station had to do little more than select a frequency to go into business. Soon stations operating on the same frequency were broadcasting overlapping signals. Chaos resulted. Strong demands from radio stations themselves and from the general public resulted in the Federal Radio Act of 1927, which established the Federal Radio Commission as the chief regulator of the broadcast industry. Since that time, the **Federal Communication Commission (FCC)**, as the agency was renamed, has attempted to regulate the broadcast industry "in the public interest, convenience and necessity." Despite this mandate, however, the media have rarely been run "in the public interest, convenience and necessity." The main reasons are economic and political.

Several economic factors influence functioning of the media. The broadcast media, for example, operate on a fairly narrow spectrum of frequencies. The result is a scarcity of a marketable commodity (which is changing with the establishment of cable and satellite services). Furthermore, the power of the broadcast media to reach large numbers of consumers makes transmission a precious economic resource.

Regulation of the media brings two American values into opposition—freedom of speech and expression frequently conflict with the "public good," especially when sex and violence are explicitly portrayed during prime time. Finally, technological innovations such as cable have led to conflicting interests that the FCC did not foresee, thus creating regulatory problems.

All these economic variables have created a political climate within which the FCC must attempt to operate "in the public interest." Pressures are brought to bear on the FCC from a variety of sources. As a creation of the U.S. Congress, the FCC receives pressure not only through official action but also from individual Congressmembers. Various segments of the executive branch also exert pressure. In addition, decisions by the FCC can be reviewed by the courts. And pressure also comes from the broadcast industry itself. Influential lobbyists are paid by the networks—as well as by other large corporations that have an interest in media regulation—to circulate among FCC members and Congressmembers in order to influence FCC decisions. In recent years citizens' groups with special interests have increasingly been able to make their opinions felt. Nonetheless, citizens who are not associated with such groups remain unrepresented.

Another reason for the "wasteland" image of the media is the industry's economic motivation. Every corporation is in business to make money. In the broadcast industry, the more viewers who watch a particular program or time segment, the more the networks and stations can charge sponsors for advertising time. For example, thirty seconds of television commercial time during the 1995 premier of "Jurassic Park" cost $650,000. This means that the networks watch the various ratings very closely; a drop of one or two percentage points may result in the loss of many thousands of dollars in advertising time and, perhaps, the cancellation of a program. In a sense the American public receives the kind of programming people want—or at least are willing to watch. Although a few substantive series such as *60 Minutes* and *Nova* have attracted a significant number of viewers, in general the "wasteland" of programming about which so many people complain is, in fact, what Americans make economically feasible by watching in large numbers.

As we have seen, policy and programming decisions affecting the broadcast industry tend to be made not according to artistic or cultural criteria but more on the basis of economic and political pressures. If neither the industry nor the government evaluates broadcast programming for us, what can we, as individuals, do to evaluate mediated messages for ourselves? We return to this question later in the chapter.

Uses and Effects of Mass Media

One long-time theory of mass communication has been called the hypodermic needle approach: the media inject the public with a dose of something, and the public responds in unison. The theory is passé, however, because it is overly simple and denies the transactional nature

Sometimes a news story presents only one side's data, especially if that group stages a "media event."

of communication. Yet this theory has led to a plethora of research studies about media effects. For example, how does television violence affect society? Does pornography increase sex crimes? How effective is political advertising? Research into such questions has not uncovered generalizations. Almost always, the answer has been, "It depends."

The public is not single-minded. Various audiences use media in different ways, and not all audiences depend equally on media information. People often select programming to meet their needs. In other words, people actively use media rather than passively receiving media messages. This may explain why media tend to reinforce rather than change attitudes.

The degree to which a given group relies on a medium for its information depends on two factors.[2] First, a group becomes more dependent on a given medium when that medium supplies information that is central to the group's needs. For example, every month or so, faculty members at one university receive a legislative news bulletin that they do not normally consider very important and often ignore. Once, however, the legislature was working on a salary plan that would give each faculty member a substantial retroactive payment. Suddenly the legislative bulletin took on new significance as faculty members depended on it for important information.

The second factor that affects a group's dependency on media is the group's social stability. When a group is undergoing change, conflict is high as norms and values change. At such times, media seem to have more influence.

Because groups vary in their media dependency, media affect different segments of society in a number of ways. First, media information can serve to reduce ambiguity. When people are confused about events, they often turn to the media for clarification. Second, media can influence attitudes, especially among people who are neutral about an issue. Third, media communications can set agendas; people use media to decide which issues are more or less important. Fourth, media can expand people's belief systems, adding new beliefs to old. Finally, media can clarify values, giving people a more distinct sense of what is important to them personally. This effect may come into play when major events such as abortion protests create conflict and precipitate self-examination.

IMPROVING MEDIA RECEIVERSHIP

Theoretically, this section could have been placed almost anywhere in the book, because reception is an integral part of all communication transactions. For that reason, many of the principles discussed here should help you in interpersonal, group, and public settings as well as with public media. Yet this discussion most belongs here because reception is absolutely central to the consumption of mass communication. It is just about the only aspect of the mass communication transaction that most of us can control.

Basically, reception of messages includes four aspects: assimilation, comprehension, retention, and critical evaluation. **Assimilation** is the process of getting the message into your nervous system and registering it. Our concern here is not with the mechanics of seeing or hearing, which are physiological processes outside the scope of this text. Rather, we are interested in the psychological and social processes that contribute to taking a message into the nervous system.

Perhaps you have heard children repeat something you have said perfectly, only to learn later that they did not understand a single word they were saying. This is pure assimilation, without the other aspects of the listening process. It involves focusing attention on the message, perceiving it as accurately and as objectively as possible, and processing it with an open mind so as not to exclude information.

After assimilation comes **comprehension**, the degree to which one person's image or concept corresponds to that of other communicators. This involves decoding and conceptualizing the message in the same way the transmitter does. Relatively full comprehension usually includes grasping the central idea or theme of the message as well as the structure or interrelationships of its components. The degree to which the other communicator can say "you seem to understand" is the degree to which comprehension has occurred.

Retention is another term for **memory**. Assimilating and comprehending a message is not much use if you forget it immediately. Retention can be enhanced by repetition, a common practice in media advertising.

The final aspect of the listening process is critical evaluation. This is the process by which you analyze the components of the message in terms of their consistency and reasonableness.

These four aspects of the receiving process are usually sequential, but not always. For instance, you might assimilate and retain a message without comprehending it. And any of these processes can occur in varying degrees of efficiency. However, your skill as a media receiver depends largely on the competence with which you assimilate, comprehend, retain, and critically evaluate the messages to which you are exposed.

Improving Assimilation

There are two general approaches to media consumption. The first, which we call nonselection, consists of thoughtlessly consuming whatever programming is available at the moment, just to pass the time. If no programs are desirable, you select whichever one is least objectionable. If you have your television or radio on all the time, you probably are a nonselecting receiver. Most of us are nonselectors from time to time, but productive assimilation can be achieved through channeled consumption. Following are some guidelines for achieving this healthier kind of media consumption.

First, be sensitive to the functions of various programs in your own life. Assess your needs, and seek programming that will fulfill them at a given time. After a hard day's work, for example, a light, even silly television show may be just what you need to relax. At other times, you may seek the function of surveillance, and *Dave's World* simply will not do. Don't be a slave to programming; let it be a slave to you.

Second, be an active program chooser. If you find yourself checking the television listings each week and noting which programs you want to see, you are on the right track.

Third, be open to new kinds of programming. Millions of people have never seen a program on PBS because they automatically dismiss this network as being "educational." Other people never watch locally produced programs simply because they think the shows will not be entertaining.

Finally, remember that mass communication, like communication in all settings, is transaction. You have to give as well as receive; you have to participate by thinking.

Improving Comprehension and Retention

Comprehension and retention are especially important when you use the mass media for other than entertainment purposes. Have you ever been driving along in your car with the radio on, your mind wandering, when a newscast caught your attention? As you focused on the program, you probably became concerned about understanding the message clearly and remembering its important points to tell others later. Mostly, good listening is a matter of concentration and motivation. Here are some guidelines for improving your listening habits:

1. Be mentally and physically prepared to listen.
2. Stop talking.
3. Develop a desire to listen.
4. Think about the topic in advance, when possible.
5. Start listening immediately.
6. Determine the personal value of the topic for you.
7. Be courteous.
8. Listen and evaluate the content of the message, instead of judging the speaker's appearance or delivery.
9. Avoid stereotyping the speaker.
10. Hear the speaker out before you judge.
11. Try to determine the speaker's intent or purpose.
12. Listen for main ideas, principles, and concepts.
13. Look for relationships among ideas.
14. Take notes.
15. Concentrate to avoid distractions.
16. Do not allow emotions to reduce your concentration on content.
17. Listen with empathy.

Basically, these principles indicate that good listening is not passive; it requires concentration and active mental participation. This is true of listening in all settings, including media programming.

Another method of improving comprehension and retention is to bolster your reception of the message through interpersonal transaction. In other words, talk with others about the programs and information you receive through the media. Contrary to popular belief, watching television and listening to the radio can be highly social. The authors have had many stimulating discussions—not only during commercials but sometimes for days afterward—about what they have seen on television. If you are like most people, much of your conversation during automobile trips probably deals with what you hear on the radio while driving.

Finally, rely on multiple media accounts. The best consumers of the mass media expose themselves to all forms—films, newspapers, periodicals (mass and specialized), radio and television broadcasts, and books. Your comprehension of messages and your retention of information will be enhanced by comparing and contrasting ideas from different media. For example, you could compare a news event as reported in newspapers, on television news shows, in weekly news magazines, and on radio talk shows.

Improving Critical Evaluation

The study of media appeals has generally focused on two major areas: content and technique. Traditionally, people have been more concerned with evaluating the content of mediated messages—the data provided and the claims that are made. Just as important, however, are the techniques used to produce those messages. Lighting, camera angles, the size of images, and other technical considerations can be evaluated in terms of their effects on media consumers. We believe that the best way to evaluate mediated messages is to develop competence in both areas—content and techniques.

In a sense, everything people know about the communication process enables them to evaluate messages—mediated and otherwise—more effectively. Virtually every concept and principle discussed in this book should enhance your critical evaluation of communicative behavior. However, because our particular focus in this section concerns receiving messages, we will examine the critical thinking process as it relates to testing data, claims, and techniques.

Evaluation of Content: Data. There are some questions that people should ask about any evidence. Perhaps the first question to ask about data is "Are the data consistent with themselves and with other data?" Have you ever had the feeling that a "fact" you have heard does not sound right? Children sometimes quote their teachers as having said something that parents are certain could not be accurate because it conflicts with dependable data they already know. This sense of consistency is usually based on a somewhat informal test, and it can be misleading. Sometimes what we think we "know" is itself inaccurate. Many scientific discoveries at first seem to violate all the laws of nature and people; consider what happened to the first people to claim the earth was round. Nonetheless, a sense of inconsistency—whether an informal feeling or one based upon a rigorous search for conflicting data—is frequently the first clue that data may be spurious.

You should also consider whether the data are described in sufficient detail to be meaningful and should ask "Are the data specific?" You should automatically discount such general references to authority as "Everyone knows . . ." or "Psychologists have proved . . ." Such vague references should make you wonder whether the communicator really knows something or is making it up. Likewise, in the use of examples and statistics, references to vague cases often seem more hypothetical than real. Imprecise references that do not describe the population, sampling procedures, methods of analysis, or conclusions in precise terms should cause suspicion. Even a seemingly precise word like average can mean very different things depending on how normally the population is distributed and whether the reporter is using the mean, median, or mode to represent the average.

In the discussion of stereotyping in Chapter 3 we observed that everyone generalizes. Clustering data is a necessary way of processing information. When confronted with generalized messages, however, the receiver must probe for specific information. For example, many advertisers claim, "Our product is better." Better than what? The implication is that the product is better than every other competing product. When pressed, however, the advertisers may have to admit that the product is only better than one other (very bad) product or only better than it was before, which could still be relatively inferior. Another familiar generality takes a form like "Scientists say . . ." What specific scientist says so? Only a qualified scientist can reasonably claim that "scientists say."

A final general test of data is "How current are the data?" Though there are significant exceptions to this generalization, the more current the data, the more dependable they tend to be. Given the exponential rate of change in our understanding of the world, information rapidly becomes obsolete.

During his term as governor of California, Ronald Reagan was quoted as saying, "If you've seen one redwood tree, you've seen them all." But have you? Imagine that you have two large vases, or urns, in front of you. One contains a hundred glass marbles, and the other contains a hundred tablespoons of vegetable soup. You take one marble out of the first urn and find that the marble is white. What color are the other ninety-nine marbles? You can infer that they are all white, but that is a tenuous conclusion. You take out a second marble, which is blue. Are the marbles half white and half blue? A third marble is white. Are they two-thirds white and one-third blue? With each marble your concept of the color of all the marbles becomes more accurate—that is, your inference becomes more dependable.

Now turn to the urn of soup. Stir it vigorously and taste one tablespoon of the mixture. How will the other ninety-nine tablespoons of soup taste? You can dependably infer that they will taste very much like the single tablespoon you tasted.

This example of the marbles and the soup illustrates our three concerns about statistics and examples as data. The critical question concerns representativeness of samples. Obviously, one spoonful of soup tells us almost all we need to know about the taste of the soup. But one marble does not tell us about the other ninety-nine marbles. The difference is that the spoonful of soup is an accurate sample of the entire urn—at least in terms of the relevant variable, taste. When dealing with most life situations, however, one example does not accurately represent a large population of people, social problems, or events. Like the marbles, human events are distinct; one example cannot represent all possibilities.

Achieving a reasonable or approximate representativeness requires an adequate number of either examples or subjects. If a margarine salesperson asks one or even a half-dozen shoppers to compare the tastes of margarine and butter, will their comparisons accurately represent those of two hundred million Americans? Probably not; as in the case of the marbles, usually the larger the sample, the more accurate the inference. On the other hand, if the representativeness of the sample can be increased, dependable inferences can be drawn from a relatively small number of instances. Consider the accuracy with which political commentators predict the outcome of an election on the basis of a few key voting districts.

Of course, there are almost always exceptions to any rule. You can usually find oddball examples to prove almost anything. When you sample the soup, for instance, you might come up with the only onion in the entire urn, "proving" that it is an urn full of onion soup. As a transmitter you should account for exceptional cases by saying something like, "Of course, you will find a few cases of (such and such), but generally . . ." As a receiver you must assess whether the examples or statistics you receive are based on the typical majority or on the atypical exceptions.

Because of the aura of credibility surrounding statistics and examples, more and more mass media commercials use such data to make claims of superiority. No doubt some of these statistical studies are carefully conducted, and some of the case studies are authentic and typical. Many more, unfortunately, are conducted by biased sources. Contrary examples and statistical results may be suppressed, and often the advertising claims are based on inadequate data. Consumers should be suspicious enough to seek corroborative data that support the examples and statistics in media advertisements as well as in other communication contexts.

When Crest toothpaste was introduced, it received the endorsement of the American Dental Association, and its sales soared. One of the most frequent techniques of media advertising involves endorsement by a famous person, usually a sports figure or an entertainment celebrity. Magic Johnson, Bill Cosby, Madonna, and Michael J. Fox have endorsed products by appearing in their commercials. It is apparently necessary to remind ourselves of what almost everyone should know: that is, celebrities are paid to communicate endorsements, which are usually written by someone else, for products that the celebrities may know little about.

Some endorsements are legitimate, of course, but most testimonials raise serious questions. For example, is the quoted authority competent in the relevant field? Although it may seem obvious that athletes are more competent to tell how to hit a baseball or tennis ball than to evaluate, say, stereo equipment, many people are taken in by such testimonial ads. To obtain an objective, comparative analysis of coffee makers, you might consult *Consumer Reports* rather than relying on the word of an actor who claims to have "tried them all." Indeed, any homemaker would probably have more competence in such matters. But advertisers have become more subtle. Now an actress poses as a competent homemaker and then endorses a coffee maker.

Another question to consider is whether a quoted authority has had sufficient opportunity to observe the data. Even a competent authority may not have been close enough to the event to observe the data firsthand. For example, the witness of a traffic accident is surely more authoritative about that particular accident than the police chief in an office miles from the scene of the accident. Some people with authoritative titles or reputations may actually be less current in their field and less aware of the particular issues than someone who is less well known but better qualified.

You also should consider whether the source is biased. Always ask, "What's in it for this person?" As we have pointed out, most celebrities who offer testimonials are paid for their efforts. Similarly, in political campaigns endorsements may be given in exchange for future favors. We noted in Chapter 3 that people actually process what should be "objective" observations in very selective ways. Thus, sources with a strong bias may report what they think is an objective observation but which is in fact an inference that has been distorted or screened by bias.

Evaluation of Content: Claims. Messages can be tested not only by their data but also by the care with which claims are drawn from those data. Here we will focus on two special classes of faulty claims: (1) faulty causal claims and (2) diversions or substitutions.

Many claims attempt to establish a relationship between an effect and a cause. Such causal claims can result from the attempt to infer a purported cause from an observed effect; a projected effect from an observable cause; or an unobserved effect from an observed effect,

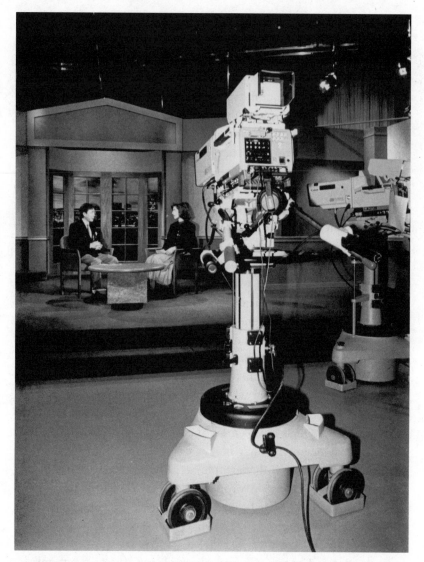

A person being interviewed on a television broadcast usually has goals besides just offering information. Viewers need to employ critical evaluation in order to ascertain those goals.

both of which have the same cause. We will discuss three types of faulty causal claims: part (or insufficient) cause, post hoc, and non sequitur.

The fallacy of part cause results from the false assumption that an effect in some complex process results from only one cause rather than several causes. How often do we hear either labor or management blaming the other's demands as the single cause of inflation, when any economist can list dozens of factors that contribute to inflation? Much difficulty can be avoided if you remember that in most cases the effects of complex social problems cannot be attributed to a single cause but frequently result from several variables or causes.

Post hoc ergo propter hoc is a Latin phrase that means "after this, therefore because of this." Suppose a black cat crosses the road in front of you on the way to class and you fail an examination that day. Does it make sense to blame the black cat? Most superstitions are based on the post hoc fallacy. Although effects naturally follow causes, not everything that follows a particular act or event results from that phenomenon; most effects, in fact, are coincidental.

Non sequitur is the formal term that logicians have given to causal reasoning in which the effect simply does not follow from the purported cause. For example, a radio commercial recently asserted, "Buying a used car deserves as much care and attention as buying a new car; so come to our dealership and look over our selection of quality used cars."

Diversionary claims are among the most common found in media appeals. These claims divert attention from the data or subject at hand by substituting an irrelevant claim that on the surface seems germane.

Name calling has been referred to as the **ad hominem** fallacy. It involves diverting attention by substituting a personal attack for an answer to the relevant claims. For example, someone who is criticizing a politician may be challenged by the rejoinder, "You have no right to talk; you didn't even vote in the last election!" But the speaker's voting record is completely irrelevant to the topic of the politician's competence.

Many of us are familiar with such pejorative terms as "redneck," "knee-jerk liberal," and "pointy-headed intellectual," as well as ethnic slurs. On the other hand, honorific terms can also be used as labels, such as "well educated," "equalitarian," "good family man," "loving mother," and "patriot." We must probe beyond such diversionary labels, good or bad, and ask, "What does the label really say about the person? Is it accurate? To what degree is it comprehensive?"

Appeal to tradition or custom is another diversion or substitution. When young people challenge an institutionalized act or event, they are frequently silenced by "Well, we've always done it this way." Although it is reasonable to favor existing methods or tried-and-true products, a relevant challenge should be met with substantive data and claims rather than merely with tradition.

Repeated affirmation is another frequently used media appeal. It reflects the idea that if you repeat a lie often enough, people will believe it. Essentially the argument goes: "It is so, because it is so, because it is so," and so on. People who are not careful to ask for the data may respond to such repeated affirmation as though it were based on data.

Another way to divert attention from the question is to substitute irrelevant emotional messages (verbal and nonverbal) for relevant data in support of claims. Virtually every advertisement attempts to elicit noncritical response on the basis of beliefs, attitudes, values, or motives in the absence of data—and frequently contrary to existing data. This approach is epitomized in cigarette advertisements that suggest both verbally and nonverbally that smoking is cool, clean, and fresh, even though most people experience cigarette smoke as hot, contaminated, and stale.

Another diversion or substitution is the use of **transfer** or (negatively) guilt by association. With this technique, competing products or people are discredited on the basis of associations with friends, relatives, organizations, or personal characteristics: "She must be immoral; just look at the crowd she runs with." Transfer is also used to build up a product. For example, automobiles are presented in luxurious or scenic surroundings, and mattresses are demonstrated by beautiful women in evening gowns.

A final diversion or substitution is that of psychological appeals. Most motivation theorists agree that people share a desire to belong, to be accepted by their peer group. The **bandwagon technique** plays on this basic human desire by suggesting that "everyone is doing it." Almost every advertiser would like to be able to claim, "More people buy our product than any other; shouldn't you?" When confronted with the bandwagon technique, always ask, "Yes, but does this meet my individual needs? Does it stand the test of evaluation by objective criteria to which I personally have given priority?"

Plain folks is in one sense an extension of the bandwagon idea of not being too different. It also contains elements of the general public's latent distrust of excellence in general and intellectuality in particular. Notice how many politicians try to come off as "just a common person." In any political campaign you will see candidates of great reputation and sophistication kissing babies, riding horses, eating local ethnic foods, and playing softball in an attempt to demonstrate that even though they aspire to lead the city, state, or nation, they are just "plain folks."

Card stacking is the term commonly used to refer to one-sided arguments. That is, the message stacks all the arguments in favor of the desired point of view and ignores the arguments on the opposite side of the question. Research has indicated that one-sided arguments are not universally effective, however. With listeners who are initially favorable or neutral, one-sided messages can be effective. But with listeners who are initially opposed to the proposal, a balanced argument tends to be more effective. This is one characteristic of the so-called soft sell as opposed to the lopsided hard sell. The advertisement or salesperson will say, "Our product does not work perfectly, of course, but it is still the best." Remember that even apparently "fair" disclaimers are still a form of card stacking in that they do not list all or even as many of the product's disadvantages as they do advantages. Basically, a weak

Sources with a strong bias often make appeals that lack objective support.

disclaimer is made in order to enhance credibility without destroying the essential one-sided nature of the argument.

We have seen that media content can be effectively evaluated by looking critically at both data and claims. Now let us turn to the evaluation of media techniques.

Evaluation of Technique. In Chapter 3 we discussed the process of abstracting through the use of language. We noted that human beings perceive the world subjectively and selectively. The intervention of media greatly exacerbates this tendency. Here we will examine three processes that influence the reception of content: (1) the willingness to suspend disbelief when receiving mediated messages, (2) the filtering of message content, and (3) the alteration of the messages that are transmitted.

Although people tend to blame the media for misunderstandings and misrepresentations, an important part of that process is our own attitude or mind-set. When we watch a movie or a play, we learn very early that it is not "for real"—that we must suspend disbelief and accept certain illusions in order to enjoy the experience. From willing suspension of disbelief it is only a short step to the uncritical acceptance of television and radio entertainment. Broadcast documentaries and news shows carry an even greater image of "reality" or "truth," and even well-educated adults accept most of what they read in books, magazines, and newspapers. Of course, much of this information is based on actual events, but the objectivity and accuracy with which it is reported varies widely, and different slants or perspectives are inevitable. It is easy to find conflicting accounts of public events in newspapers and magazines with different editorial perspectives. Realize, however, that the question "Is it fact or fantasy?" is not a yes-or-no question. All mediated messages are to a degree fantasy; at best they represent only a selective presentation of the "facts."

Before you observe or read any mediated message, it has been filtered, or screened, by a number of people. The first filtering occurs at the point of initial collection of information. Any newsworthy event is covered by reporters from newspapers and magazines as well as radio and television stations and also, if the event is big enough, from international news services. These reporters wield great power over

Reporters are the first in a chain of media representatives to filter information before it reaches the public.

your transaction with the media. Out of a plethora of possibilities, whom do they choose to photograph or record? A political rally can appear to be deserted or crowded, depending on whether the camera operator photographs vacant seats or filled ones. Presumption of guilt or innocence can be created depending on whether the reporter interviews a sobbing relative of the victim or an equally distraught loved one of the accused criminal.

Next, the writer or writing team filters the message content. Not all data can be included in a news story or even in a lengthy documentary or book. Choices are made about what to include and what to leave out. Even historians—who use a supposedly objective, scholarly approach—can represent events very differently from one another.

The message is next examined by a series of editors who further filter what is transmitted. Stories are shortened, rewritten, and even eliminated. Decisions are made about the priority and position that news stories will have in the newspaper, magazine, or newscast. Film editors cut and paste footage, altering or eliminating scenes.

It is always wise to pay as much attention to what is not represented in mediated messages as to what is represented. Remember that the message has been filtered through countless reporters, camera operators, writers, directors, and editors. Consider the broader context of each picture or statement. Have all sides been fairly represented?

Not only are mediated messages filtered by a variety of individuals, but the technology of the media itself provides several ways of altering the message.

The first method of altering the transmission is through the compression or extension of visual and aural space and time. Virtually every television or film drama condenses space and time to fit the artistic needs of the plot. A zoom lens can shift the perspective from foreground to background or from panorama to closeup while people watch, almost unaware. Directional microphones pick up minute sounds at great distances while excluding other sounds nearby. Segments of life are distorted by eliminating the boring or the mundane. Frequently, when people experience in real life what they have experienced only vicariously through the media, they are let down and disappointed because the real-life experience does not move as rapidly and thus is not as exciting as the mediated image.

Time and space can also be expanded. Several cameras can be used to film a segment of life, and the film can then be edited to repeat the event, often from different perspectives. Instant replays of spectacular performances in sporting events are a familiar case in point. Events that may pass in a fleeting moment in real life may be stretched into a full-length television show, novel, or movie.

In the case of either the compression or extension of time, remember that the image of reality is being distorted. The assumption that the image even approximates reality can lead to significant difficulties in both judgment and behavior.

Another way that the transmission can be altered is by manipulating the juxtaposition of images and events. This screening is done in many ways. People are most aware of the editorial process, in which the editor, perhaps responding to constraints of space and cost, cuts certain portions of a story and emphasizes others. Once the administration building of a university was the scene of a demonstration by a few hundred students, less than two percent of the student body. One of the authors was working in a nearby building and would not have been aware of the event if he had not inadvertently glanced out the window. It seemed a minor matter at the time. But on the evening news, close-up photographs of the shouting and speeches made the demonstration look almost like a riot. The ninety-eight percent of the students who were quietly attending classes were not pictured; their story went unreported.

During any movie your mood will be influenced by the music that accompanies the images on the screen. Similarly, during a newscast, the pictures accompanying the story can create a context that constitutes an essentially different transaction than the same story read in the daily newspaper. Finally, entire stories as well as events and images can be so arranged during the editing process that relationships can be suggested that do not actually exist. This is particularly true of causal relationships.

One important aspect of the relationship between images and events is the interruption of broadcast programming by commercial messages. Many commercial television and radio stations plan the flow of their regular programming with great care, paying special attention to the relationship between the programming and the content or image depicted in the commercials.

In most television programs, too, there is an interesting relationship between the aural track and the visual images. The aural track is used primarily to communicate plot information, while the visual track is used to develop such affective dimensions as color, impact, and excitement. More conventional dramatic continuity is maintained by what is heard; the visual track can be a somewhat disjointed collage of images that reinforce the aural message. The exception to this general rule is the use of music, which is overlaid on both the dialogue and the visual image.

A final and very significant way in which technique can manipulate impression is through animation and electronic alteration of image. Computer animation techniques are so impressive now that extremely realistic images can be created from scratch, as any viewer of the film *The Mask* can testify. More alarming and potentially dangerous than animation are techniques for altering audio and video images. With the digitization of sound and video, false impressions can be made to seem very real.

In digitized video, for example, one can easily change individual pixels of a video display image by computer to change some aspect of the picture. For example, an object in the original video might be removed or placed in a different location. One of the authors recently saw a demonstration in which the face of a counselor in a videotaped group therapy session was altered to look like the actor Billy Crystal. The message is clear: Don't assume that what you see or hear on audiotape or videotape is real.

Seeing through the Cultural Production. The various methods discussed above—the use of certain forms of data, claims, and techniques—enable producers to arrange symbols in a way that creates a certain meaning or impression. These images—whether in commercials, news programs, documentaries, or entertainment media—constitute an important part of our cultural reality.[3] In other words, our beliefs about what is real and right is heavily influenced by media messages.

This does not mean that media producers are solely responsible for our cultural images. As we have seen, producers too are influenced by a host of transactional factors beyond their control. Nor does it mean that there is some kind of conscious conspiracy or intent to do harm. When an advertiser, for example, makes a commercial, the aim is to depict the product in as positive a light as possible and to make money, not to hurt anybody.

Still, when media producers create a message, certain meanings are dominant and intended to influence us in certain ways, and often these meanings contribute to and reflect the dominant interests of powerful groups. Even though producers do not mean to do so, they almost always promote the interests of powerful groups over those of less powerful ones, sometimes even to the detriment of certain groups of people.

It is vital for citizens to realize that the images and meanings projected in media messages are not the only way to read those messages. Other, often very important images can also come through if you are willing to suspend your belief long enough to look for them. We call the intended message of a media producer the **dominant reading** and alternative meanings **oppositional readings.** This distinction just refers to the fact that a message can be deliberately read or understood in a way that opposes the dominant interests being promoted by the producers.

For example, a beautiful and nearly naked woman may attract attention to a car in a magazine advertisement. The advertiser's intention is to appeal to male audience members and to sell the car, pure and simple. A feminist group, however, may read the message in an entirely different way. A news reporter may state that a "black" man was observed running from the scene of a crime, and civil rights groups may read this news report in a way that the reporter never intended. A movie may tell the story of a company town and logging operations in rural America, and ecologists may read the film in ways that ordinary citizens do not. All of these are oppositional readings.

There are two important reasons to look for opposing meanings and images in media messages. First, this kind of reception makes people constantly aware that more than one reading is always possible. It sensitizes us to the effects created by the data, claims, and techniques of media producers, and we become less susceptible to them. In other words, we become good critics. Second, oppositional readings expose the dominant interests of media producers and some of the ways that people can be hurt by these messages.

In a remarkable and dramatic documentary entitled *Dreamworlds,* filmmaker Sut Jhally presents an oppositional reading of rock music videos. By carefully taking apart the images and techniques of these productions, the filmmaker shows how they fulfill an adolescent sexual fantasy in which women are objectified and depersonalized. He goes on to show persuasively how these media messages are part of a larger cultural construction that can and does lead to violence against women.

When we show this film in our classes, students are skeptical at first, thinking the documentary to be some silly "political correctness" thing, but by the end of the program, they are almost universally persuaded about the importance of the filmmaker's oppositional reading in uncovering important meanings that would otherwise go unnoticed.

SUMMARY

In this chapter we have looked at the mass media of communication from the standpoint of improving the consumption of mediated messages. You will be a more competent consumer of the media if you approach them from the transactional perspective rather than from the one-step flow model, the two-step flow model, or the multistep flow model. The media serve several functions (and can create dysfunctions) in our society. The main functions are surveillance, correlation, education, entertainment, and advertising. Awareness of the political and economic influences on the media, along with an understanding of the uses and effects of media, will enhance your ability to evaluate messages.

Receivership skills can be improved by understanding the listening process and improving assimilation. Skills can be developed further by increasing comprehension and retention, which involve listening actively, attending to the interpersonal transaction, and using multiple media.

Finally, receivership skills can be enhanced through critical evaluation of the media. This can be accomplished by evaluating both content and techniques. Content is evaluated by testing a variety of claims and the data upon which claims are based. Techniques are evaluated by being sensitive to the willing suspension of disbelief and by examining the various ways in which the message content is filtered and the message is altered during transmission. Finally, receivership skills are enhanced by the realization that a media message can be read in several legitimate ways, and that the intended meaning may not be the best one for society.

Notes

CHAPTER ONE

1. This term was created by philosopher Juergen Habermas. See, for example, Sonja K. Foss, Karen A. Foss, and Robert Trapp, *Contemporary Perspectives on Rhetoric* (Prospect Heights, Ill.: Waveland Press, 1991), pp. 262–266.

2. *McGraw-Hill Encyclopedia of Science and Technology* (New York: McGraw-Hill, 1966), p. 137.

3. D. Larsen, *The Flow of Information* (New York: Harper & Row, 1958), p. 5.

4. M. P. Andersen, "What Is Communication? *Journal of Communication*, 9 (1959), p. 5.

5. Dale Hample, "Argument: Public, Private, Social and Cognitive," *Argumentation and Advocacy* 25 (1988): 13–19.

6. Deborah Tannen, *You Just Don't Understand: Women and Men in Conversation* (New York: Ballantine, 1994).

7. This section on process is drawn heavily from L. Hawes, "Elements of a Model for Communication Processes," *Quarterly Journal of Speech*, 59 (1973), pp. 11–21.

8. For more detailed discussion of social construction, see Stephen W. Littlejohn, *Theories of Human Communication* (Belmont, Calif.: Wadsworth Publishing, 1996), chap. 8–9.

9. This discussion of functionality is drawn from Frank Dance and Carl Larson, (New York: Holt, 1976), and from Hawes (note 7).

10. Pamela Benoit, et al. "From 'Jet Screaming Hootie Queen' to 'Talking to Ralph': An Undergraduate Slang Dictionary" (paper presented at the Speech Communication Association meeting, Chicago, October 1992).

11. René Descartes, *Second Meditation.*

12. For a good general discussion of cognitivism, see Vincent R. Waldron and Donald J. Cegala, "Assessing Conversational Cognition: Levels of Theory and Associated Methodological Requirements," *Human Communication Research*, 18 (1992): 599–622.

13. Leslie A. White, "The Symbol: The Origin and Basis of Human Behavior," in *The Science of Culture*, ed. Leslie White (New York: Farrar, Straus & Cudahy, 1949), p. 34.

14. Example from Stanley Deetz, *Democracy in an Age of Corporate Colonization: Developments in Communication and the Politics of Everyday Life* (Albany: State University of New York Press, 1992), p. 127.

CHAPTER TWO

1. Dyirbal categories are discussed in George Lakoff, *Women, Fire and Dangerous Things: What Categories Reveal about the Mind* (Chicago: University of Chicago Press, 1987), pp. 92–96.

2. The study of signs is called semiotics. For an introduction, see Arthur Asa Berger, *Signs in Contemporary Culture: An Introduction to Semiotics* (Salem, Wis.: Sheffield Publishing, 1989). See also Stephen W. Littlejohn, *Theories of Human Communication* (Belmont, Calif.: Wadsworth, 1996), chap. 4.

3. Gerard Egan, *Encounters* (Belmont, Calif.: Brooks/Cole, 1970), p. 248.

4. Paul Watzlawick, Janet Beavin, and Don Jackson, *Pragmatics of Human Communication* (New York: Norton, 1967).

5. For a good introduction to discourse, see Jonathan Potter and Margaret Wetherell, *Discourse and Social Psychology: Beyond Attitudes and Behavior* (London: Sage Publications, 1987). See also Littlejohn, *Theories*, chap. 5.

6. See, for example, Michael Motley, "On Whether One Can(not) Not Communicate: An Examination via Traditional Communication Postulates," *Western Journal of*

Speech Communication, 54 (1990): 1–20; and Peter A. Andersen, "When One Cannot Not Communicate: A Challenge to Motley's Traditional Communication Postulates," *Communication Studies*, 42 (1991), pp. 309–325.

7. Watzlawick, Beavin, and Jackson, *Pragmatics*.

8. Quoted in B. L. Whorf, *Language, Thought, and Reality* (New York: Wiley, 1956), p. 134.

9. Examples from Joseph Devito, *The Psychology of Speech and Language* (New York: Random House, 1970), pp. 203–204.

10. For a general introduction to nonverbal communication, see Mark L. Knapp and Judith A. Hall, *Nonverbal Communication in Human Interaction* (Fort Worth, Tex.: Holt, Rinehart, & Winston, 1992).

11. Judee K. Burgoon and Thomas Saine, *The Unspoken Dialogue* (Boston: Houghton Mifflin, 1978), p. 54.

12. Ashley Montagu, *Touching: The Significance of the Human Skin* (New York: Columbia University Press, 1971).

13. Edward T. Hall, "Proxemics," *Current Anthropology*, 9 (1968).

14. Ursula Le Guin, *Dancing at the Edge of the World* (New York: Grove Press, 1989), p. 142.

15. Edward T. Hall, *Beyond Culture* (Garden City, N.Y.: Anchor, 1977).

C H A P T E R   T H R E E

1. Willa Cather, *Death Comes for the Archbishop* (New York: Alfred A. Knopf, 1927, p. 274.

2. *Intelligence in the Modern World*. ed. Joseph Ratner (New York: Random House, 1939), p. 813.

3. The fallacy of monousage is discussed by William Haney in *Communication and Organizational Behavior* (Homewood, Ill.: Irwin, 1973).

4. Sut Jhallyn, *Dreamworlds: Desire/Sex/Power in Rock Video* (Amherst: University of Massachusetts, 1990).

5. Hans Georg Gadamer, *Truth and Method* (New York: Seabury Press, 1975).

6. Doug Losee, "Communication within a County Sheriff's Department," International Communication Association, 1975.

7. *The Roosevelt Reader: Selected Speeches, Messages, Press Conferences, and Letters of Franklin D. Roosevelt*, ed. Basil Rauch (New York: Holt, 1964), p. 301.

8. Stephen Toulmin, *The Uses of Argument* (New York: Cambridge University Press, 1964).

9. Stella Vosniadou and Andrew Ortony, *Similarity and Analogical Reasoning* (Cambridge: Cambridge University Press, 1989).

10. For a more complete treatment of this subject, see Walter R. Fisher, *Human Communication as Narration: Toward a Philosophy of Reason, Value, and Action* (Columbia: University of South Carolina Press, 1987).

11. John Dewey, *How We Think* (Boston: Heath, 1933).

12. Several of the problems discussed in this section, including inference-observation confusion, stereotyping, allness, and bypassing, are elaborated in Haney, *Communication and Organizational Behavior*.

13. The obstacles to good problem solving are discussed by Dennis S. Gouran, Randy Y. Hirokawa, Kelly M. Julian, and Geoff B. Leatham, "The Evolution and Current Status of the Functional Perspective on Communication in Decision-Making and Problem-Solving Groups," in *Communication Yearbook 16*, Stanley Deetz, ed. (Newbury Park, Calif.: Sage Publications, 1993), pp. 573–600.

C H A P T E R   F O U R

1. A classic book on this subject is Kenneth Boulding, *The Image* (Ann Arbor: University of Michigan Press, 1956).

2. The idea of information as reducing uncertainty is adapted from technical aspects of information theory. For a recent sum-

mary, see Klaus Krippendorff, "Information Theory," in *International Encyclopedia of Communications*, ed. Erik Barnouw, et al (New York: Oxford University Press, 1989), pp. 214–320.

3. See Janet Beavin Bavelas, Alex Black, Nicole Chovil, and Jennifer Mullett, *Equivocal Communication* (Newbury Park, Calif.: Sage Publications, 1990).

4. Dean E. Hewes and Sally Planalp, "The Individual's Place in Communication Science," in *Handbook of Communication Science*, eds. C. R. Berger and S. H. Chaffee (Newbury Park, Calif.: Sage Publications, 1987), pp. 146–183; Sally Planalp and Dean E. Hewes, "A Cognitive Approach to Communication Theory: *Cogito Ergo Dico?*" in *Communication Yearbook*, ed. M. Burgoon (New Brunswick, N.J.: Transaction, 1982), pp. 49–78.

5. This subject is developed in Dan Sperber and Deirdre Wilson, *Relevance: Communication and Cognition* (Cambridge, Mass.: Harvard University Press, 1986).

6. Sonja Foss and Karen Foss, *Inviting Transformation: Presentational Speaking for a Changing World* (Prospect Heights, Ill.: Waveland Press, 1994), p. 4.

7. These three concepts are discussed in the foundational work: Milton Rokeach, *Beliefs, Attitudes, and Values: A Theory of Organization and Change* (San Francisco: Jossey-Bass, 1968). See also Milton Rokeach, *The Nature of Human Values* (New York: Free Press, 1973), pp. 57–58.

8. For a recent summary of conceptions of attitude, see James Price Dillard, "Persuasion Past and Present: Attitudes Aren't What They Used to Be," *Communication Monographs*, 60 (1993): 90–97; Daniel J. O'Keefe, *Persuasion: Theory and Practice* (Newbury Park: Sage Publications, 1990), pp. 13–27; Richard P. Bagozzi, "Attitudes," in *International Encyclopedia of Communications*, ed. Erik Barnouw et al. (New York: Oxford University Press, 1989), vol. 1, pp. 147–152.

9. For an overview of learning theory, see Stephen B. Klein and Robert R. Mowrer, eds., *Contemporary Learning Theories* (Hillsdale, N.J.: Lawrence Erlbaum Associates, 1989).

10. Kenneth Burke, *Rhetoric of Motives* (Berkeley: University of California Press, 1969).

11. See, for example, O'Keefe, *Persuasion*.

12. Abraham Maslow, *Motivation and Personality* (New York: Harper & Row, 1970).

13. For a more complete discussion of these 7 principles, see Leon Festinger, *A Theory of Cognitive Dissonance* (Stanford, Calif.: Stanford University Press, 1957).

14. Muzafer Sherif, Carolyn Sherif, and Roger Nebergall, *Attitude and Attitude Change: The Social Judgment-Involvement Approach* (Philadelphia: Saunders, 1965); see also O'Keefe, , pp. 29–44.

15. For a general discussion of attribution theory, see Brant R. Burleson, "Attribution Schemes and Causal Inference in Natural Conversations," in *Contemporary Issues in Language and Discourse Processes*, ed. D. G. Ellis and W. A. Donohue (Hillsdale, N.J.: Erlbaum, 1986), pp. 63–86.

16. For an overview, see Mary John Smith, *Persuasion and Human Action: A Review and Critique of Social Influence Theories* (Belmont, Calif.: Wadsworth Publishing, 1982).

17. Martin Fishbein and Icek Ajzen, *Belief, Attitude, Intention, and Behavior* (Reading, Mass.: Addison-Wesley, 1975). See also Bagozzi, "Attitudes."

18. Richard E. Petty and John T. Cacioppo, *Communication and Persuasion: Central and Peripheral Routes to Attitude Change* (New York: Springer-Verlag, 1986); Richard E. Petty and John T. Cacioppo, "The Elaboration Likelihood Model of Persuasion," in *Advances in Experimental Social Psychology*, ed. Leonard Berkowitz, (New York: Academic Press, 1986), pp. 123–205.

For an excellent brief summary, see O'Keefe, *Persuasion*, pp. 95–116.

19. Lane Cooper, *The Rhetoric of Aristotle* (Englewood Cliffs, N.J.: Prentice-Hall, 1932).

20. O'Keefe, *Persuasion*, pp. 130–145.

21. A foundational study on this topic is Kim Giffin, "The Contribution of Studies of Source Credibility to a Theory of Interpersonal Trust in the Communication Process," *Psychological Bulletin*, 68 (1967), pp. 104–120.

22. For a more complete discussion of inducing resistance to change, see Philip G. Zimbardo and Michael R. Leippe, *The Psychology of Attitude Change and Social Influence* (Philadelphia: Temple University Press, 1991), pp. 202–243.

23. Originally attributed to William McGuire, in "Inducing Resistance to Persuasion: Some Contemporary Approaches," in *Advances in Experimental Social Psychology*, ed. L. Berkowitz (New York: Academic Press, 1964), vol. 1, pp. 191–229.

C H A P T E R   F I V E

1. For a good overview of this approach, see Stephen W. Littlejohn, *Theories of Human Communication* (Belmont, Calif.: Wadsworth Publishing, 1996), pp. 86, 186–195.

2. The importance of relationship in interpersonal communication is discussed in a classic treatment by Paul Watzlawick, Janet Beavin, and Dan Jackson in *Pragmatics of Human Communication* (New York: Norton, 1967); see also Steve Duck, *Meaningful Relationships: Talking, Sense, and Relating* (Thousand Oaks, Calif.: Sage Publications, 1994).

3. W. Barnett Pearce, *Communication and the Human Condition* (Carbondale: Southern Illinois University Press, 1989).

4. These three needs have been noted repeatedly in the interpersonal communication literature. They were originally proposed by William Schutz, *FIRO: A Three-Dimensional Theory of Interpersonal Behavior* (New York: Rinehart, 1958).

5. See John A. Daly and James C. McCroskey, eds., *Avoiding Communication: Shyness, Reticence, and Communication Apprehension* (Beverly Hills: Sage Publications, 1984).

6. James C. McCroskey, "Oral Communication Apprehension: A Summary of Recent Theory and Research," *Human Communication Research*, 4 (1977), p. 88.

7. William R. Cupach and Sandra Metts, *Facework* (Thousand Oaks, Calif.: Sage Publications, 1994).

8. Penelope Brown and Stephen Levinson, *Politeness: Some Universals in Language Usage* (Cambridge: Cambridge University Press, 1987).

9. Among the best work on the control dimension is that of Frank E. Millar and L. Edna Rogers, "A Relational Approach to Interpersonal Communication," in *Explorations in Interpersonal Communication*, ed. Gerald Miller (Beverly Hills, Calif.: Sage Publications, 1976), pp. 87–103.

10. For an overview, see Steve Duck and Garth Pittman, "Social and Personal Relationships," in *Handbook of Interpersonal Communication* (Thousand Oaks, Calif.: Sage Publications, 1994), pp. 687–691.

11. Sandra Petronio, "Communication Boundary Management: A Theoretical Model of Managing Disclosure of Private Information between Marital Couples," *Communication Theory*, 1 (1991), pp. 311–335.

12. Dalmas A. Taylor and Irwin Altman, "Communication in Interpersonal Relationships: Social Penetration Theory," in *Interpersonal Processes: New Directions in Communication Research*, ed. M. E. Roloff and G. R. Miller (Newbury Park, Calif.: Sage Publications, 1987), pp. 257–277.

13. Adapted from Kim Giffin and Robert Patton, "Personal Trust in Human Interaction," in *Basic Readings in Interpersonal*

Communication, ed. Giffin and Patton (New York: Harper & Row, 1971), pp. 375–391.

14. For a recent overview of this subject, see William A. Donohue and Robert Kolt, *Managing Interpersonal Conflict* (Newbury Park, Calif.: Sage Publications, 1992).

15. Ralph Kilmann and Kenneth Thomas, "Interpersonal Conflict-Handling Behavior as Reflections of Jungian Personality Dimensions," *Psychological Reports*, 37 (1975), pp. 971–980.

16. Roger Fisher and William Ury, *Getting to Yes: Negotiating Agreement Without Giving In* (New York: Penguin Books, 1991).

17. William K. Rawlins, *Friendship Matters: Communication, Dialectics, and the Life Course* (Hawthorne, N.Y.: Aldine de Gruyter, 1992).

18. Leslie A. Baxter, "Dialectical Contradictions in Relationship Development," *Journal of Social a;nd Personal Relations*, 7 (1990), pp. 69–88.)

19. See Richard J. Johanneson, "Communication as Dialogue," *Quarterly Journal of Speech*, 62 (1971), pp. 373–382.

20. Martin Buber, *I and Thou* (New York: Scribner's, 1970).

21. Carl R. Rogers and Richard Farson, "Active Listening," in *Readings in Interpersonal and Organizational Communication*, ed. Richard Huseman, Cal Logue, and Dwight Freshley (Boston: Holbrook, 1973), pp. 541–557.

22. This section based primarily on Virginia Satir, "You as Change Agent," in *Helping Families to Change* (New York: Aronson, 1975), pp. 37–62.

23. Thomas Harris, *I'm O.K.; You're O.K.* (New York: Harper & ow, 1969).

C H A P T E R   S I X

1. Dennis C. Alexander, Don F. Faules, and David M. Jabusch, "The Effects of the Basic Speech Course Training on Ability to Role-Play an Employment Interview," *Communication Studies* 25 (1974): 303–306.

2. For a more complete discussion, see Charles Stewart and William Cash, *Interviewing: Principles and Practices* (Dubuque, Iowa: W. C. Brown, 1978).

3. For a more thorough discussion of decision making in the interview, see Don F. Faules and Dennis C. Alexander, *Communication and Social Behavior: A Symbolic Interaction Perspective* (Reading, Mass.: Addison Wesley, 1978), pp. 181–182.

4. This section based primarily on Jack Gibb, "Defensive Communication," *Journal of Communication*, 11 (1961), pp. 141–148.

5. Gibb, "Defensive Communication," p. 147.

6. Susan Schenkel, *Giving Away Success* (NY: Random House, 1991), pp. 76–77.

C H A P T E R   S E V E N

1. For a detailed account of this group, see Irving Janis, *Victims of Groupthink: Psychological Studies of Policy Decisions and Fiascoes* (Boston: Houghton Mifflin, 1982).

2. Adapted from Raymond Cattell, "Concepts and Methods in the Measurement of Group Syntality," *Psychological Review*, 55 (1948), 48–63.

3. This distinction has permeated the literature on small group communication to the present time. It was probably created by Robert F. Bales, *Interaction Process Analysis: A Method for the Study of Small Groups* (Reading, MA: Addison-Wesley, 1950); and *Personality and Interpersonal Behavior* (New York: Holt, 1970). For a more recent discussion, see Marshall Scott Poole and Jonelle Roth, "Decision Development in Small Groups IV: A Typology of Group Decision Paths," *Human Communication Research* 15 (1989): 323–356.

4. This still-useful concept goes back to the classic studies of Bavelas and Leavitt. See, for example, A. Bavelas, "Communication Patterns in Task-Oriented Groups," *Journal of Acoustical Society of America* 22 (1950): 725–730; H. Leavitt, "Some Effects

of Certain Communication Patterns on Group Performance," *Journal of Abnormal and Social Psychology* 46 (1951): 38–50.

5. Adapted from Kenneth Benne and Paul Sheats, "Functional Roles of Group Members," *Journal of Social Issues*, 4 (1958): 41–49.

6. For a review of various approaches to leadership, see J. Kevin Barge and Randy Y. Hirokawa, "Toward a Comunication Competency Model of Group Leadership," *Small Group Behavior* 20 (1989): 167–189.

7. Herbert C. Kelman, "Compliance, Identification, and Internalization: Three Processes of Attitude Change," *Journal of Conflict Resolution*, 2 (1958): 51–60.

8. Marvin Shaw, *Group Dynamics: The Psychology of Small Group Behavior* (New York: (McGraw-Hill, 1981).

9. Janis, *Victims*.

10. Norman R. F. Maier, *Problem-Solving Discussions and Conferences* (New York: McGraw-Hill, 1963), pp. 76-97.

11. Adapted from Lawrence Rosenfeld, *Human Interaction in the Small Group Setting* (Columbus, Ohio: Merrill, 1973), pp. 91–92.

12. Irving Janis and Leon Mann, *Decision Making* (New York: Macmillan, 1977), pp. 91–92.

13. Randy Y. Hirokawa and Dirk R. Scheerhorn, "Comunication in Faulty Group Decision-Making," in *Communication and Group Decision-Making*, eds. R. Y. Hirokawa and M. S. Poole (Beverly Hills: Sage, 1986), pp. 63–80.

Adapted from Janis and Mann, , p. 11.

14. Janis, *Victims*.

15. Adapted from Harold P. Zelko, "When You are 'In Conference,'" *Supervision* (June, 1965), pp. 4–6, 19.

16. Zelko, "In Conference."

17. Lawrence N. Loban, "Questions: The Answer to Meeting Participation," *Supervision (January, 1972)*, pp. 11–13.

18. For a review of this literature, see Judith Hall and Mark Knapp, Nonverbal Communication in Human Interaction (New York: Holte, Rinehart & Winston, 1992).

19. Lawrence B. Rosenfeld and Jean M. Civikly, With Words Unspoken: The Nonverbal Expreience (New York: Holt, 1976), p. 161.

C H A P T E R   E I G H T

1. Public speaking as elevated conversation is not a new idea. See James Winsns, *Public Speaking* (New York: Century, 1917).

2. Lloyd F. Bitzer, "The Rhetorical Situation," *Philosophy and Rhetoric* (1968).

3. *Wold Book Encyclopedia* (Chicago: World Book, Inc., 1994), vol. 5, p. 253.

4. Bitzer, "The Rhetorical Situation," p. 8.

5. Bitzer, "The Rhetorical Situation."

6. Kenneth Boulding, *The Image: Knowledge in Life and Society* (Ann Arbor: University of Michigan Press, 1975).

7. William Norwood Brigance, *Speech: Its Techniques and Disciplines in a Free Society*, 2nd ed. (New York: Apleton Century Crofts, 1961), p. 193.

8. Gary Cronkhite, *Persuasion, Speech, and Behavior Change* (New York: Bobbs-Merrill, 1969), pp. 13–14.

9. Sonja K. Foss and Karen A. Foss, *Inviting Transformation: Presentational Speaking for a Changing World* (Prospect Heights, Ill.: Waveland Press, 1994), p. 12.

10. Foss and Foss, *Invitation Transformation*.

11. John Wesley Powell, *Exploration of the Colorado and Its Canyons* (New York: Dover Publications, Inc., 1895), p. 274.

12. John Douglas Gibb, *An Experimental Comparison of the Humorous Lecture and the Non-humorous Lecture in Informative Speaking*, unpublished master's thesis, University of Utah, 1964.

13. Foss and Foss, *Inviting Transformation*, p. 44.

14. James H. McBath and Walter R. Fisher, *British Public Addresses: 1828–1960* (boston: Houghton Mifflin, 1971), p. 494.

15. Foss and Foss, *Inviting Transformation*, pp. 30–51.

C H A P T E R   N I N E

1. This pattern was introduced by Sonja K. Foss & Karen A. Foss, *Inviting Transformation: Presentational Speaking for a Changing World* (Prospect Heights, Ill.: Waveland Press, 1994).

2. The stock issues approach is well established in the literature. See, for example, James A. Herrick, *Critical Thinking: The Analysis of Argument* (Scottsdale, AZ: Gorsuch Scarisbrick, 1991), pp. 63–72; John C. Reinard, *Foundations of Argument* (Dubuque, IA: Wm C. Brown, 1991), pp. 256–271.

3. Foss and Foss, *Inviting Transformation*, p. 52.

4. From James H. McBath and Walter R. Fisher, *British Public Address: 1828–1960* (Boston: Houghton Mifflin, 1971), p. 513.

C H A P T E R   T E N

1. Jan Work and William Work, *Relating: Everyday Communication* (Boston: Houghton Mifflin, 1975), p. 99.

2. Robert Famighetti, *The World Almanac and Book of Facts* (Mahwah, NJ: Funk and Wagnalls, 1995), p. 310.

3. For a more detailed discussion of media audiences, see Stephen W. Littlejohn, *Theories of Human Communication* (Belmont, Calif.: Wadsworth Publishing, 1996), chap. 15.

4. These functions have been discussed by numerous sources. See, for example, Everett M. Rogers, *A History of Comunication Study: A Biographical Approach* (New York: Free Press, 1994), p. 223.

5. See Sam Donaldson, *Hold On, Mr. President* (New York: Fawcett Crest, 1987).

6. Marshall McLuhan and Quentin Fiore, *The Medium Is the Message* (New York: Bantama, 1967).

7. "Bay City Best," *San Francisco Examiner* Magazine (May 7, 1995): 7.

8. See Alan M. Rubin, "Audience Activity and Media Use," *Communication Monographs*, 60 (1993), pp. 98–105.

9. Melvin L. DeFleur and Sandra J. Ball-Rokeach, *Theories of Mass Commuication* (New York: Longman, 1982), pp. 240–251.

10. The agenda-setting function has been widely discussed. See, for example, David Proters and Maxwell Combs, *Agenda Setting: Readings on Media, Public Opinion, and Policymaking* (Hillsdale, NJ: Erlbaum, 1991).

11. Adapted from Emil Bohn and Karen Foss, "Teaching Listening in the Classroom: An Integrated Approach" (Phoenix: Western Speech Communication Association, 1977).

12. These categories adapted from *The Way We See It* (Salt Lake City, Utah: Media Research Center, 1978).

13. For a summary of these ideas, see Littlejohn, *Theories, chap.* 11.

14. Sut Jhally, *Dreamworlds: Desire/Sex/Power in Rock Video* (Amherst: University of Massachusetts, 1990).

Glossary

A

Abstraction—A process of leaving out details in symbolization.

Accommodation—Managing conflict by giving in to others.

Active listening—A mode in which a communicator listens for more than literal meaning and suspends judgment.

Ad hominem—The fallacy of attacking the person rather than the idea.

Adaptation principle—The idea that a speaker should use supporting material that the audience can understand and appreciate.

Affect display—Vocal and facial cues used in the expression of emotion.

Affection need—The need to feel loved.

Allness—The feeling that everything that might be said about a situation has or can be said.

Analogic thinking—Making an inference about something not known based on a comparison with something known.

Analysis—Careful scrutiny of actual situations.

Anchor—A standard used by comparison in the judgment of a stimulus.

Appeal to tradition—A fallacy in which one states that a course of action should be adopted because it was used in the past.

Appraisal interview—An interview designed to evaluate the performance of an employee.

Apprehension, communication—Extreme and abnormal fear of interaction.

Art-form sequence—A series of questions arranged in an order designed to evaluate, interpret, and select.

Articulation—The production of speech sounds are produced by the anatomy of the throat and mouth.

Artifactual codes—The use of objects in the expression of meaning.

Assertiveness—Standing up for one's rights without denying the rights of others.

Assimilate—To incorporate information into the cognitive system.

Assimilation effect—Judging a stimulus to be closer to a comparison stimulus than it actually is.

Attitude—A cluster of beliefs about an object, person, or situation that predisposes to act in a positive or negative way toward the object, person, or situation.

Attribution—The process of explaining one's own or others' actions.

Autocratic style—A style of group leadership in which one person exerts most of the control within the group.

Avoidance-avoidance situation—A situation in which each option is unpleasant in some way.

Avoiding—Managing conflict by disengaging from a dispute or potential dispute.

B

Bandwagon technique—The fallacy in which one states that a course of action should be adopted because it is popular.

Belief—An accepted datum about the world.

Bipolar question—A question that requires the respondent to select one of two options, such as yes and no.

Bolstering tactics—Behaviors that justify or rationalize the decisions of a group.

Bypassing—A miscommunication caused by communicators' using different meanings for terms.

C

Card stacking—Making a claim with one-sided arguments.

Central idea—The main point, or thesis, of a speech.

Central route—The process by which messages are weighed critically.

Centrality—The relative extent to which person communicates with others in a group, the inverse of peripherality.

Charting—A method for structuring messages in a speech.

Claim—A conclusion stated as a sentence.

Closed question—A question that asks for a very particular piece of information such as one's address.

Coalition—A subgroup within a larger group that joins together through a tight network of communication.

Coding—The process of using signs to create and understand messages.

Cognitive flexibility—The ability to assign a number of meanings or interpretations to a message or sign.

Cognitive processes—The mechanisms or operations required to manage and use information.

Cognitive system—The interrelated set of attitudes, beliefs, and values comprising a person's thoughts.

Cohesiveness—A feeling of connection or identification among the members of a group.

Collaboration—Managing conflict by working with others to create a win-win solution.

Communication apprehension—Extreme and abnormal fear of interaction.

Communication competence—The ability to communicate well, deriving from understanding, sensitivity, skill, and ethical responsibility.

Comparison—Pointing out the similarities between two things.

Competence, communication—The ability to communicate well, deriving from understanding, sensitivity, skill, and ethical responsibility.

Competition—Managing conflict by trying to win over others.

Complementary interaction—An exchange in which control moves are accepted or granted as intended.

Compliance—Acting publicly in a way that conforms to a group's expectation.

Comprehension—The process of making sense of information in the environment.

Compromise—Managing conflict by making trade-offs.

Concept—A labeled group of things distinguished by common qualities.

Concern, principle of—Communicating with concern for the well-being of all the participants.

Conflict—A clash, disagreement, or difference that is significant to the parties and expressed in communication.

Conformity—Acceptance of group norms.

Connotation—The subjective meanings of a symbol.

Consensus—Making a decision within a group by general agreement.

Content level of meaning—The topical information contained within a message.

Context—The historical, sociocultural, physical, and psychological situation within which a communication event occurs.

Contradiction—A state in which two valued things are inconsistent with one another.

Contrast—Pointing out the difference between two things.

Contrast effect—Judging a stimulus to be more distant from a comparison stimulus than it actually is.

Control need—The need to feel competent and responsible.

Coordination—A state in which two or more individuals' behaviors are meshed or organized in such a way that all believe their actions are consistent with the rules.

Correctional interview—An interview designed to change undesirable behavior.

Correlation function—The function of the mass media in showing the public the significance and connection among events.

Counseling (interview)—A type of interviewing designed to help people understand themselves and arrive at appropriate decisions in their lives.

Counterattitudinal advocacy—A method of persuasion in which attitude change is achieved by inducing a person to advocate a position they do not initially believe in.

Created group—A group formulated to accomplish a purpose.

Culture—A large community that shares common beliefs, values, and norms.

D

Data—The information used as the basis of a claim.

Decisional interview—An interview designed to affect a one's own or another's decision.

Decode—Use of signs to understand meanings in messages.

Deductive approach—Establishing the content of a speech by moving from general ideas to more specific points and information.

Deductive reasoning—Reaching conclusions of a specific nature based on observations or statements of a general nature.

Defensive climate—An atmosphere in which communicators feel self-protective and guarded.

Democratic style—A style of group leadership relying on the joint decisions of the members of the group.

Denotation—The objective referent of a symbol.

Depth-breadth principle—The idea that a speaker should demonstrate both the extent of the problem or situation being discussed and its significance in particular cases.

Developmental interview—An interview designed to help a person in his or her life.

Diagnostic interview—An interview designed to analyze a problem.

Dialogue—A type of communication in which parties are just as interested in listening as in talking.

Directed question—A question that restricts the form of the answer.

Discourse—A message or set of related messages.

Dispositional attributions—Explaining an action on the basis of factors within a person's control.

Disruptive conflict—Disagreement marked by defensiveness and disrespect.

Dissonance—A tension arising from inconsistency in the cognitive system.

Diversionary claim—A claim that diverts one's attention from the real issue at hand.

Division—Conscious points of difference between groups or persons.

Dominant reading—The meaning intended by the producers of a media message.

Drive—Internal, physiological states of tension leading to the desire to reduce or resolve the tension.

E

Ego involvement—The degree to which a subject or position is considered important to one's self interest.

Elaboration likelihood—The probability that one will weigh arguments critically.

Employment interview—An interview designed to evaluate an applicant for employment.

Encode—Use of signs to express meanings in messages.

Enthymeme—A rhetorical device for engaging an audience in deduction by presenting only a portion of the deduction and relying on the audience to provide the missing statements.

Equal access—Helping to provide the conditions in which all points of view can be heard and interests expressed equally.

Equivocation—Communicating ambiguously.

Ethical responsibility—Communication that attempts to embody concern, shared responsibility, and equal access.

Extemporaneous speaking—Speaking in a conversational style with or without brief notes after substantial preparation.

External rules—Expectations about behavior shared across a wide spectrum of groups.

F

Face—Personal identity, which is in need of protection.

Facework—Communicating in a fashion that helps another person save face.

Fact, issue of—A point of disagreement about a state of affairs.

Fallacy of monousage—The belief that a symbol has just one meaning.

Federal Communication Commission (FCC)—An agency of the Executive Branch of the U.S. government that establishes the rules of broadcasting.

Feedback—Verbal and nonverbal cues given to a speaker by a listener.

Focusing—Attending to the details of information.

Foot-in-the-door—Getting a person to agree to a more extreme position by first getting them to agree to a less extreme one.

Funnel sequence—A series of questions arranged in order from general to specific.

G

Grammar—The rules by which a set of signs relate to one another, usually applied to language; the rules used in generating and understanding sentences.

Groupthink—A pattern of behavior in which a group fails to think critically about ideas suggested by powerful members.

H

Hierarchy of needs—A series of needs from basic (e.g., food) to higher (e.g., self-actualization) in which the fulfillment of lower-level needs is required before higher-level ones can be fulfilled.

High-context culture—A culture in which most of the meaning of messages is gained from the situation and the nonverbal behaviors of the communicators.

I

Ideal speech situation—The set of conditions in which ethical responsibility can be achieved, including the principles of concern, shared responsibility, and equal access.

Identification—Believing privately, as well as behaving publicly, in a way that is consistent with a group's expectations; Points of similarity between groups or persons that become known to them.

Image—One's personal mental world of space, time, interpersonal relations, nature, and feeling.

Implementing—Carrying through with a chosen action.

Impromptu speaking—Speaking "off the cuff" with little or no preparation time.

Inclusion need—The need to feel accepted.

Individualistic perspective—That point of view focusing on the psychology of the person.

Inductive approach—Establishing the content of the speech by moving from specific data and ideas to more general points.

Inductive reasoning—Reaching conclusions of a general nature based on observations or statements of a specific nature.

Inference—The process of filling in missing details on the basis of what you do know.

Inference-observation confusion—Mistaking a conclusion drawn from reasoning with an event actually observed.

Inferential thinking—Making conclusions about something that has not been observed based on what has been observed.

Information—The measure of uncertainty in a situation.

Information capacity—The amount of information that can be processed by a person in a particular time period.

Information load—The amount of information that must be processed in a given time.

Informational interview—An interview designed to share or gain information about a subject.

Inoculation—Providing a mild argument against a person's point of view so that he or she will become more resistant to the opposing point of view.

Integration—Making connections among pieces of information.

Intellectualization—In reflective thinking, the careful definition of a problem.

Interactional perspective—That point of view focusing on the feedback and mutual response among communicators.

Internal rules—Expectations about behavior unique to a particular relationship.

Internalization—Integration of a group's norms into an individual's value system.

Interpersonal energy—The effort of a group toward maintaining the relationships among its members.

Interview—A formal communication event, relying mostly on questions and answers, in which at least one of the participants has a preconceived purpose.

Interview schedule—An outline or list of questions to be asked in an interview.

Intimate distance—The distance at which intimate verbal and nonverbal messages are exchanged.

Inverted-funnel sequence—A series of questions arranged in order from specific to general.

Investigative interview—An interview designed to get information that another person may be trying to hide.

Issue of fact—A point of disagreement about a state of affairs.

Issue of policy—A point of disagreement about a course of action.

Issue of value—A point of disagreement about a matter of judgment.

K

Kinesics—The study of body motion in communication.

Knowledge structures—The patterns into which an individual organizes his or her information.

L

Laissez-faire style—A style of group leadership in which the leadership functions are diffused among the membership.

Leadership—A set of functions that individuals can assume in order to help a group accomplish its goals.

Leading question—A question that is stated in such a way that it tells the respondent what answer to give.

Learning—Change resulting from new information, rewards, and punishments received from the environment.

Limited-option question—A question that requires the respondent to select from a short list of options.

Linking—Connecting one aspect of the cognitive system to another.

Loaded question—A question that is stated in such a way that no matter how the respondent answers, the answer will look bad.

Low-context culture—A culture in which most of the meaning of messages is gained from the language in the message itself.

M

Meaning—The relationship between symbols and objects; the image that arises in a person's mind in response to a symbol, speech act, or message.

Memory—The process of storing and retrieving information in the cognitive system.

Message—A set of interrelated signs used to exchange meanings.

Metacommunication—Communication about communication; subtle, usually nonverbal signs related to the relationship between communicators.

Metalevel—A perspective or view of something that provides a context for understanding that thing.

Metaphor—An implied or implicit comparison.

Method of residues—An approach to argument in which one eliminates all but one course of action.

Monologue—A type of communication in which talking, rather than listening, is the preferred mode.

Multistep flow model—The idea that the media influence certain individuals who pass on the message to others, who in turn pass it on to even more people.

N

Narrative—A progression of ideas following the events of a story.

Natural social group—An unplanned group emerging from ordinary interaction.

Negative facework—Communicating in a fashion that avoids hurting another person's feelings.

Network—A series of connections via communication between individuals or groups in a system.

Non sequitur—Irrelevant reasoning.

Nonscreener—A person who has difficulty focusing on some aspects of a field of stimulation and tuning out unwanted stimulation.

Norm—A group's expectation for the behavior of all members.

O

One-across message—A message that neither asserts nor accepts control.

One-down message—A message that accepts the control of another person.

One-step flow model—The idea that the media influence the public in one step.

One-up message—A message that asserts control.

Open question—A question that allows a respondent to answer in any form.

Openness—A willingness to disclose information about the self and a sensitivity to the disclosures of others.

Oppositional reading—Disclosing the hidden and oppressive meanings within a media message.

Paralanguage—Meaningful vocal cues used in the utterance of language.

Peripheral route—The process by which messages are received without critical evaluation.

Peripherality—The relative extent to which one is not connected to others in a group, the inverse of centrality.

Personal distance—The distance at which conversation of a personal nature occurs.

P

Personal space—The area around one's body serving as a psychological buffer zone.

Perspective—A point of view.

Persuasion—A transactional process by which people are influenced by messages to make choices consistent with other communicator's intentions.

Placement interview—An interview designed to determine the position a person should be given in a job or at school.

Plain folks—The fallacy that something must be true because common people know it to be true, or false because "experts" say that it is true.

Planned coding—Using signs and messages intentionally.

Policy, issue of—A point of disagreement about a course of action.

Positive facework—Saying things that make others feel good about themselves.

Post hoc ergo propter hoc—Latin for "Before the fact, therefore because of the fact;" the fallacy of false cause.

Practice—Engaging in communication activities.

Principle of concern—Communicating with regard for the well-being of all the participants.

Principle of equal access—Helping to provide the conditions in which all points of view can be heard and interests expressed equally.

Principle of shared responsibility—A willingness to allow others to participate in determining the outcome of the communication transaction and to provide the information necessary for them to do so.

Proattitudinal advocacy—A method of persuasion in which one's attitudes are strengthened by inducing the person to advocate a favorable position.

Process—The aspect of communication characterized by change, effects, simultaneous action, and social understanding.

Productive conflict—Disagreement in an atmosphere of respect.

Psychological context—The personal ways of thinking by which a communicator understands messages.

Public distance—The distance at which public business is conducted.

Q

Qualifier—A statement of probability attached to a claim.

R

Quintamensional sequence—A series of questions arranged in an order designed to determine the intensity of the respondent's opinions.

Reasoning—Reaching conclusions on the basis of other stated claims.

Recruitment interview—An interview designed to evaluate an applicant for employment.

Redundancy—Predictability or pattern in a situation.

Reflective thinking—A sequence of considerations involved in careful analysis of and solution to a problem.

Relationship level of meaning—Implicit meanings within messages that define the relationship.

Relevancy—A condition in which the receiver is able to connect information with what is already known.

Repeated affirmation—The fallacy of repeating a claim rather than giving logical reasons.

Reservation—A contingency or exception to a claim.

Residues, method of—An approach to argument in which one eliminates all but one course of action.

Responsibility, ethical—Communication that attempts to embody concern, shared responsibility, and equal access.

Résumé—A document outlining one's qualifications for employment.

Retrieval—A term used in cognitive theory to designate remembering.

Role—The expectations that a group has for a member's behavior.

Rules—Expectations about how people should behave within a relationship.

S

Sales interview—An interview designed to sell a product or service.

Screener—A person who can focus on some aspects of a field of stimulation while tuning out unwanted stimulation.

Selection—In cognitive theory, choosing appropriate behaviors in response to a situation

Selective perception—Noticing certain aspects of a stimulus and not others.

Self-actualization—Fulfilling one's highest potential.

Self-disclosure—Revealing things about oneself.

Shared centrality—The degree to which the members of a group are connected through communication with one another.

Shared responsibility—A willingness to allow others to participate in determining the outcome of the communication transaction and to provide the information necessary for them to do so.

Sign—A stimulus taken to represent something other than itself.

Situational attribution—Explaining an action on the basis of factors beyond the person's control.

Social construction—The co-creation of meaning within a group.

Social-consultative distance—The distance at which conversation of a non-personal nature occurs.

Socioemotional leader—A person who assumes functions that enable a group to maintain its interpersonal relationships.

Sociocultural situation—The events and shared meanings within a society that affect the communication within that society.

Spontaneous coding—Using signs and messages on the spur of the moment without advanced planning.

Stereotyping—Applying a generalization to every member of the group on which the generalization has been made.

Stimuli—Events that have the potential for eliciting a reaction.

Stock questions—Standard questions often answered in the development of an argument.

Storage—A term used in cognitive theory to designate the placement of information into memory.

Subjective norm—One's assessment of what other people think should be done.

Supportive climate—An atmosphere in which communicators feel open and not defensive.

Surveillance function—The function of the mass media in keeping track of what is going on in the world.

Syllogism—A formal device for deduction including a major premise, a minor premise, and a conclusion.

Symbol—A sign that represents a concept and is used in conscious thought.

Symmetrical interaction—An exchange in which control is neither accepted nor granted.

Symptomatic coding—Assigning meaning to the behavior of oneself or another.

Synergy—The output, or total energy, of a group.

T

Task energy—The effort of a group toward accomplishing its task.

Task group—A group formulated to solve a problem.

Task leader—A person who assumes functions that enable a group to accomplish its task.

Territoriality—The tendency of animals and humans to mark and guard spaces.

Theory—An explanation based on systematic observation and research.

Toulmin model—A set of categories for analyzing an argument, outlining the stages between data and claim.

Tradition, appeal to—A fallacy in which one states that a course of action should be adopted because it was used in the past.

Transactional perspective—That point of view stressing the interrelated nature of feelings, meanings, behavior, and situations involved in a communication event.

Transactional purpose—The response desired during or after a speech.

Transfer—The fallacy of guilt by association.

Transmissional perspective—That point of view focusing on the sending and receiving of messages.

Trust—A state in which one person relies on another and risks something of value to help achieve a goal.

Tunnel sequence—A series of questions of the same order of generality.

Two-step flow model—The idea that the media influence opinion leaders, who in turn influence others.

U

Unwanted repetitive pattern—A highly coordinated but negative pattern of communication.

V

Value—A highly central belief used as a guideline for living; according to Fishbein and Aizen, the positive or negative weighting of a belief.
Value, issue of—A point of disagreement about a matter of judgment.

Variety principle—The idea that a speaker should include a variety of types of supporting material.

W

Warrant—The logical link between data and claim.

Web pattern—A method of organizing a speech in which one moves from the central idea out to a series of related ideas and then back to the central idea again.
Weight—The credibility assigned by a person to a statement.

Index